FROMMER'S
1987-1988 GUIDE TO CANCÚN, COZUMEL & THE YUCATÁN

by Tom Brosnahan

Published by Prentice Hall Press
A Division of Simon & Schuster, Inc.
Gulf + Western Building
One Gulf + Western Plaza
New York, NY 10023

ISBN 0–671–62432-6

Manufactured in the United States of America

Although every effort was made to ensure the accuracy
of price information appearing in this book
it should be kept in mind that prices
can and do fluctuate in the course of time.

CONTENTS

MAPS

A Word About Prices: You're liable to get your first unpleasant shock in Mexico when you sit down to survey a restaurant menu and see "Tacos —$500." The wave of relief comes as you realize that the dollar sign "$" is used to indicate *pesos* in Mexico, and that your 500-dollar plate of tacos actually only costs 500 pesos, or about a dollar. To avoid confusion in this book, we use the dollar sign *only* to indicate U.S. dollars; peso amounts are written as just figures alone, or are qualified by the word "pesos."

Sometimes Mexican establishments will quote prices in U.S. dollars, usually written "$1 Dlls."; for the peso price, then, they may write "$500 m.n.," meaning 500 pesos, *moneda nacional* (that is, Mexican national currency).

Although every effort is made to ensure that the information given is accurate and up-to-date at press time, keep in mind that some transportation schedules, museum opening hours, telephone numbers, and other such data may change by the time you reach Mexico.

Note also that Mexico has a Value-Added Tax, or "Impuesto de Valor Agregado." Abbreviated "IVA," (*ee*-bah), the 15% tax is already included in most prices you'll see in Mexico: hotels, restaurants, rental cars, souvenirs, transportation tickets. Essentials such as medicines are exempt. Some modest hotels and restaurants get away with not charging IVA. Always ask whether IVA has been included.

Converting Pesos to Dollars: As this book goes to press, the Mexican economy is undergoing a painful period of reconstruction. This is bad news for Mexicans but very good news for foreign tourists. You may find that you'll pay even *less* than the prices indicated in this book, in terms of dollars for rooms and meals.

With inflation in Mexico running at 100% per year and the peso fluctuating wildly, our dollar prices (figured at U.S. $1 = 500 pesos), may be your best guide to actual costs. The peso prices will undoubtedly be higher, but that won't really matter to you.

To help you get used to spending Mexican money, here's a blank currency exchange table. Fill in the dollar values after you change money.

Pesos	U.S.$	Pesos	U.S.$
1		75	
5		100	
10		250	
15		500	
20		1,000	
25		5,000	
50		9,000	

Chapter I

YUCATÁN: AN INTRODUCTION

A LIMITLESS SWATH of emerald jungle, bounded by sand beaches of the purest white, bordered by palm trees swaying lazily in a freshening breeze, all surrounded by water so intensely blue it seems a great liquid jewel—that's the Yucatán.

But no simple description can encompass this fascinating area, the very heart of Mesoamerica, where the ancient Mayas lifted great monuments of enduring beauty above the dense carpet of vegetation, and built a civilization which reverberates in this land even today. Although the earth here is of such poor quality that only the mat of jungle grows without toil, and the population must struggle even to feed itself, the Mayas developed a rich and advanced civilization, the Spanish Conquistadores built beautiful cities, and the Roman Catholic Church raised huge churches that had to be fortresses, so fiercely did the Mayas hold to their ancient religious rites. Though the coasts present the perfect picture of tropical paradise, ruthless pirates used to cruise the sea lanes here, pillaging coastal towns that were not completely walled and heavily defended.

Always there has been a spirit of adventure, of something unexpected and unusual, like the priceless sacrificial treasures drawn by archeologists from the great well at Chichén-Itzá, or the irridescent colors of a school of fish seen by a diver near the Palancar Reef off Cozumel. You feel this spirit as you drive along a flat, dead-straight Yucatecan highway, with nothing ahead for miles except the monotony of the jungle, when, all at once, a cloud of butterflies, brilliantly yellow, will block your way. And you feel it as you penetrate the jungle at Xcaret, stumble upon a miniature Mayan temple, and then come across a crystal-clear natural swimming pool of limpid water, half sheltered by a cave.

Yucatán is in Mexico, and yet Yucatán and its people, the

Mayas, do not really look upon themselves merely as Mexicans. Yucatán is different, they will tell you. Yucatán is special. It is not simply Mexican, nor just Caribbean, not Mayan nor Spanish. You will feel this special spirit when you meet the Mayas, speaking Spanish and Mayan, wearing traditional costumes or modern fashions, living in thatched cottages or in air-conditioned bungalows.

Whatever happens here, you're in for an adventure. As far as I'm concerned, you couldn't have picked a better place for it, whether your idea of adventure is surfing or archeology, cuisine or architecture, diving or folk art, or meeting new people. Yucatán has enough to keep you happy and adventuring for years, not just for weeks, whatever your desires.

Perhaps the way to start your adventure is with a summary of Yucatán's past, a story which seems more fitting in a spellbinding novel than in a history book. After that, let's go on to some less romantic, but more practical, details of planning your trip.

Yucatán's Fascinating History

Yucatán's history has fascinated the rest of the world since Lord Kingsborough published a study of its ruins in 1831. Just a few years later, New York lawyer John L. Stephens and artist Frederick Catherwood made several trips through Yucatán and Central America. Stephens recorded his adventures in a fascinating series of travel books, decorated by Catherwood's superb drawings, which achieved great, immediate, and lasting popularity. The books still make for wonderful reading, and are available from Dover Publications, 31 E. 2nd St., Mineola, NY 11501-3582, or through bookstores in North America and Mexico.

Ever since Stephens's adventures, foreigners have been touring the Yucatán to view its vast crumbling cities and ponder the fall of a once truly great civilization. The Mayas, though they practiced human sacrifice and self-mutilation, developed mathematical theories far in advance of European thought, and perfected a calendar even more accurate than the Gregorian one we use today.

Here is a summary of Maya history so you can comprehend the importance of the archeological sites you're about to visit.

THE EARLY TIMES: The years 1500 B.C. to A.D. 320, the Preclassic Period, are thought to be the time when Maya civilization began and was shaped. It may be that the Mayas learned a good deal from the mysterious Olmecs, whose great monolithic head sculptures are preserved in the Parque La Venta at Villahermosa and in the Museo de Antropología in Mexico City. Or it may be that the Mayas developed from wandering tribes in what is now Guatemala's vast low-lying jungle province of El Petén.

Little is known about the first thousand years of Maya culture, except that they discovered how to cultivate corn (maize), the food—to them even a religious symbol—which was to shape their lives for thousands of years, and which still influences them strongly today.

In any case, by 500 B.C. the Mayas were making great strides.

The Formative Period

The time from 500 B.C. until the end of the Preclassic Period is sometimes called the Formative Period because this is when they developed their calendar, their complex and beautiful system of hieroglyphic writing, and their early architecture. The Maya religion, with its 166 known deities, was also being shaped in these early centuries.

While the Mayas were doing these things in the yet-to-be-"discovered" New World, the following events took place in the Old World: the Second Temple was built in Jerusalem; the Roman Empire reached the height of its power and influence; Jesus carried out his ministry; Jerusalem was destroyed and the Jewish Diaspora took place; and Constantine the Great was preparing to found his new imperial capital of Constantinople, now Istanbul.

THE CLASSIC YEARS: The great years of Maya culture were from A.D. 320 to 925, called the Classic Period. When Rome was falling to the barbarians and the Dark Ages were spreading over Europe, the Mayas were consolidating their cultural gains, wiping out pockets of backwardness, and connecting their ceremonial centers by means of great roads. The finest examples of Mayan architecture were conceived and constructed during these years, well before the Gothic style made its appearance in Europe. You can see these supreme achievements of Mayan art at Palenque (near Villahermosa), at Copán in Honduras, and at Quiriguá in Guatemala. All these sites flourished during the last part of the Classic Period, in the 700s.

The End of the Great Era

The Classic Period closes with a century of degradation and collapse, roughly equivalent to the A.D. 800s. By the early 900s, the great ceremonial centers mentioned above were abandoned, the jungle moving in to cover them after not much more than one short century of florescence. Why classic Maya culture collapsed so quickly, we don't really know. Epidemic? Earthquake? Overpopulation? A breakdown of society?

In Europe at the time of the Maya collapse, it was the Middle Ages. Charlemagne was building his empire, an Umayyad Muslim prince reigned in Spain, the Anglo-Saxon King Alfred the Great ruled England, and the iconoclastic controversy raged in the Byzantine Middle East.

INTERREGNUM: With the collapse of Maya civilization, the Mayas seem to have migrated from their historic home in Guatemala and Chiapas into the northern lowlands of the Yucatán, roughly the modern states of Yucatán and Campeche. After their arrival around A.D. 900, they spent three centuries (till 1200) growing into an inferior copy of their former greatness.

Puuc Architecture

The cities near Yucatán's low western hills were built in this period in the style now called Puuc ("hills"). These include Kabah, Sayil, Labná, and Xlapak. Even though Mayan architecture never regained the heights achieved at Palenque or Tikal, the Puuc buildings, such as the Codz Poop at Kabah and the palaces at Sayil and Labná are quite beautiful and impressive.

The Putún Maya

After the Puuc period in architecture, Yucatán was profoundly affected by a strong influence from mainland Mexico. Some theories now hold that a distantly related branch of the Mayan people, called the Putún Maya, were the ones who came from the borders of Mexico and crowded into the Yucatán during the Interregnum, developing a civilization of their own, heavily influenced by the cultures of mainland Mexico. The Putún Maya had been traders and navigators, controlling the coastal and riverine trade routes between mainland Mexico and the classic Mayan lands in Petén and Chiapas. They spoke the Mayan language badly, using many Nahuatl (Aztec) words.

QUETZALCÓATL: The legend of Quetzalcóatl, a holy man who appeared during the time of troubles at the end of the Classic Period, is one of the most important tales in Mexican history and folklore. Quetzalcóatl means "feathered serpent," but seems to have been a religious title during later Maya times. Like the young Jesus, wise and learned beyond his years, he became the high priest and leader of the Toltecs at Tula, and did a good deal to "civilize" them and stop or ameliorate the bad effects of sacrifice. He stopped human sacrifice altogether. His influence completely changed the Toltecs from a group of spartan warriors to peaceful and fabulously productive farmers, artisans, and craftspeople. But his success upset the old priests who had depended on human sacrifice for their own importance, and they called upon their ancient god of darkness, Texcatlipoca, to degrade Quetzalcóatl in the eyes of the people. One night the priests conspired to dress Quetzalcóatl in a ridiculous garb, get him drunk, and tempt him to break his vow of chastity. The next morning they offered him a mirror, and the horror of what he saw after this night of debauch drove him in shame out of his own land and into the wilderness, where he lived for 20 years. He emerged in Coatzacoalcos, in the Isthmus of Tehuantepec, constructed a boat of feathers, bade his few followers farewell, and sailed away, having promised to return in a future age. But artistic influences noted at Chichén-Itzá in the Yucatán suggest that in fact he landed there and began his "ministry" again, which may in fact have been the Itzáes invasion (see below). He died there, but the legend of his return in a future age remained.

The Itzáes

When the Putún Maya left their ships and joined the Toltecs to overrun Yucatán, the invaders became known as the Itzáes.

It is thought that the semi-legendary god-man Quetzalcóatl (in Nahuatl; Kukulcán in Maya) was the leader of the invasion. With a band of Toltecs, and the support of the Putún Maya, he conquered the town which he called Chichén-Itzá ("In the mouth of the well of the Itzá"). It became his chief city until he founded Mayapán.

Uxmal was founded during this same period (around A.D. 1000), according to some authorities, by the tribe known as the Tutul Xiú. Other scholars think that the Xiú took over from some earlier builders.

The three great centers of Chichén-Itzá, Mayapán, and Uxmal lived in peace under a confederation: the Itzá ruled in Chichén-Itzá, the Cocom tribe in Mayapán, and the Xiú in Uxmal. But in 1194 the people of Mayapán overthrew the confederation, sacked Chichén-Itzá, conquered Uxmal, and captured the leaders of the Itzá and the Xiú. Held in Mayapán, the Itzá and Xiú princes reigned over, but did not rule, their former cities.

The Xiú took their revenge in 1441 when they marched from

Uxmal on Mayapán, capturing the city, destroying it, and putting the Cocom rulers to death. They thereupon founded a new city at Maní. Thereafter the Mayan lands suffered from a series of battles and skirmishes, and were to know no peace until it was brought forcibly by the Spanish Conquistadores.

THE SPANISH CONQUISTADORES: When Hernán Cortés and his men landed in 1519 in what would become Veracruz, the Aztec empire was ruled by Moctezuma (also, misspelled, Montezuma) in great splendor. The emperor thought the strangers might be Quetzalcóatl and his followers, returning at last, in which case no resistance must be offered; on the other hand, if the strangers were not Quetzalcóatl and his followers, they might be a threat to his empire. Moctezuma tried to bribe them with gold to go away, but this only whetted their appetites. Despite the fact that Moctezuma and his ministers received the Conquistadores with full pomp and glory when they reached Mexico City, Cortés pronounced the Aztec chief to be under arrest and had him tortured. Moctezuma never did reveal where he had hidden his fabulous treasure, which had been seen by a Spaniard earlier.

Actually the Spaniards were living on bravado at this point, for they were no match for the hundreds of thousands of Aztecs; but they skillfully kept things under their control until a revolt threatened Cortés's entire enterprise. He retired to the countryside, made alliances with non-Aztec tribes, and finally marched on the empire when it was governed by the last Aztec emperor, Cuauhtémoc. He was victorious; Cuauhtémoc defended himself and his people furiously, but was finally captured, tortured, and made a prisoner. He was ultimately executed.

The Spanish conquest had started out as an adventure by Cortés and his men, unauthorized by the Spanish crown or its governor in Cuba, but the conquest was not to be reversed and soon Christianity was being spread through "New Spain." Guatemala and Honduras were explored and conquered, and by 1540 the territory of New Spain included Spanish possessions from Vancouver to Panama. In the two centuries that followed, Franciscan and Augustinian friars converted great numbers of Indians to Christianity, and the Spanish lords built up huge feudal estates on which the Indian farmers were little more than serfs. The silver and gold which Cortés had sought made Spain the richest country in Europe.

THE CONQUEST OF YUCATÁN: Francisco de Montejo, the Spaniard who led the conquest of Yucatán, was actually three men. The adventure was begun by Francisco de Montejo the Elder, a member of the lesser Spanish nobility, who had petitioned the crown for the right to conquer Yucatán at his own expense in exchange for a lifetime appointment as its governor.

"El Adelantado"

The conquest of Yucatán took a full 20 years. Montejo sailed from Spain in 1527 with 400 soldiers, landed at Cozumel, then proceeded to the mainland at Xel-ha. After scouting the terrain and plumbing the depths of the Mayas' wrath, he decided to re-launch his campaign from the western coast, where he could more easily receive supplies from New Spain (Mexico).

Having regrouped in Mexico, Montejo the Elder (El Adelantado, "the pioneer") conquered what is now the state of Tabasco (1530), and then pushed onward to Yucatán. At first his campaign was successful, but Maya resistance increased along with his success, and after four difficult years (1531–1535) he was forced to return to Mexico a failure, out of money and out of energy. His soldiers had found little in the way of gold, and when stories began to arrive of the vast treasures up for grabs in newly conquered Peru, they deserted the Montejo cause en masse.

"El Mozo"

Montejo's son, Francisco Montejo the Younger (El Mozo, "the lad"), had accompanied him on this expedition, and in 1540 the father turned over his cause and his hope to the son. Montejo the Younger, bringing new vigor and his cousin (another Francisco de Montejo) to the cause, was successful in firmly establishing a town at Campeche, and another at Mérida (1542), and by 1546 (the year Martin Luther died in Germany) virtually all of the peninsula was under his control.

A few weeks after the founding of Mérida, the greatest of the several Maya leaders, Ah Kukum Xiú, head of the Xiú people, offered himself as Montejo's vassal, and was baptized. As was the custom, upon being baptized he took a new Christian name. Choosing what must have been the most popular name in the entire 16th century, he became—yes!—Francisco de Montejo Xiú. With the help of Montejo's troops he then accomplished his real objective, the defeat of the Cocoms. By allying his people with the Spaniards, Xiú signed the Cocoms' death warrant—but also his own and that of the Yucatecan Mayas as a free people.

The Fruits of Conquest

The population of the peninsula declined drastically in the following centuries as the result of warfare, disease, slavery and emigration.

Fray Diego de Landa, second bishop of Yucatán, studied the Mayan culture and language and, thus equipped, used this knowledge to eradicate as much of it as possible. It was he who ordered the mass destruction of the priceless Mayan codices, or "painted books," at Maní in 1562, only three of which survived.

INDEPENDENCE: Yucatán, controlled directly from Spain rather than from Mexico City, struggled along under the heavy yoke of Spanish colonial administration until the era of Mexican independence. In 1810 the Mexican War of Independence began with Father Hidalgo's famous "Cry of Dolores." With the success of the revolutionary effort in 1821, Spain signed a treaty with the newly independent country of Mexico. In that same year, the Spanish governor of Yucatán resigned, and Yucatán too became an independent country. Though it decided to join in a union with Mexico two years later, this period of Yucatecan sovereignty is an indication of the local spirit. That same spirit arose again in 1845 when Yucatán seceded from Mexico, unhappy with close control from Mexico City.

Rise of the Haciendas

With independence came important changes in landholding practices, and thus in the economy. Sugarcane and henequen cultivation were introduced on a large scale, and soon there arose a culture of vast landed estates, each of which employed hundreds of Mayas. The trick, according to the hacienda owners, was to keep them in debt, so much debt that they could never work their way out of it, and that is precisely what the owners did.

The same Mayas who provided virtual slave labor on the haciendas also served in Yucatán's armed forces which, in the light of later events, was very poor planning on the part of the oppressive hacienda owners. Having been issued weapons with which to defend independent Yucatán against attack from Mexico or the United States, the Mayas instead attacked their local oppressors. Thus, in 1847, began the War of the Castes.

WAR OF THE CASTES: The first target was Valladolid, which was attacked, looted, and sacked by the rebellious Mayas in the most horrible manner. It soon became apparent to all concerned that this was a race war, and the line was drawn between the Mayas on one side and those of Spanish blood on the other.

The Mayas, increasing their numbers with every victory, bought more guns and ammunition from British merchants in Belize (British Honduras). By June 1848 they held virtually all of

Yucatán except Mérida and Campeche—and Mérida's governor had already decided to abandon the city. Feeling sure they had won the war, the rebel fighters went off to do something equally important: plant the corn. In the meantime reinforcements arrived from Mexico, which sent this aid in exchange for Yucatán's resubmission to Mexican authority. Government troops took the offensive, and things went badly for the Mayas. Many retreated to the wilds of Quintana Roo, in the southeastern reaches of the peninsula.

The Talking Crosses

Then came the Talking Crosses. Massed in southern Quintana Roo, the Mayas needed inspiration in their war effort. It came in the form of a cross that "spoke." The cult was begun in 1850 by a Mayan ventriloquist and a mestizo "priest," and carried on a tradition of "talking idols" which had flourished for centuries in several places, including the sacred Mayan island of Cozumel. The first appearance of the loquacious symbol was at a place which later became the town of Chan Santa Cruz, named "Little Holy Cross" in its honor. Soon several crosses were talking, inspiring the Mayas to go out and get the whites.

This worked pretty well until about 1866, when the fighting subsided. The Yucatecan authorities seemed content to let the rebels and their talking crosses rule the southern Caribbean coast, which they did with only minor skirmishes until the late 1800s. The rebel government received arms from the British in Belize, and in return allowed the British to cut lumber in rebel territory.

The End

But at the turn of the century, Mexican troops with modern weapons penetrated the rebel territory, soon putting an end to this bizarre, if romantic, episode of Yucatecan history. The town of Chan Santa Cruz was renamed in honor of a Yucatecan governor, Felipe Carrillo Puerto, and Yucatán was finally a full and integral part of Mexico, just in time for the Mexican Revolution.

THE MEXICAN REVOLUTION: From 1877 to 1911 the prime role in the drama of Mexico was played by an emotional strongman named Porfirio Díaz. Hailed by some as a modernizer, he was a terror to his enemies and to anyone who stood in his way or challenged his absolute power. He was finally forced to step down in 1911 by Francisco Madero and the greater part of public opinion.

The fall of the Porfirist dictatorship only led to more trouble, however. The country was split among several factions, including those led by "Pancho Villa" (real name Doroteo Arango), Alvaro Obregón, Venustiano Carranza, and Emiliano Zapata. The turbulent era from the fall of Porfirio Díaz through the next ten years is referred to as the Mexican Revolution. Drastic reforms were proposed and carried out by the leaders in this period, and the surge of vitality and progress from this exciting if turbulent time has inspired Mexicans down to the present day. Succeeding presidents have invoked the spirit of the Revolution, and it is still studied and discussed.

THE 20th CENTURY: After the turmoil of the revolution, Mexico sought stability. It came in the form of the *Partido Revolutionario Institutional (el PRI,* pronounced ell-*pree),* the country's dominant political party. With the aim of "institutionalizing the revolution," the PRI literally engulfed Mexican society, leaving little room for vigorous, independent opposition. For over half a century, the monolithic party has had control of the government, labor unions, trade organizations, and other centers of power in Mexican society.

The most outstanding Mexican president (1934–1940) of the century is without doubt General Lázaro Cárdenas. A vigorous and effective leader, Cárdenas broke up vast tracts of agricultural land and distributed parcels to small cooperative farms called *ejidos;* reorganized the labor unions along democratic lines; and provided funding for village schools. His most famous action was the expropriation of Mexico's oil industry from U.S. and European interests. The expropriated assets became Petroleros Mexicanos (Pemex), the enormous government petroleum monopoly.

The PRI has selected Mexico's president (and, in fact, virtually everyone else on the government payroll) from its own ranks after Cárdenas, the national election being only a confirmation of the choice. Among these men have been Avila Camacho, who continued many of Cárdenas's policies; Miguel Alemán, who expanded national industrial and infrastructural development; Adolfo López Mateos, who expanded the highway system and increased hydroelectric power sources; and Gustavo Díaz Ordaz, who provided credit and technical help to the agricultural sector.

In 1970, Luis Echeverría came to power, followed in 1978 by José López Portillo. During their presidencies there emerged a studied coolness in relations with the United States and an activist role in international affairs. This period also saw an increase in charges of large-scale corruption in the upper echelons of Mexican society. The corruption, though endemic to the system, may have been fostered by the river of money that began to flow into Mexican banks (and Mexican pockets) because of the precipitous rise in oil prices. As oil income skyrocketed, Mexican borrowing and spending did likewise. Virtually all bankers, economists, and politicians saw the rise in oil prices as permanent. When, in the 1980s, oil prices dropped as fast as they had risen, Mexico was left with an enormous debt to foreign banks, and serious deficiencies in its infrastructure.

MEXICAN FACTS AND FIGURES: The United Mexican States today is headed by an elected president and a bicameral legislature. It's divided into 31 states, plus the Federal District (Mexico City). The population of about 70 million is 15% white (descendants of the Spaniards); 60% mestizo, or mixed Spanish and Indian blood; and 25% pure Indian (descendants of the Mayas, Aztecs, and other peoples). Although Spanish is the official language, about 50 Indian languages are still spoken, mostly in the Yucatán peninsula and the mountainous region of Oaxaca. Economically, Mexico is not by any means a poor country. Only about a sixth of the economy is in agriculture. Mining, which made the Spanish colonists and their king fabulously rich, is still fairly important. Gold and silver account for some of it, and there are many other important minerals still mined, but the big industry today is oil. Mexico is also well industrialized, manufacturing textiles, food products, everything from tape cassettes to automobiles.

In short, Mexico is well into the 20th century, with all the benefits and problems that contemporary life brings, and although vast sums are spent on education and public welfare (much, much more than is spent on implements of war), a high birth rate, high unemployment, and unequal distribution of wealth show that much remains to be done.

ABOUT YUCATÁN: Contrary to popular belief, which places Yucatán in the extreme southeast of Mexico, the land of the Mayas forms the far east-central part of the Republic. A look at the map reveals that the Yucatecan capital, Mérida, is north of such major population centers as Mexico City, Guadalajara, Puebla, and Veracruz. Mérida is also surprisingly close to the tip of Florida: from Mexico City to Mérida it's about 600 miles as the crow flies, and from Mérida to Miami it's a mere 675 miles.

Actually there are two Yucatáns—the peninsula and the state.

The peninsula is the piece of land north of Hwy. 186 which extends from Francisco Escárcega to Chetumal, and includes part of the state of Campeche and all of the state of Yucatán, plus most of the state of Quintana Roo. The Yucatán state is a wedge-shaped entity that includes Mérida and many of the best archeological sites.

Preparing for Your Trip

LEGAL DOCUMENTS: You'll need a Mexican Tourist Card, issued free, available at the border, at a Mexican consulate, or at any of the Mexican tourist offices listed below. Those flying to Mexico can ask their travel agent or airline to get them a Tourist Card; most agents will do so at no extra charge.

The Tourist Card is more important than a passport in Mexico, so hold onto it carefully—if you lose it, you may not be able to leave the country until you can replace it, and that bureaucratic hassle takes several days or a week at least.

To get your Tourist Card, be sure to bring along a birth certificate, passport, or naturalization papers when you apply, and when you travel in Mexico. You'll also need this proof of citizenship to reenter the U.S. or Canada. Minors under the age of 18 when traveling alone must have a notarized statement of parental consent *signed by both parents* before they can get a permit. One parent entering Mexico with a minor child must have written consent from the other parent. Check with the nearest Mexican tourist office for details.

Important Note: A Mexican Tourist Card can be issued for up to 180 days, and although your stay south of the border will doubtless be less than that, you should get the card for the maximum time, just in case. When the official who fills out your card asks you how long you intend to stay, say "six months," or at least *twice* as long as you really plan to be there. Who knows? You may find the perfect stretch of beach and not want to leave, or you may have to stay for some reason, and you'll save yourself *a lot* of hassle if you don't have to renew your papers. This hint is especially important for people who take cars into Mexico.

Mexican government tourist offices abroad include those in the following cities in the United States and Canada:

Chicago: 2 Illinois Center, 233 N. Michigan Ave., Suite 1413, Chicago IL 60601 (tel. 312/565-2785).

Houston: 2707 N. Loop West, Suite 450, Houston TX 77008 (tel. 713/880-5153).

Los Angeles: 10100 Santa Monica Blvd., Suite 225, Los Angeles CA 90067 (tel. 213/203-8151).

Montréal: 1 Place Villa-Marie, Suite 2409, Montréal PQ H3B 3M9 (tel. 514/871-1052).

Toronto: 181 University Ave., Suite 1112, Toronto ON M5H 3M7 (tel. 416/364-2455).

RESERVE IN ADVANCE FOR HOLIDAYS: Those planning to be in the Yucatán on major holidays (Mexican as well as international) should definitely write ahead for hotel reservations. Christmas and New Year's are the worst for crowding. If you discover you're up against a holiday when you're almost there, plan to arrive in the resort early in the day—before noon—and see what you can find. Here's a suggestion: write for reservations in plenty of time, saying in your letter that you'll forward a deposit upon receipt of a confirmation. Or, instead, place a telephone call to the hotel concerned, make the reservation, get the name of the person who takes the reservation, and then send your deposit by registered mail, return receipt requested. Remember that the process can take a good deal of time.

WEATHER, CLOTHING, PACKING: Virtually every day, Yucatán is hot. During the dry season (late October through mid- or late May), the days start out hot and get hotter so that by midafternoon the only place to be is on the beach or in an air-conditioned room. April is definitely the hottest month of the year.

During the rainy season (mid-May through mid-October), there are often daily showers, usually in the afternoon, but these bring little relief from the heat; rather, they add high humidity to the hot air. Since virtually all of Yucatán is flat jungle, there's no escaping to the mountains for a breath of cool air.

Light, airy cotton clothing should make up most of your wardrobe. Though visitors to Cancún like to dress up in the evening, jacket-and-tie formality is almost unheard of. Instead, men wear the dressy square-tailed shirt called *guayabera,* which is not tucked into the trousers. It's cool, handsome, and on sale throughout Yucatán. Women will likewise find lots of cotton fashions on sale, in case your wardrobe has a preponderance of winter woolens.

Everyone who visits Yucatán should have a hat, plus suntan lotion, without fail. The sun is relentless, and you will be spending lots of time bathed in it, whether you want to or not, clambering up Maya temples, strolling the shopping streets, relaxing on the beach, waiting for buses or taxis, or on boats. You've got to have protection. Also bring some insect repellant. If you spend most of your time at the beach in Cancún you may not need it, but if you venture into the jungle at all (which you will), it'll come in handy.

As for shoes, sandals are the footwear of choice, but you should also have sneakers or running shoes which cover your whole foot. You'll need them when you climb those temples, or stroll into the jungle for a look around. All sorts of shoes and sandals are readily available at shops throughout Yucatán.

Will you need a sweater? Believe it or not, you might. In the evening, with a sea breeze blowing, it can become cool. After a day in the sun the contrast can be striking, and you'll want a light sweater to stay warm.

TRAVELING WITH CHILDREN: With Mexico's high birth rate, small children make up a large part of the population. The Mexican government has big programs to promote children's well-being. You should check with your doctor at home, and get advice on medicines to combat diarrhea, etc. Bring a supply, just to be sure. If your child is an infant, you'll be happy to know that disposable diapers are made and sold in Mexico (one popular brand is Kleen Bebé). The price is about the same as at home, though the quality is not quite so high. Also, Gerber's baby foods are on sale in many stores. In addition to the foods you're used to, you'll see "exotic" ones such as mango and papaya! Dry cereals, powdered formulas, baby bottles, purified water—they're all available easily in the larger cities.

The one problem you may encounter is with cribs. Except for the largest and most luxurious hotels, few Mexican hotels will have cribs, so you should be prepared to manage some other way.

HEALTH AND MEDICAMENTS: Of course, the very best ways to avoid illness or to mitigate its effects are to make sure that you're in top health and that you *don't overdo it*. Travel, strange foods, upset schedules, overambitious sightseeing tend to take more of your energy than a normal working day, and missed meals provide less of the nutrition you need. Make sure you get three good, wholesome meals a day, get *more* rest than you normally do, don't push yourself if you're not feeling in top form, and you'll be able to fight off Traveler's Diarrhea.

How to Prevent Traveler's Diarrhea

Traveler's Diarrhea is the name given to the pervasive diarrhea, often accompanied by fever, nausea, and vomiting, that attacks so many visitors to Mexico on their first trip. Doctors say it's not just one "bug," or factor, but a combination of different food and water, upset schedules, overtiring, and the stresses that accompany travel. I've found that I get it when I'm tired and careless about what I eat and drink. A good high-potency (or "therapeutic") vitamin supplement, and even extra vitamin C, is a help; yogurt is good for a healthy digestion, but it is not available everywhere in Mexico.

The U.S. Public Health Service recommends the following measures for prevention of Traveler's Diarrhea:

Drink Only Purified Water: This means tea, coffee, and other beverages made with boiled water; canned or bottled carbonated beverages, including carbonated water; beer and wine; or water that you yourself have brought to a rolling boil or otherwise purified. To purify water you can add five drops of 2% tincture of iodine to clear water; for cloudy water, strain it through a clean cloth, then add ten drops of 2% tincture of iodine. You can also purify water with tetraglycine hydroperiodide tablets sold under brand names such as Globaline, Potable-Agua, or Coughlan's. Pick them up in a pharmacy or sporting goods store.

Choose Food Carefully: In general, avoid salads, uncooked vegetables, and unpasteurized milk or milk products (including cheese). Choose food that is freshly cooked and still hot. Peel fruit yourself. Don't eat undercooked meat, fish, or shellfish.

What To Do If You Get It

The Public Health Service does not recommend that you take any medicines as preventatives. All the applicable medicines, including antibiotics, bismuth subsalicylate (as in Pepto-Bismol) and difenoxine (as in Lomotil) can have nasty side-effects if taken for long periods of several weeks. The best way to prevent illness is to take care with food and water, get rest, and don't overdo it.

Should you get sick, there are lots of medicines available in Mexico which can harm more than help. You should talk with your doctor before you go, and ask what medicine he recommends for Traveler's Diarrhea. Ask the doctor's opinion of these treatments:

Bismuth subsalicylate ("Pepto-Bismol"), one ounce of liquid or the equivalent in tablets, every half hour, for four hours (if you have kidney problems, or are allergic to salicylates, this can be dangerous).

Diphenoxylate and loperamide (Lomotil, Imodium), synthetic

opiates known as antimotility agents, should not be used if you have a high fever, or blood in the stool, and should not be used longer than two full days.

As for antibiotics, the Public Health Service guidelines are these: if there are three or more loose stools in an eight-hour period, especially with other symptoms such as nausea, vomiting, abdominal cramps, and fever, it might be time to go to a doctor and get an antibiotic. The ones usually prescribed, both available in Mexico if you haven't brought a supply, are doxycycline (100 mg twice daily); or trimethoprim (160 mg) / sulfamethoxazole (800 mg), known as TMP/SMX and sold in Mexico as Bactrim F (Roche), taken twice daily.

If someone recommends any other drug, be suspicious and get another opinion. These antibiotics are strong medicine; they can have significant and even dangerous side-effects, which is why you should consult with a doctor before taking them. Remember that what you have may not be Traveler's Diarrhea at all, and that such an antibiotic might not be the appropriate treatment. Also, antibiotics can cause reactions such as painful rashes when the skin is exposed to sunlight. In sunny Mexico, the last thing you want is hands that can't be exposed to the sun.

How To Get Well

Should you come down with Traveler's Diarrhea, the first thing to do is go to bed, stay there, and don't move on until it runs its course. Traveling with the illness only makes it last longer, whereas you can be over it in a day or so if you take it easy. Drink lots of liquids: tea without milk or sugar, or the Mexican *té de manzanilla* (chamomile tea), is best. Eat only *pan tostada* (dry toast rusks), sold in grocery stores and *panaderías* (bakeries). Keep to this diet for at least 24 hours, and you'll be well over the worst of it. If you fool yourself into thinking that a plate of enchiladas can't hurt, you'll be back at square one as far as the Traveler's Diarrhea is concerned.

The Public Health Service advises that you be especially careful to replace fluids and electrolytes (potassium, sodium, etc.) during a bout of diarrhea. Do this by drinking glasses of fruit juice (high in potassium) with honey and a pinch of salt added; and also a glass of pure water with one-quarter teaspoon of sodium bicarbonate (baking soda) added.

Bugs and Bites

Another thing you should consider is the bugs and bites. Mosquitoes and gnats are quite prevalent along the coast and in the lowlands of Yucatán. Insect repellent (*rapellante contra insectos*) is a must, and it's not always available in Mexico. Also, those sensitive to bites should pick up some antihistamine cream from a drugstore at home ("Di-Delamine" is available without a prescription). Rubbed on a fresh mosquito bite, the cream keeps down the swelling and reduces the itch. In Mexico, ask for "Camfo-Fenicol" (Camphophenique), a second-best remedy.

Most readers won't ever see a scorpion, but they are found in most parts of Mexico. Stings can be painful to dangerous (if you're particularly sensitive to the venom), and it's best to go to a doctor if you get stung.

THE LANGUAGE: Of course, not everyone in Yucatán speaks English (this isn't as silly as it sounds; these days English is taught in most Mexican schools), so it helps tremendously to have some basic vocabulary at your fingertips. For this, the Berlitz *Latin American Spanish for Travellers* Phrase Book, available at most bookstores, cannot be recommended highly enough. Frommer's *Fast 'n Easy Phrase Book* offers the best bargain of all—four languages (French, German, Italian, and Spanish) in one handy pocket-size book. *The American Express Pocket Guide to Spanish* is another useful possibility.

THE WAGES OF CHANGE: On the subject of money, it might be good to put in a word about prices and inflation. Back in the halcyon days (several decades ago) when prices throughout the world changed at a rate of about 3% a year, a traveler could take dad's copy of a good travel book abroad and make a mental adjustment for a small price rise. But recently the inflation rate for Mexico has been in the neighborhood of 100% per annum; some businesses (hotels and restaurants included) will hold off as long as they can, perhaps two years, and then raise prices by even more than this factor to compensate for *future* inflation! Every effort is made to provide the most accurate and up-to-date information in this book, even to the point of predicting price increases that I feel are on the way and that will arrive before the book reaches the reader's hands; but changes are inevitable and uncontrollable with inflation. Keep in mind when you look at price lists that even though the peso price may have risen over that given in the book, the dollar price will still be fairly accurate, and *the establishments recommended will still be the best value for the money*.

Speaking of currency, don't forget that the dollar sign ($) is used by Mexicans and some other Latin Americans to denote their own national currencies, and thus a Mexican menu will have "$300" for a glass of orange juice and mean 300 pesos. To avoid confusion I will use the dollar sign in this book *only* to denote U.S. currency. Peso prices will be listed merely with figures or with the qualifying word "pesos."

Chapter II

GETTING THERE AND GETTING AROUND

GETTING TO YUCATÁN is easy and not really very expensive. The peninsula is closer to many American cities than it is to many Mexican ones: it's almost as easy, and quick, to fly from Miami to Cancún or Cozumel as it is to fly from Mexico City to those same Yucatecan resort destinations.

Air travel is the method of choice for getting to Yucatán. The Mexican railroads south and east of the Isthmus of Tehuantepec run chronically behind schedule, the trains are uncomfortable, and incidents of theft are common. Though bus routes are operated efficiently, and ticket prices are surprisingly low, it's a very long haul of some 1,500 miles (2,300 km) along the shortest route from the border (Brownsville, Texas) to Mérida. The long, hot drive is the prime reason not to come by private car, also. And as of this writing, there are no regular passenger boat or car ferry services from, say, New Orleans or Florida to the Yucatán peninsula. So you'll probably get to Yucatán by air.

Going by Air

Air fares to Yucatán are an indisputable bargain, and you have a virtual smörgåsbord of opportunities from which to choose.

SCHEDULED FLIGHTS: Many scheduled airlines, including Aero-México, American, Continental, Lacsa, Mexicana, Republic and United, operate direct or nonstop flights to Cancún, Cozumel, and Mérida from Atlanta, Chicago, Dallas / Fort Worth, Denver, Houston, Los Angeles, Miami, New Orleans, New York, Philadelphia, San Antonio, San Diego, Washington, D.C., and Wichita. From many other cities there are convenient connecting flights.

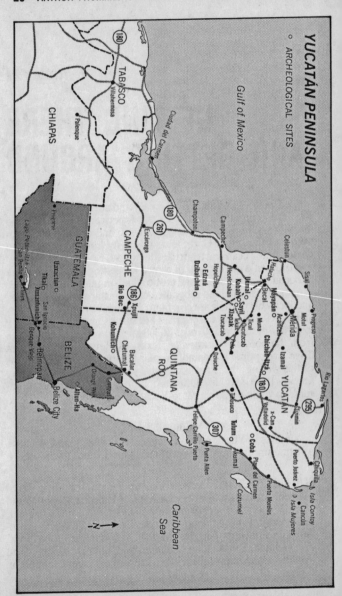

Excursions and package plans are offered for any preference, from a one-week, all-expenses-paid vacation to a two-month vagabond tour.

The Mexican national carriers, AeroMéxico and Mexicana, are both top-flight operations with high standards. Of the two, Mexicana is the smaller airline, and may have the edge on inflight service. These two companies are marketing their sunny destinations very aggressively, at very good prices for you. A travel agent can give you all the latest details, prices, and schedules at no cost.

THE HALF-AND-HALF ITINERARY: In these days of airline deregulation, it's not unusual to find very low fares in effect between two American cities. You can use this to your advantage. As airfares within Mexico are surprisingly cheap, you might be able to fly to a town on the U.S. side of the border (El Paso, Texas, for example, or San Diego, California), cross the border, and catch a domestic Mexican flight from Ciudad Juárez (or Tijuana) to Cancún. This sort of planning requires a cooperative travel agent, a willingness to experiment, and a sense of adventure, but airfare savings can be substantial. If your travel agent is unfamiliar with the procedure, you might call an airline directly for a reservation to the border, then call AeroMéxico or Mexicana for a reservation on the Mexican portion of your trip.

CHARTER FLIGHTS: Besides the scheduled flights, you should be aware that dozens of charter flights depart each week from many North American cities for Yucatán, and in many cases you can get in on the low charter fares whether or not you participate in a package tour. Here's how it works:

A company that organizes package tours signs a contract with an airline (either a scheduled carrier or a charter airline) to provide a certain number of seats on a particular date. The tour company then tries to fill the seats with its tour participants, but in many cases there are empty seats. Though the company would prefer that you buy the package deal, it prefers even more strongly that the seats in the plane not go empty, so the company will sell you a seat at a very, very good price.

Price is the advantage; the disadvantage is that you cannot easily change your mind. In most cases, once you've signed up for such a flight, you must depart and return on the dates designated. If you miss your flight, you cannot use your ticket on another flight. Your ticket becomes a worthless slip of paper. Let me hasten to add that tour companies which buy many seats on a regular basis (perhaps even one planeload a week) sometimes permit you to change your mind, and your travel dates, as long as you fly only on one of the company's flights.

PACKAGE TOURS: Speaking of package tour companies brings up the question of package tours: should you take one? The answer is a resounding "yes," if the tour resembles fairly closely the itinerary you desire. You could never equal the value of the services provided by arranging your own itinerary and staying in the same hotels. Tour companies bargain for wholesale rates on flights, hotels, meals, transfers, and sightseeing tours, and they pass some of these wholesale savings on to tour participants. A luxury hotel which charges $100 a night to the individual traveler may charge a tour company only $50 for the very same room on the very same day. So package tours can provide you with the most cost-effective way to see Yucatán.

I must add that signing up for a package tour can limit you to certain cities. If, for instance, you buy a package tour to Cancún, but you want to take an overnight trip to, say, Cozumel or Mérida, you'll have to pay out of your own pocket for hotels and meals in those places. Surprisingly, a package tour is often so cheap that it remains a bargain, even if you pay some of your own off-the-route expenses.

Some tour companies will sell you only those features of a tour which you desire. For instance, you can purchase the inexpensive charter air travel for a two-week trip, and four nights' hotel lodging in Cancún. On the fifth night you must pay for your own hotel, but by then you may be out on the road, visiting the ruins at Chichén-Itzá, shopping in Mérida's bustling market, or lazing on the beach in Cozumel. As tour companies tend to work with the more expensive hotels, you can often realize big savings by staying at more modest hostelries. Check with your travel agent for details of all these options. If you want to look into the details of charter flights and package tours yourself, get hold of a copy of *JAXFAX Travel Marketing Magazine,* the monthly "bible" of the charter air travel business. A travel agent may show you a current issue, or give you a past issue, or you can order a year's subscription for only $12 from the publisher, Jet Air Transport Exchange Inc., 280 Tokeneke Road, Darien, CT 06820.

Here are some examples of package tours to **Cancún,** offered from major U.S. cities by various tour companies. All include round-trip airfare and a week's lodging in a comfortable hotel, plus one or two meals a day. The lower price is charged during the summer, the higher price during the winter:

Atlanta	$459 to $759
Boston	$399 to $699
Chicago	$469 to $769
Dallas	$359 to $659
Los Angeles	$439 to $739
Philadelphia	$329 to $769
Washington, D.C.	$299 to $684

ARRIVING IN YUCATÁN: Arrival in Yucatán couldn't be easier. As you step out of the airplane and feel the warm Caribbean sun on your face, you'll know you've come to the right place.

Cancún, Cozumel, and Mérida all have attractive modern, efficient airports. The first Mexican official you'll encounter is the Immigration officer *(Migración),* who will stamp your Tourist Card and ask you to sign it on the back (you can save time by signing it in advance—he doesn't have to witness your signature). The official will keep one copy of the form, and you'll keep the other. Safeguard it carefully.

Next comes the Customs *(Aduana)* inspection, which is usually nothing more than spot checking. You may not even have to open your bags.

Currency exchange counters are often located within the Customs area (that is, in the same room in which you pick up your luggage). You cannot return to this room once you leave it, so decide now if you want to change some money into pesos. I suggest changing at least $50 into pesos to cover transportation, tips, and incidentals until you can get to a bank in town. If it's a holiday or a weekend, change more money because the banks will be closed. You can always change money at your hotel, but the exchange rate will be much worse than at a bank.

Rental car desks are located in the arrivals hall of each airport. You will also see a desk at which you can purchase tickets for seats in a minibus that drops passengers at any hotel or in the center of town. See the chapter on a particular destination for details and prices of this service.

THE DEPARTURE TAX: While on the subject of airports, you should be aware that Mexico levies a Departure Tax on all visitors who leave the country by air. It's roughly equivalent to US$10, and is payable after check-in and before security clearance on your return flight. Remember to save enough pesos to pay the tax. You can always exchange leftover pesos for dollars in the departure lounge after you've paid the tax, cleared security, and handed in your tourist card.

NOW THAT YOU'RE HERE: Having arrived safely in Yucatán, let's explore the possibilities of where to go, how to get there, and what to do. Here are some examples of how to see the fascinating dominion of the Mayas.

Touring Yucatán: Itineraries

Any good itinerary of Yucatán would involve the following elements:

Mérida: Spend at least overnight here; two full days to see the city would be much better. You can also use Mérida as your base for visits to Chichén-Itzá, Uxmal, Kabah, Sayil, Xlapak, Labná, and Loltún, taking organized tours or renting a car to tour on your own.

Uxmal: If you get as far as Mérida, seeing Uxmal is an absolute must! Traveling from Mérida, touring the ruins, and returning to the city will take the best part of a day. There are hotels at Uxmal where you can spend the night. Though well worth the money, they do exceed our daily budget limit.

Kabah, Sayil, Labná, Xlapak, Loltún: These Maya cities, south of Uxmal, demand another full day of touring time. If you stay overnight at Uxmal, you'll save travel time from Mérida.

Campeche, Edzná, Dzibilnocac, Hochob: Campeche, capital of the state of the same name, is a pleasant city with a charming walled colonial center. It's not a necessity on your Yucatán itinerary, but you may want to stay the night here if you're en route between Palenque and Mérida. Campeche is also the most convenient place to stay for those visiting the Maya sites at Edzná and Dzibalchén (Dzibilnocac and Hochob).

Chichén-Itzá: This is another must-see, the most impressive Maya city in Yucatán. You'd be well-advised to spend the night here, as there is a good range of hotels, with several in the budget category. If you take a day tour from Mérida or Cancún, you'll arrive and begin to climb pyramids at the very hottest, most crowded time of day, and you'll climb back into your bus for the two-hour return ride just when the light on the ruins is prettiest and the heat is abating. Plan to spend the night at Chichén-Itzá.

Cancún: You'll want to see this world-class resort, but you needn't plan to spend all of your beach time here. Prices are lower on nearby Isla Mujeres, and the skindiving and snorkeling are best on Cozumel (though Cozumel prices rival—even exceed —those of Cancún at times).

Isla Mujeres: Easily accessible from Cancún by city bus and ferry boat, this small island is great for a day-trip, or even for a stay of several days.

Caribbean coast: You'll certainly want to take a trip along the coast south of Cancún, certainly as far as the beautiful cove of Xel-ha and the Mayan seaport of Tulum. Inland from Tulum lies the ancient city of Cobá, well worth the detour if you have the time.

Cozumel: Mexico's entry into the Caribbean islands competition, it's a skindiver's paradise, which drives up prices in winter. Though larger than Isla Mujeres, Cozumel does not offer a greater variety of activities, and it's farther from the mainland.

TIME AND DISTANCE: You must become aware of the distances involved in a trip to Yucatán. For instance, a trip to Yucatán's nicest colonial city, Mérida, from the peninsula's premier resort, Cancún, involves a bus ride of five or six hours.

To help specifically in planning your trips **from Cancún,** here are some distances from that city to other Yucatecan points:

Belize City, 610 km (378 miles)
Chetumal, 390 km (242 miles)
Chichén-Itzá, 200 km (124 miles)
Cobá, 175 km (109 miles)
Felipe Carrillo Puerto, 230 km (143 miles)
Isla Mujeres Ferry Dock (Punta Sam), 10 km (6 miles)
Mérida, 320 km (199 miles)
Palenque, via Chetumal, 895 km (555 miles)
Palenque, via Mérida, 940 km (583 miles)
Playa del Carmen (Cozumel passenger dock), 68 km (42 miles)
Puerto Morelos (Cozumel car-ferry dock), 36 km (22 miles)
Tulum and Xel-Ha, 130 km (81 miles)
Uxmal, 400 km (248 miles)
Valladolid, 160 km (99 miles)
Villahermosa, via Chetumal, 1,200 km (744 miles)
Villahermosa, via Mérida, 1,240 km (769 miles)

You can touch on all the high points of Yucatán in a week of touring by rental car, but you'll be traveling fast. Ten days is a more reasonable period to spend, and two weeks is excellent. You can easily spend three weeks and even more if you plan to explore ruined Maya cities off the beaten track, or put in several hours of beach or pool time every day.

TEN DAYS TO TWO WEEKS: Here is a sample itinerary for a visit of ten days to two weeks, starting on the day you arrive in Mérida:

Day 1, Mérida: On the day of arrival, plan to settle in, get your bearings, perhaps change some money and adjust to the heat.

Day 2, Mérida: Tour the city, stopping at each of the historic buildings near the Plaza Mayor, and along the Paseo de Montejo. Save some time for the market!

Day 3, Uxmal: If you're driving, you can stop at Mayapán on your way to Uxmal. These two sites, and perhaps a quick stop in Ticul, will fill your day. Return to Mérida for the night, or stay at Uxmal.

Day 4, Kabah, etc.: Spend the day touring sites of Kabah, Sayil, Labná, Xlapak, and the Grutas (caves) de Loltún. If you're absolutely fascinated by ruins and can't get enough, head for Campeche to spend the night, then spend the next day at Edzná, Dzibilnocac, and Hochob. Otherwise return to Mérida.

Day 5, Chichén-Itzá: Ride from Mérida through henequen country to Chichén-Itzá. Find a hotel room, have lunch, perhaps take a nap, then hike out to the ruins and tour until closing time.

Day 6, Cancún: Spend the morning at the ruins of Chichén-Itzá, then ride to Cancún in the afternoon. Find a hotel and settle in.

Day 7, Cancún: Put on your bathing suit, catch a city bus, and head out to the Zona Hotelera. Spend the day on one of Cancún's fine beaches. In the evening, wander around the restaurants in town.

Day 8, Isla Mujeres: Get an early start, and spend the day on Isla Mujeres's beaches, especially Garrafón, with its good snorkeling and diving. Perhaps stay the night.

Day 9, Caribbean coast: Using Cancún or Cozumel as your base, visit Tulum, Xel-ha, and perhaps other beaches and sites along the coast between Tulum and Cancún. If you have a car, drive inland to Cobá also. By bus or hitchhiking, Cobá will take at least a full day by itself.

Day 10, Cozumel: Spend a day on Cozumel, taking the passenger ferry or the shuttle flight from Playa del Carmen, or a flight from Cancún.

BEST MEANS OF TRANSPORT: Touring Yucatán is best done by car, though this presents several problems. First and foremost, rental cars in Mexico as of this writing are breathtakingly expensive. For a week's rental of a VW Beetle, adding in the costs of unlimited mileage, insurance, tax, and gas, you might pay $300 to $350! If you have several people to share the cost, if you shop around and haggle a bit, and if it's not high season, the price becomes more reasonable.

Another caution is that roads are narrow, with virtually no shoulders or rest stops—just jungle on both sides. Though daytime driving is all right, you should not drive at night. I mean this! A way to cut the high cost of renting a car is to rent one only on certain days. For instance, touring from Mérida to Uxmal and Kabah, rent a car. But from Mérida to Chichén-Itzá and Cancún, take the bus—or even fly. From Cancún, take the ferry to Isla Mujeres, or the bus to the ferry for Cozumel, but rent a car for a day to see Xel-ha, Tulum, and Cobá. This involves more paperwork, but if a car costs $50 or $60 per day, you don't want it sitting around unused. For more detailed information on car rentals, see Chapter XIII.

Of course, the bus is by far the most economical transport. Prices are incredibly low, less than $1 for an hour's travel. Although the buses go everywhere, you will spend a lot of time waiting at highway intersections, particularly near Uxmal, Kabah, etc., and along the Caribbean coast. Hitchhiking doesn't help too much, as traffic is usually light. If you plan to take buses exclusively, you must allow at least two weeks to see Yucatán thoroughly.

DRIVING IN MEXICO: Cardinal rule: **Never drive at night if you can avoid it.** The roads aren't good enough, the trucks and carts and pedestrians and bicycles usually have no lights, you can hit potholes, animals, rocks, dead ends, bridges out with no warning. Enough said.

Indeed, get used to the fact that people in the countryside are not good at judging the speed of an approaching car, and often panic in the middle of the road even though they could easily have reached the shoulder. It's not rude to use your horn if it may save someone from injury.

Road Signs

Here are the most common ones:

Camino en Reparación	Road Repairs
Conserva Su Derecha	Keep Right
Cuidado con el Ganado, el Tren	Watch Out for Cattle, Trains
Curva Peligrosa	Dangerous Curve
Derrumbes	Earthquake Zone
Despacio	Slow
Desviación	Detour
Disminuya Su Velocidad	Slow Down
Entronque	Highway Junction

Escuela	School (Zone)
Grava Suelta	Loose Gravel
Hombres Trabajando	Men Working
No Hay Paso	Road Closed
Peligro	Danger
Puente Angosto	Narrow Bridge
Raya Continua	Continuous [solid] White Line
Tramo en Reparación	Road Under Construction
Un Solo Carril a 100 m.	One-lane Road 100 Meters Ahead
Zona Escolar	School Zone

Also *Topes,* or a sign with a drawing of a row of little bumps on it, means that there's a row of speed bumps across the road placed there by the authorities to slow you down through towns or villages. Slow down when coming to a village whether you see the sign or not—sometimes they install the bumps but not the sign!

Kilometer stones on main highways register the distance from local population centers. There is always a shortage of directional signs, so check quite frequently that you are going on the right road.

The Green Patrols

The Mexican government sponsors an admirable service whereby green, radio-equipped repair trucks manned by uniformed, English-speaking officers patrol the major highways during daylight hours to aid motorists with troubles. Minor repairs and adjustments should be free of charge, although you pay for parts and materials if you have need of these "Green Angels."

Minor Accidents

Most motorists think it best to drive away from minor accidents if possible. You are at a distinct disadvantage without fluent Spanish when it comes to describing your version of what happened. Sometimes the other descriptions border on mythology, and you may end up spending days straightening out things that were not even your fault. In fact, fault often has nothing to do with it.

Parking

I use pay parking lots in cities, especially at night, to avoid annoyances such as broken antennas, swiped emblems, or break-ins. Never leave anything within view inside your locked car on the street (day or night), for Mexico has thieves like everyplace else. Another good reason to use pay parking lots is that you avoid parking violations, and when a cop in Mexico finds you parked illegally, and knows you may ignore a ticket, he'll take out his pliers and screwdriver and remove your license plate and take it to the station house. When pay lots are not available, dozens of small boys will surround you as you stop, wanting to "watch your car for you." Pick the leader of the group, let him know you want him to guard it, and give him a peso or two when you leave. Kids may be very curious about the car and may look in, crawl underneath, or even climb on top, but they rarely do any damage.

Mexican Roads

Most Mexican roads, although quite sufficient, are not up to northern standards of smoothness, hardness, width of curve or grade of hill, or safety marking. You will have to get used to the spirited Latin methods, which tend to depend more on flair and good reflexes than on system and prudence. Be prepared for new procedures, as when a truck flips on his left-turn signal when there's not a crossroad for miles. He's probably telling you that the road's clear ahead for you to pass—after all, he's in a position to see better than you are. How do you tell that's what he means, and not that he intends to pull over on the left-hand shoulder? Hard to say.

Getting Gas

Along with Mexico's economic difficulties has come a return to highway robbery at the pumps. Though many service station attendants are honest and above-board, a surprising number are not. Here's what to do when you have to fuel up:

Drive up to the pump and get close enough so that you will be able to watch the pump run as your tank is being filled. Check that the pump is turned back to zero, go to your fuel filler cap and unlock it yourself, and watch the pump and the attendant as the gas goes in. By the way, it's good to ask for a specific peso amount rather than saying "full." This is because the attendants tend to overfill, splashing gas on the car and anything within range.

As there are always lines at the gas pumps, attendants often finish fueling one vehicle, turn the pump back quickly (or don't turn it back at all), and start on another vehicle. You've got to be looking at the pump when the fueling is finished, because it may show the amount for only a few seconds. This "quick draw" from car to car is another good reason to ask for a certain peso-amount of gas. If you've asked for 3,000 pesos' worth, the attendant can't charge you 3,500 for it.

Once the fueling is complete, *then* you can let the attendant check your oil, or radiator, or put air in the tires. Do only one thing at a time, be with him as he does it, and don't let him rush you. Get into these habits, or it'll cost you.

If you get oil, make sure that the can that is tipped into your engine is a full one. If in doubt, have the attendant check the dipstick again after the oil has supposedly been put in.

Check your change, and don't let them rush you.

Check that your locking gas cap is back in place.

Don't depart from a major town or city except with a full or near-full tank of gas. Yucatán is a big area, and service stations are not quite as frequent as in other countries. It's wise to keep the gas tank pretty full at all times.

All gasoline in Mexico is sold by the government-owned **Pemex** (Petroleras Mexicanas) company. Nova (81 octane) costs about 70¢ per gallon. Nova is leaded gasoline *(con plomo)*, and comes from the blue pump; Extra is a high-octane unleaded *(sin plomo)* gasoline, from the silver pump, but you will rarely find it available; the red pump is for diesel fuel, which costs about 45¢ a gallon. In Mexico fuel and oil are sold by the liter, so, a liter being slightly more than a quart, 40 liters equal about 10½ gallons.

No credit cards are accepted for gas purchases, so be prepared to pay in cash.

Chapter III

CANCÚN:
THE MEGA-RESORT

A VIEW OF CANCÚN from the air reveals a vast country-club layout: wide tree-lined streets, golf courses, emerald lawns, yachts at anchor. But not too long ago this huge and phenomenally successful resort was nothing more than unbroken jungle, wide unpopulated beaches, and crystalline blue water.

The Mexican government, having seen how successful Acapulco was in luring foreign visitors (and their dollars) south of the border, decided to build a brand-new world-class resort from scratch. Government planners fed data about various sites into a computer, and out popped the magic word: Cancún.

Plans for the resort were ambitious, and thoroughly Mexican in their audacity. The resort's "Touristic Zone," where most of the development would take place, was to be a 14-mile-long spit of sand called Isla Cancún, just off the coast near the sleepy village of Puerto Juárez. To house the workers (and later the resort's service personnel), a modern planned town for 70,000 people would be built on the mainland at the northern end of the sand spit. The southern end of the sand spit would be connected to the mainland by a causeway. On the mainland where the causeway came ashore would be an international airport capable of taking wide-body jets.

That was the dream, and it all came true in an astoundingly short period of time. Crowds of sunseekers flocked to Cancún as soon as the airport was finished and the first hotels opened, and the flocks have now turned to a flood. The influx has changed the whole vacation travel pattern in Yucatán. Whereas most visitors used to begin their Yucatecan adventure in Mérida, most now head for Cancún first.

What makes Cancún the perfect site for a resort? The land is the beautiful Yucatecan jungle, the long sand spit is perfect for seaside hotels, and the beaches are covered in a very fine sand that has been called "air-conditioned" by its ingenious promoters. Mayan ruins at Tulum, Chichén-Itzá, and Cobá are a short drive away, and for a change of scene the older resorts of Isla Mujeres and Cozumel are close at hand. The Caribbean waters are incredibly blue and limpid, temperatures (both air and water) are just right, and the coral reefs and tropical climate guarantee brilliant underwater life, good snorkeling, and fine scuba-diving.

GETTING AROUND: Though it costs more here than in most Mexican cities, there's plenty of transport available.

From the Airport

Special minibuses run from Cancún's international airport into town for 830 pesos ($1.66) per person. As of this writing, minibus service is one way only, and you'll have to hire a taxi for twice that amount to get back to the airport.

Note that if you are in a group or family of more than two people, you can do better by taking a taxi instead of a minibus. Rates for a cab from the airport to the Zona Hotelera are 1,800 pesos ($3.60) for one person, 2,000 pesos ($4) for up to four persons.

By Bus

In town, almost everything's within easy walking distance. The only places you need take buses to are the beaches near the luxury hotels in the Zona Turística, and to Puerto Juárez / Punta Sam for ferries to Isla Mujeres. City buses will trundle you from your in-town hotel out to the beaches of the Zona Turística for a ridiculously low fare. These "Ruta 1" buses operate every 15 minutes or so along the Avenida Tulum, Ciudad Cancún's main street, all the way to Punta Nizuc at the far end of the Zona Turística.

As for Puerto Juárez / Punta Sam, catch a Ruta 8 (to Puerto Juárez and Punta Sam) bus along Cancún's main street, Avenida Tulum, and the bus will take you straight to the ferry docks for 80 pesos (16¢). A taxi costs 600 pesos ($1.20).

By Taxi

The city fathers have instituted an authorized table of taxi fares, but in any case it's best to make a deal on a fare in advance. From Ciudad Cancún out to, say, the Hotel Camino Real should cost 500 pesos ($1); a short ride between two of the big hotels, less than 350 pesos (70¢); from Ciudad Cancún to the airport, 450 pesos ($2.90).

By Moped

You'll see lots of moped (motorbike) rental places in Cancún, particularly out in the Zona Hotelera. Fees for a day's rental can range from 3,000 to 6,000 pesos ($6 to $12). The lowest rates come from the guys who have set up shop on a piece of sidewalk: no phone, no desk, no address, just a few mopeds and a folding chair. Highest rates are from legitimate agencies with a phone number you can call in case of emergency or breakdown. They usually have newer bikes in better repair.

When you rent, try to get a discount if it looks like business is slow. You will have to pay the estimated rental in advance, and perhaps leave your driver's license as security for the moped. You should receive a crash helmet and a lock and chain with the rental.

Mopeds are a fine way to cruise around the Zona Hotelera, but they're not really good for trips to and from town, or for any distances over a few kilometers. The bike path which borders the roadway between the Zona Hotelera and the town is in bad disrepair in many spots, so you must ride cautiously and slowly. The alternative—riding in the roadway itself—pits you against hundreds of would-be Latin Grand Prix racers in beat-up Datsuns, not a cheery prospect.

By Calesa

An alternative to the expensive car and the somewhat dangerous and unwieldy moped is the *calesa,* which in Cancún means a little two- or four-person horseless carriage. These antique-style putt-putts rent for 5,800 or 7,650 pesos ($11.60 or $15.30) per hour, up to 15,750 or 21,150 pesos ($31.50 or $42.30) for a full day until 6 p.m. These prices, for two- and four-seat models respectively, include gas, mileage, tax, and insurance. Rent one in the parking lot next to the Plaza Caracol shopping mall, between the Viva and Krystal hotels (no phone).

ORIENTATION: Here's the layout. Ciudad Cancún, the new town on the mainland, has banks, travel and airline agencies, car rental firms, restaurants, hotels, and shops, all within an area about nine blocks square. The main thoroughfare is Avenida Tulum. Heading south, Avenida Tulum becomes the highway to the airport, Tulum, and Chetumal; heading north, it joins the Mérida–Puerto Juárez highway.

The Zona Hotelera, or Zona Turistica, stretches out along the former Isla Cancún (Cancún Island), a sandy strip 14 miles long,

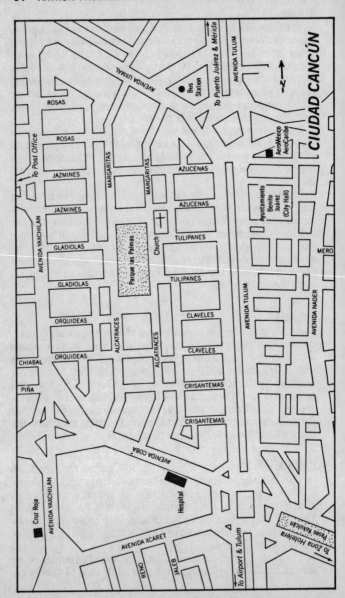

shaped like a "7." Now joined by bridges to the mainland at north and south, it is an island no longer. Cancún's international airport is just inland from the base of the "7."

A Note on Addresses

Starting with a clean slate, one would think the city fathers of Ciudad Cancún would have laid out a street-numbering system that was simple and easy to use, but such has not been the case. Addresses are still often given by the number of the building lot and by the *manzana* (city block). Some streets have signs with names on, although the establishments along the street may refer to the street only by its number, as Retorno 3, etc. In short, it is very difficult to find a place in Ciudad Cancún just by the numbers. Luckily, the city is still relatively small and the downtown section can easily be covered on foot. I've tried to be very specific in my directions to recommended establishments. Your best companion in confusing Cancún is the map in this book.

USEFUL FACTS: The information below covers not only the location of banks, etc., but also transportation to and from Cancún. (See also Chapter 11.)

Airlines: Here's where to find them, and where they'll take you: **AeroMéxico** (tel. 988/4-2728 or 4-2639) is located at Avenida Tulum, corner of Avenida Uxmal, and they also have an office in the Centro Comercial El Parián, near the Convention Center; they operate daily flights between Cancún and Houston, Mérida, Mexico City, Monterrey, New York, and Villahermosa. **Mexicana** (tel. 988/4-1423) at Avenida Cobá 13, has daily non-stops between Cancún and Chicago, Dallas / Fort Worth, Guadalajara, Miami, Mexico City, and Philadelphia. **AeroCaribe** (tel. 988/ 4-1231 or 4-1364), in the same building as AeroMéxico, has six daily flights to Cozumel, so you can whiz over and back in a day easily; round-trip fare is 14,000 pesos ($28). **Aero Cozumel** (tel. 988/4-2562 at the airport) has a number of small prop planes that make trips between Cozumel and Cancún; see the section on Cozumel (below) for full details. **Lacsa,** the Costa Rican airline, has offices at Avenida Yaxchilan 5 (tel. 988/4-1276), in the Centro Comercial El Parián (tel. 988/4-2617), and at the airport (tel. 988/ 3-0103); go here for flights to New Orleans and to Central American destinations.

Banks: Most are downtown along the Avenida Tulum. There are also a few *casas de cambio* (exchange houses). In addition, you'll find downtown merchants particularly eager to change cash dollars, sometimes at very advantageous rates. In Cancún it's important to shop around for a good exchange rate. Many places, particularly hotels, will offer you absolutely terrible rates of exchange.

Buses (Intercity): Autotransportes del Caribe (BUS) is located across the street from the Hotel Plaza Caribe, downtown in Ciudad Cancún at the intersection of Avenidas Tulum and Uxmal. They run buses almost hourly from 6 a.m. to midnight on the route between Cancún and Mérida, stopping at Valladolid and Chichén-Itzá. There are both first- and second-class buses (each has its own ticket window and waiting room). Though second class is a bit cheaper, the buses are slower.

Consulates: The U.S. Consular Agent (tel. 988/4-2411) is in the office of Intercaribe Real Estate, Avenida Cobá 86, a block off Avenida Tulum going toward the Zona Hotelera. The agent's hours are Tuesday through Saturday from 10 a.m. to 2 p.m.; the office is open from 9 a.m. to 2 p.m. and from 4 to 8 p.m., Monday through Friday. In an emergency, call the U.S. Consulate in Mérida (tel. 992/5-5011).

Medical Care: Cruz Roja (Red Cross; tel. 4-1616), good for first aid, is on Avenida Yaxchilán near the intersection with Avenida Xcaret. For more serious ailments, head for the IMSS (Mexican Social Security Institute) Hospital (tel. 4-1108 or 4-1907), on Avenida Cobá at Avenida Tulum.

Post Office: The main post office (tel. 4-1418) is at the intersection of Avenidas Sunyaxchen and Xel-Ha, open 9 a.m. to 7 p.m. except Sunday.

Rental Cars: If you plan to visit other cities and beaches, plus major Maya ruins, the way to do it is to rent the cheapest car, a VW Beetle, for a week at the unlimited-mileage rate. Total cost for the week, including gas, insurance, rental fee, and IVA tax, might be $300, which comes out to $42.85 per day. As of this writing, only two companies—**Budget Rent-A-Car** and **Dollar Rent-A-Car**—offer this weekly unlimited-mileage rate, and in fact both of these franchises are owned and operated by the same Mexican firm. They have an office at the airport, and another downtown at the corner of Avenidas Tulum and Uxmal (tel. 988/4-1709), across from the Autobuses del Caribe bus terminal.

TOURIST INFORMATION: The official tourist office is in the City Hall ("Ayuntamiento Benito Juárez") on Avenida Tulum. You may find one of the several little information kiosks set up on busy sidewalks downtown attended by a helpful person as well. Lots of other people will offer to give you information, usually in exchange for listening to a spiel about the wonders of a Cancún time-sharing or condo purchase.

Pick up a copy of the monthly pocket-sized publication called *Cancún Tips*. It's handed out for free at the airport when you arrive, and is available downtown in several places. It's got lots of useful information, as well as fine maps. The publication sponsors information offices in several locations, stocked with well-informed personnel, brochures, and a collection of restaurant menus for browsing. The scheme is designed to benefit the publication's advertisers, of course, but these people and their booklet are very helpful nonetheless.

Where to Stay in Cancún

Despite its reputation for glamour, Cancún actually has a full range of accommodations, from the sybaritic high-rise right on the beach to tiny, spartan pensions. Prices, likewise, go from $200 per night right down to $2 per night. And luckily for the visitor, there are no gaps in this vast range. No matter how much you plan to spend on a room, you'll find a place that's exactly right for you.

Though your chosen hotel may have rooms at your price, you must make sure they also have a room reserved in your name. This is not much of a problem during the summer, which is off-season, when lots of rooms are available. But in December, January, and February, rooms in many hotels can be in short supply. If you plan to stay at one of the fancier places costing, say, $50 or more per night, you can have your travel agent make the reservation at no extra charge to you. As for the less expensive places, you'll have to make reservations yourself, by mail—allow lots of time!—or by phone.

Pricing details: Cancún, like other Mexican resorts, has a two-season price structure. December through April is the busy season, when prices are higher; during holiday periods (Christmas, New Year's, Easter) surcharges are added to the already high winter prices. You may get a slight reduction from the regular winter rates during the "mini-off-season" from January 2 through 21. True off-season is the warm period from May through November, when prices (especially in the most expensive hotels) are 25% to 40% lower than during the winter. Note also that the 15% Value-Added Tax (*Impuesto de Valor Agregado,* or IVA, pronounced "*ee*-bah") has already been included in the prices quoted below.

As Cancún is a planned resort aimed directly at the package-tour market, most of the larger hotels have similar services. In any hotel charging US$90 or more for a double room in winter ($65 in summer), you can expect to find several restaurants and

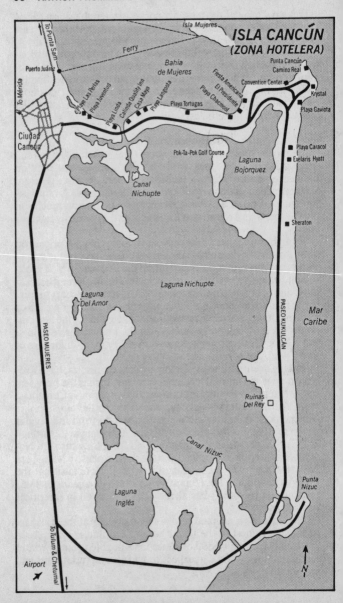

bars, a swimming pool with a swim-up bar, a beachfront location, air conditioning, color cable TV with satellite dish to receive U.S. programs, a balcony or terrace with water view on each room, and perhaps a self-serve "pay as you go" refrigerator bar in each room.

By the way, many of the most luxurious hotels quote their prices in U.S. dollars rather than in pesos.

THE TOP HOTELS (Doubles from $140): At the pinnacle of Cancún's lodging structure are these few luxurious places, ready, willing, and able to provide every service and comfort you might desire on a beach resort vacation.

Camino Real Cancún, Box 14, Cancún, Q. Roo 77500 (tel. 988/ 3-0100, or toll free 800/228-3000 in U.S.), right at the tip of Punta Cancún, is this resort's premier place to stay. Though it has a choice location, a lavish country-club layout, and dramatic architecture which inspired many other buildings at Cancún, it is not an enormous hotel. With 300 rooms, it is actually a bit smaller than some of its neighbors. Swimming and paddling possibilities include a beautiful fresh-water pool, a private salt-water lagoon, and a more or less private surf beach. The hotel has its own sailing pier and water sports center for sailboard and boat rentals, and other water sports, and also four of its own tennis courts. There's a bar for every mood: a swim-up bar in the pool, a lobby bar for people-watching, another for gazing at the Caribbean, yet another beneath a thatched roof for lazy afternoon cocktails. As for restaurants, you can choose from continental, Mexican, or Yucatecan cuisines. The rooms in the vaguely Mayan or Mycenaean slope-sided hotel are in lanai style, each with its own semi-private terrace. The price for all this luxury? Package deals give you the best value, but if you come on your own, you'll pay US$150 double in winter, $100 double in summer.

Cancún Sheraton Resort, Paseo Kukulcán, Cancún, Q. Roo 77500 (tel. 988/3-1988, or toll free 800/325-3535 in U.S.), a Mayan step-pyramid on its own vast stretch of surf beach south of Punta Cancún, has 476 luxurious rooms and suites, plus its own lighted tennis courts, fitness center, three swimming pools (one indoors), and shuffleboard. For sustenance, the Sheraton offers three restaurants and two bars, including a lobby bar with music for dancing. Rooms have views of the Caribbean (to the east) or of the lagoon (to the west); if you choose one of the suites, you'll find a private whirlpool bath waiting. For a standard room, the price is US$150 double in winter, US$104 in summer.

Exelaris Hyatt Regency Cancún, Box 1201, Cancún, Q. Roo 77500 (tel. 988/3-0966, or toll free 800/228-9000 in U.S.), at Punta

Cancún, has this resort's most dramatic architecture. Handsome but unremarkable from the outside, when you enter the hotel you'll find yourself at the bottom of a vast cylindrical court, the walls of which are festooned with greenery. The 300 guest rooms are entered from walkways overlooking the central space; once in your room, you'll head straight for the balcony to take in the sea view—every room has it. The list of services here is long: movies on closed-circuit TV, a nursery to look after the children, telex station, several bars, an Italian restaurant, and another restaurant specializing in seafood. The location at Punta Cancún puts you at the center of the action, within walking distance of the convention center, archeological museum, and many nightclubs, restaurants, and shops. The beach here is perhaps not as commodious as at other locations, but you needn't go far to find a better one. Rooms, single or double, cost US$150 in winter, $104 in summer. Note that there are two Hyatt hotels in Cancún.

Exelaris Hyatt Cancún Caribe, Paseo Kukulcán, Cancún, Q. Roo 77500 (tel. 988/3-0044, or toll free 800/228-9000 in U.S.), is the other Hyatt hotel in this resort, south of Punta Cancún. Because of its dramatic crescent shape, all rooms in this 202-room hotel face the sparkling Caribbean, and have terraces on which to enjoy the view. Between the hotel and the beach is a pool complex built to resemble a Mayan village—a very, very posh one! A replica of chac-mool gazes out to sea, like any sunbather. Though the other Hyatt is generally thought to be the snazzier place, the Cancún Caribe has recently renovated its lobby and restaurant. Prices here are almost the same as those at its sister establishment mentioned above.

Fiesta Americana Cancún, Paseo Kukulcán, Cancún, Q. Roo 77500 (tel. 988/3-1400, or toll free 800/223-2332 in U.S.), is unique among Cancún hotels. Instead of the up-to-the-minute architecture found in most Cancún buildings, the Americana is built to resemble the charming jumbled design of an Old World city street. Balconies and windows of different styles are placed at random on the façade, and a ground-floor arcade simulates a row of shops. Though the hotel is new and thoroughly luxurious and up-to-date, it echoes the charm of another time and place. All services are provided in the 286 guest rooms, including in-room movies, self-serve bar, Caribbean views, and purified water. The beach here is surf, but there's a veritable system of swimming pools (lots for kids), with one pool large enough to boast its own little island. Room rates in winter are US$140 single or double; in summer, $98.

Villas Tacul, Paseo Kukulcán (reservations: 924 Farmington Avenue, West Hartford, CT 06107; tel. 203/523-1609) is unique among Cancún hostelries. Here you find a private compound wonderfully landscaped with tropical flowers and shrubs. Accommodations are in private villas with two to five bedrooms. Facilities include a quiet stretch of beach and a lagoon-like swimming pool. You can have breakfast prepared for you in your villa each morning. For other meals, you visit independent restaurants nearby. Rates depend on the size of the villa (how many bedrooms) and the number of guests, but start at US$193 double, breakfast and tax included.

UPPER-BRACKET HOTELS (Doubles from $90):
Not as well known as the top hotels, yet in most respects just as comfortable and well-located, the following hotels charge slightly less for their rooms.

Krystal Cancún, Paseo Kukulcán, Cancún, Q. Roo 77500 (tel. 988/3-1133, or toll free 800/231-9860 in U.S., 800/521-2431 in Canada, 800/392-4671 in Texas), is right on Punta Cancún with the Camino Real and Exelaris Hyatt Regency, near the convention center and archeological museum, many shops, restaurants, and clubs. The 325 guest rooms have luxury appointments and water views. Should you decide to rent one of the penthouse suites, you'll get your own private swimming pool. The Krystal has lots of luscious, cool marble used in its decoration, a big swimming pool overlooking the Caribbean, several restaurants (including a Moroccan one), and Christine, one of the most popular discos in town. Other attractions include a health club, whirlpool bath, and racquetball court. For all this, and the convenient location, you pay US$138 single or double in winter, $92 in summer.

Hotel Beach Club Cancún, Paseo Kukulcán, Cancún, Q. Roo 77500 (tel. 988/4-1643), is not a hotel, not a condominium complex, not an apartment building, but a little bit of each. From the outside, it looks like a smaller but handsome and comfortable hotel, with a fine stretch of beach, swimming pools, health club, tennis courts, and the other diversions important to daily life in Cancún. In the lobby, it resembles a hotel, with shops, restaurants, and several bars (including that Cancún essential, a swim-up pool bar). But in the guest rooms, it resembles an apartment building, for each has a water view, whirlpool bath, kitchenette with refrigerator, color TV, and balcony. You can choose from four sizes of accommodations: standard rooms are the size of other hotels' junior suites, and rent for US$110 double; studios have two double beds in the bedroom, and a separate living room / kitchenette, for a few dollars more; two-bedroom apartments have separate living and dining rooms and two baths for US$173; and duplex penthouses have an upstairs master bedroom with private bath and large terrace, plus a downstairs bedroom with bath, a living room, and kitchenette, all for US$201. The Beach Club Cancún is just south of the Sheraton.

Casa Maya Hotel, Paseo Kukulcán, Cancún, Q. Roo 77500 (tel. 3-0555, or toll free 800/854-2026 in U.S.), is huge, dramatic, and imposing, a cross between a modern high-rise hotel and a Mayan pyramid. It's a popular lodging-place for tour groups, with the bustle and activity that groups bring. The 356 rooms are more like junior suites, each with its balcony, color cable TV featuring U.S. stations, and tropical decor. You can swim in the hotel's own huge pool, or on its beach, or play tennis on its own courts. Prices at the Casa Maya are $119 for a standard room, $159 for a suite.

Hotel Miramar Misión, Paseo Kukulcán, Cancún, Q. Roo 77500 (tel. 3-1755, or toll free 800/854-2026 in U.S., 800/542-6028 in California), is the Cancún incarnation of a popular Mexican hotel chain, a moderate-sized (225-room) hotel where, because of ingenious siting, each room has views of both the Caribbean and the lagoon. Two big swimming pools are right next to the beach (which bears several signs warning about undertow). One of the pools, the longest one in Cancún, has clever sunken lounge-chairs so you can lie back and relax right in the water; there's even a little sunken pedestal on which to perch your drink! Besides the necessary restaurants and bars, the Misión has a feature unique to the resort: an 18-hole miniature golf course. Rates here are US$111 in winter, $98 in summer.

Hotel Cancún Viva, Paseo Kukulcán, Cancún, Q. Roo 77500 (tel. 3-0108 or 3-0019, 905/553-5444 in Mexico City, or toll free 800/221-6509 in U.S.), member of a Mexican chain, has a blockhouse look from the street side. But on the ocean side you'll find a small but pretty patio garden and a beach which is fairly safe for swimming as the surf breaks farther out. All of the rooms face the sea, and have private balconies so you can enjoy the view. The 162 rooms at the Viva have all the little luxuries, from color cable TV through self-service refrigerator-bars, and the hotel has a pair of its own lighted tennis courts. The price for a room, single or double, is US$112 ($121 triple) in winter; $58 single or double, $65 triple in summer. You may be able to bargain for a slight discount during the "mini-off-season" of early to mid-January, when occupancy is lower.

Hotel Flamingo Cancún, Paseo Kukulcán, Cancún, Q. Roo 77500 (tel. 988/3-1544), seems to have been inspired by the dramatic slope-sided architecture of the Camino Real. But the Flamingo is considerably smaller, with 90 guest rooms forming a quadrangle or courtyard in which you'll find the swimming pool. Prices are not up to Camino Real levels, thank goodness. During the winter season, you pay US$127, $11 more for a third person. Rates in summer are $96 single or double.

Hotel Calinda Cancún Quality Inn, Paseo Kukulcán, Cancún, Q. Roo 77500 (tel. 988/3-1600, or toll free 800/228-5151 in U.S.), just beyond the first bridge when coming out from Ciudad Cancún, has 280 guest rooms, two-thirds of them facing the Caribbean, the others looking across the boulevard to the lagoon. Prices for the luxury rooms are $115 double in winter, $62 in summer. You can expect, and enjoy, all of the normal Cancún luxury hotel services here.

MODERATE-PRICE HOTELS (Doubles $60 to $90 in Winter): As I mentioned above, Cancún accommodations run the full price gamut. The following hotels are comfortable in every way, and luxurious in many ways, yet they cost substantially less than those described above. Locations and facilities are still extremely good. You can't go wrong at any of these choices.

Hotel El Presidente Cancún, Paseo Kukulcán 7, Cancún, Q. Roo 77500 (tel. 988/3-0200, or toll free 800/472-2427 in U.S.), is the 337-room representative of Mexico's largest hotel chain, noted for its luxury accommodations, excellent service, and moderate prices. Modern in design, but with many colonial and Mexican folk accents, El Presidente provides all of the things you'd expect: restaurants, bars, a good nightclub, two swimming pools, a more or less private and fairly safe beach, water sports facilities, lighted tennis courts, and air-conditioned rooms with private balconies. Why does it cost only US$72 single, $75 double, $93 triple to stay here in winter? Don't wonder, reserve a room! It's a great deal. In summer, rates are lower, and equally delightful compared to the competition. Coming from Ciudad Cancún, you'll reach El Presidente before you get to Punta Cancún.

Hotel Aristos Cancún, Box 450, Cancún, Q. Roo 77500 (tel. 988/3-0011), is a member of a Mexican chain with hotels in major resorts and in Mexico City. Their Cancún establishment has 268 rooms facing either the Caribbean or the boulevard, a nice wide stretch of beach one level below the pool and lobby, a marina with water sports equipment, lighted tennis courts, and a babysitting service. Three restaurants and as many bars provide sustinence, or you can help yourself to drinks from the self-service bar in your room. Best of all, rooms are priced at US$60 to $75 in winter, $48 to $55 in summer. Ask for a room with a sea view. The rooms facing the boulevard may be noisy.

Playa Blanca Hotel and Marina, Box 107, Cancún, Q. Roo 77500 (tel. 988/3-0344, 212/697-7424 in New York, or toll free 800/221-4726 in U.S.), has the distinction of being among the "older" hotels in Cancún. As no building here is very old, that means simply that the Playa Blanca's courtyard gardens have had time to mature. You'll love the greenery. Guest rooms have all the services found at the more expensive places, and guests can avail themselves of a similar list of services, including lighted tennis court, nice swimming pool, several restaurants and bars, and a night spot that provides the setting for various theme evenings: "Pirates' Night," "Mexican Fiesta," and the like. With 160 rooms and suites, the Playa Blanca is not big, and not small, but very pleasant, and priced at US$81 single, $92 double, $104 triple in winter, $20 to $25 less in summer.

EVEN LESS EXPENSIVE (Doubles $40 to $60 in Winter): Believe it or not, there are several smaller hotels, located right out there in the Zona Hotelera along with the big places, but charging less than half of the big prices. The hotels are smaller, the rooms are smaller, there are perhaps not as many services, but the mood can be more relaxed, and the staff less busy than at the places with 600 or 700 guests. The price at the following places is low, but the beach is just as beautiful, the air just as balmy. All of these hotels provide swimming pools, restaurants and bars, opportunities for all water sports, and comfortable air-conditioned rooms, most with terraces.

Club Caribe Cancún, Paseo Kukulcán, Cancún, Q. Roo 77500 (tel. 2-0811 or 3-0567), has just 85 rooms and suites on the three floors of its all-white buildings, grouped around a courtyard with a big swimming pool (and a smaller one for the children). The beach beyond is good and safe for swimming most of the time as it's not pounded directly by the surf. Two restaurants and a bar keep you happy at mealtimes, and a beach club with water-sports rental equipment can provide for the rest of the daylight hours. The hotel has its own private dock, fishing boats, and a sailboard school. For tennis or golf, you have privileges at the nearby Pokta-Pok country club. Room rates are 20,000 pesos ($40) double in winter for standard rooms; 12,500 to 15,000 pesos ($25 to $30) in summer. Suites, which come with a kitchenette, cost about 20% more.

Hotel Carrousel Cancún, Box 407, Cancún, Q. Roo 77500 (tel. 988/3-0513 or 3-0239), on Paseo Kukulcán not far out from Ciudad Cancún, looks fairly modest and unimpressive from the boulevard. But upon entering the hotel you discover its very pleasant gardens, nice pool, another pool for kids, and good safe swimming beach (very little surf). Every one of the 111 rooms and suites in the hotel has its own little balcony facing the Caribbean. Volleyball, paddle tennis, and badminton facilities are here, as is the opportunity for parasailing. That's the exciting sport in which you strap on a parachute and are towed by a motorboat until you're hundreds of feet in the air above the water. The hotel has a beach restaurant. For one of the air-conditioned rooms, you pay 23,000 pesos ($46) in winter, 16,000 pesos ($32) in summer, single or double.

Club Verano Beat, Paseo Kukulcán, Cancún, Q. Roo 77500 (tel. 988/3-0772), has architecture inspired by the Camino Real, with the swimming pool in a courtyard surrounded by the rooms and by nice (if small) gardens. Rustic thatch here and there adds a Yucatecan touch. Rooms, as usual, are air-conditioned and have balconies, and cost 19,000 pesos ($38) double in winter, 15,000 pesos ($30) in summer.

IN CIUDAD CANCÚN (Doubles $25 to $60 in Winter): All of the aforementioned hotels are located in the Zona Turistica, or Zona Hotelera, along Paseo Kukulcán on Isla Cancún. There are almost as many hotels located on the mainland, in Ciudad Cancún. Although the town can boast no five-star places, and few hotels have views of the water, the guest rooms are comfortable, air-conditioned, and surprisingly lower in price than beachfront rooms.

The in-town hotels are not on the beach, but most of the better ones have vans to shuttle guests to and from the beaches. Other facilities may be comparable to Isla Cancún hotels: restaurants and bars, discothèques, health clubs. A bonus is the easy walk to all of the independent shops, banks, restaurants, and nightspots in town.

Hotel América, Box 600, Cancún, Q. Roo 77500 (tel. 988/4-1500), on Avenida Tulum near the intersection with Brisa, is fairly large, quite plush, and fully equipped with a nice big swimming pool, arctic central air conditioning, a restaurant, coffee shop, and several bars. Except for the absence of the surf, you'd think you were on Isla Cancún. You can be out on the beach in minutes by shuttle van to the hotel's own beach club and marina. The América is about the most expensive place downtown, charging 27,600 pesos ($55.20) single, 29,900 pesos ($59.80) double, 31,625 pesos ($63.25) triple in winter, about $20 to $25 less in summer.

Hotel Plaza del Sol, Avenida Yaxchilán 31, Cancún, Q. Roo 77500 (tel. 988/4-3888), is part of a shopping and office complex near the intersection with Avenida Sunyaxchén. The 87 rooms each have two double beds, wall-to-wall carpeting, central air conditioning, telephone, and piped-in music; some have television. A small swimming pool takes care of that urge for a quick dip, and the hotel's shuttle van can whisk you out to the hotel's beach club in about ten minutes. Other services include a restaurant, coffee shop, lobby bar, pool bar, car rental desk, travel agency, and shopping arcade; there are at least a dozen other restaurants within a few minutes' walk. Winter rates are surprisingly reasonable: 17,500 pesos ($31.50) single, 17,500 pesos ($35) double, 19,250 pesos ($38.50) triple. Summer rates, as usual, are 20% to 30% lower.

Hotel-Suites Caribe Internacional, Avenida Yaxchilán 36, Cancún, Q. Roo 77500 (tel. 988/4-3999), at the corner with Avenida Sunyaxchén, has 80 rooms, junior and master suites, a swimming pool, snack bar, lobby bar, and guarded parking lot. Each room has a balcony overlooking the grassy traffic circle and the town. The hotel is modern, comfortable, and well located, but perhaps its biggest attraction is that you can rent as much space, for as many persons, as you like. In winter, one person pays 11,500 pesos ($23); two pay 17,000 pesos ($34) in a room, 21,000 pesos ($42) in a junior suite; three people in a junior suite costs 24,000 pesos ($48); five persons in a master suite costs 31,500 pesos ($63), or a mere $12.60 per person.

BUDGET HOTELS (Doubles $10 to $25 in Winter): It is truly astounding that a visiting couple can spend the night in this billion-dollar resort for as little as $10 per night, but so it is. For $10 to $25 you can get a double room with one or two beds (perhaps two double beds), private bath, ceiling fan, and perhaps even an air conditioner. The room may have little other furniture—a telephone, table and chair, perhaps, and a place to hang your clothes (but no hangers!)—and the hotel will have few other services. You won't find a swimming pool, or whirlpool, or shuttle vans to the beach, or nightclub. In the very cheapest hotels, the management gets away with cleaning the rooms only every other day or so. But if you're traveling on a budget, the chance to see Cancún on $10 a day is an indisputable bargain.

Here are Cancún's budget hotels, grouped by area so you can walk from one to the next, inspecting rooms, until you find one you like.

On and Off Avenida Tulum

Just off Avenida Tulum, entered from Calle Claveles 37, is the new **Antillano Hotel** (tel. 988/4-1532 or 4-1244). Modern wood-and-stucco in design, the Antillano has air-conditioned rooms that overlook the busy Avenida Tulum and also the side streets. Being one of the newer hotels downtown, it's decidedly a bit fancier, and includes a swimming pool. Consider that when you study the prices: 9,200 pesos ($18.40) single, 9,775 pesos ($19.55) double, 10,580 pesos ($21.16) triple.

The seafood restaurant chain of Soberanis has both a restaurant and a hotel in Cancún. The **Hotel Soberanis**, Cobá 5, near the corner with Avenida Tulum (tel. 988/4-1125 or 4-1858), has a bright white-and-orange color scheme and some other touches such as elegant table lamps, two double beds to a room, and little balconies. All rooms are air-conditioned, of course, and are priced at 9,750 pesos ($19.50) single, 10,750 pesos ($21.50) double with one double or two twin beds, 11,250 pesos ($22.50) double with two double beds.

An Outstanding Choice All Around

An outstanding choice all around is the attractive **Novotel en Cancún** Apdo. 70, Cancún Q. Roo 77500 (tel. 988/4-2999), on Avenida Tulum at Azucenas, near the intersection with Avenida Uxmal. Though modern, it has enough traditional touches, such as white stucco walls, metalwork, and colorful craft decorations, to give it a truly Mexican spirit. The 40 air-conditioned rooms are often booked solid, and are priced at 7,130 pesos ($14.26) single, 7,333 pesos ($14.66) double, 8,740 pesos ($17.48) triple, 9,890 pesos ($19.78) for four.

Carrillo's, for which the official address is Retorno 3, Manzana 22 (tel. 988/4-1227), is on a side street called Calle Claveles which meets Avenida Tulum at two places (Claveles forms a loop). Look for the intersection of Claveles and Tulum that's right across from the Banco Nacional de México and its large statues of Tula's Atlantean men. Now that you're there, you'll find Carrillo's to be one of the strangest places in Cancún. Although a few of the hotel's rooms are older and more standard, most are finished—walls and ceiling—in a nubbly white stucco that gives the entire place a troglodytic quality. Add plywood vanities, tile showers, and individual air conditioning units and you have the standard room at Carrillo's, which rents for 7,015 pesos ($14.03) single, 8,280 pesos ($16.56) double. Besides the two-story hotel, Carrillo's building houses a seafood restaurant.

The **Hotel Cancún Handall,** at the intersection of Avenidas Tulum and Cobá (tel. 988/4-1122 or 4-1976), opened in 1980. Two wings of two floors each hold a variety of single rooms, doubles, and suites, and a pool awaits your pleasure outside. Most of the modern rooms have two double beds, and cost 11,500 pesos ($23) single, 13,800 pesos ($27.60) double, and 15,000 pesos ($30) triple.

On the Avenida Tulum right downtown is the **Hotel Rivemar** (tel. 988/4-1199), a modern but heavily used establishment right in the midst of downtown. Rooms are air-conditioned, of course, with private baths, and are priced at 1,315 pesos ($10.68) single, 6,855 pesos ($13.71) double, 8,275 pesos ($16.55) triple.

It's strange to imagine a colonial hotel in brand-new Cancún, but there is such a thing. Aptly enough, it's named the **Hotel Colonial,** Tulipanes 22 at Avenida Tulum, on a quiet side street (tel. 988/4-1535). Furnishings of the rooms around the little courtyard are, not surprisingly, colonial in inspiration. But the colonists didn't have private baths or air conditioning, yet every room in the hotel does. Price for a room, single or double, is 5,000 pesos ($10) with a fan, 5,400 pesos ($10.80) with air conditioning.

On and Off Avenida Yaxchilán

Avenida Yaxchilán, west of and parallel to Avenida Tulum, also has a good selection of hotels in all price ranges.

My favorite place in this area is the tidy, quaint little **Posada Lucy,** Calle Gladiolas 25 (tel. 988/4-4165), a half-block off Avenida Yaxchilán near the Plaza del Sol hotel and shopping complex. The dozen rooms here are jammed into a tiny space, on two levels, painted cheery blue and white, with red tile floors. It's quiet, though, and the rooms have aluminum screens on the windows, air conditioners, and even a kitchenette in some. Rates are 6,000 pesos ($12) single, 8,000 pesos ($16) double for a room, 12,000 pesos ($24) double for a room with kitchenette. Weekly rates are even cheaper.

The **Hotel Komvaser,** Avenida Yaxchilán 15 (tel. 988/4-1650), is a surprisingly open-air place with pool, bar, reception desk, etc. all right out next to the sidewalk. No big sign announces the hotel's presence, and you may find yourself waltzing right by it. The rooms, all air-conditioned and set back from the street, have one double and one single bed, and rent for 8,500 pesos ($17) single or double, 9,500 pesos ($19) triple.

For big families, the place is the **Hotel Hacienda Cancún,** Avenida Sunyaxchén 39-40, at Avenida Yaxchilán (tel. 988/4-1208 or

4-3672). The building gives a whole new dimension to the word "stucco," but some of the rooms can hold up to six persons, for 15,000 pesos ($30) total. Other rates are 6,210 pesos ($12.42) single, 7,475 pesos ($14.95) double, 8,855 pesos ($17.71) triple; continental breakfast is included in these rates. The hotel has its own parking lot, swimming pool, and restaurant.

The simple, modern **Hotel Canto,** Avenida Yaxchilán at Retorno 5 (tel. 988/4-1267), is tall enough to stand out, modern enough to satisfy, and cheap enough to please. Double rooms with ceiling fans here go for 5,570 pesos ($11.14).

The **Hotel Yaxchilán,** Avenida Yaxchilán 41-43, at the intersection with Sunyaxchén (tel. 988/4-1324), has several dozen quite plain rooms with ceiling fans for 4,500 pesos ($9) single, 5,075 pesos ($10.15) double. Avoid rooms overlooking the busy street. Housekeeping here is sporadic, but the hot water always seems to be hot.

Right around the corner is the **Hotel Marrufo,** on Calle Rosas at Avenida Yaxchilán (tel. 988/4-1334). The plain but clean rooms here cost even less: 3,900 pesos ($7.80) single, 4,400 pesos ($8.80) double, 5,000 pesos ($10) triple with fan; about 600 or 700 pesos ($1.20 or $1.40) more for a room with air conditioning, hot plate, and refrigerator.

The **Suites Residencial "Flamboyanes,"** Avenida Carlos J. Nader, no. 101-103, Super Manzana 3, just off Avenida Cobá (tel. 988/4-1503); for reservations in Mérida, call 992/1-0603 or go to Calle 65 no. 514), is a different and delightful place. There are 80 suites in a number of attractive two-story buildings surrounded by grass and trees, and equipped with a private swimming pool. All suites are air-conditioned and include a bedroom, a living room with couches to sleep two more people, fully equipped kitchen with dining area, bathroom, and terrace/porch. A suite for one or two persons costs 10,925 pesos ($21.85), plus 2,300 pesos ($4.60) for each additional person. The daily rate goes down for extended stays, of course. Remember that you are renting an *apartment* here, and not just a hotel room, and thus the prices are very reasonable for what you get.

The Youth Hostel

Cancún has a big, beautiful, comfortable, modern youth hostel right out in the expensive Zona Turística. Look for the sign that says **Albergue de la Juventud,** Paseo Kukulkán km 3.2, Apdo. 849 (tel. 988/3-1337), on the left-hand (north) side of the road as you bus out from town. Backpackers will want to know that the hostel is 4 kilometers (2½ miles) from the bus station. Inexpensive city buses ("Hoteles") go right by it. The hostel has

612 beds, a swimming pool, a fine location right near the beach, and prices like this: 1,050 pesos ($2.10) for a bed, 420 pesos (84¢) for breakfast, 540 pesos ($1.08) for lunch or dinner. It's fabulous!

Cancún's Restaurants

Dining in Cancún gives you the chance to sample many varieties of Mexican cuisine. In addition to the familiar tacos and enchiladas, you'll find restaurants specializing in seafood, steaks, and the indigenous Maya cuisine of Yucatán.

Cancún restaurant prices are higher than in places like Mérida which do not draw resort crowds, but even so, you'll probably find your dinner tab here much lower than at home. Many restaurants provide entertainment during your meal. The show might be a rope-twirling *charro* (Mexican cowboy), a guitarist or two, or even a mariachi band. For the price of a moderate dinner, you'll often get an entire night's entertainment.

Most of Cancún's independent restaurants (the ones not connected to large hotels) are downtown, in Ciudad Cancún. Virtually everyone who stays at one of the large hotels on Isla Cancún makes the trek downtown at least once during their stay. When you go, here are some places to look for:

FOR SEAFOOD: There always seems to be a line for dinner at the **Restaurant El Pescador,** Tulipanes 5, off of Avenida Tulum (tel. 4-2673). Fresh seafood excellently prepared and moderately priced (for Cancún) is the drawing card. You can sit on the rustic porch at streetside, or in an interior dining room, and feast on cocktails of shrimp, conch, lobster, fish, or octopus for 1,200 to 1,525 pesos ($2.40 to $3.05), and main fish courses priced between 2,150 and 3,000 pesos ($4.30 and $6). The specialty here is Créole cuisine, such as Créole-style shrimp (camarones alla criolla), or charcoal-broiled lobster, but these cost more. Open for dinner only, El Pescador is closed Monday.

The **Restaurant El Pirata,** Azucenas 19 off Avenida Tulum (no phone), has the proper nautical motif, long dinner hours (3 to 11 p.m., seven days a week), and seafood prices that are moderate for Cancún. For a dinner based on grilled filet of fish, expect to spend about 4,000 pesos ($8), half again as much for fancy items such as a brochette of shrimp and steak.

The local incarnation of the Soberanis seafood restaurant group is at Avenida Cobá 5 and 7, in the **Hotel Soberanis** (tel. 4-1125). The patio dining area is shaded by large awnings, and although you're not far from Avenida Tulum here, it's fairly quiet. Service is attentive, and prices are moderate considering the general range of prices in Cancún for seafood. Fish entrees are a moderate 1,750 to 3,000 pesos ($3.50 to $6), and are the best things to have. Soberanis opens about 9 in the morning (good for breakfast), and closes at 11 p.m. or midnight.

Carrillo's Restaurant (tel. 4-1227), in the hotel of the same name on Calle Claveles (see above), is a good place, whether you want to put together a light lunch for a couple of dollars, or go all-out and have lobster. A nice filet of red snapper (huachinango) will cost about 2,100 pesos ($4.20), depending on style of preparation, while a steak will cost a few dollars more. For a full meal, with wine, tax, and tip, expect to pay 4,500 to 6,000 pesos ($9 to $12) per person. The big bonus at Carrillo's, fairly rare in Cancún restaurants, is air conditioning. There's piano music every evening. In winter it's fun to sit at one of the outdoor tables, but in the heat of summer almost everyone opts for the cool indoor dining room.

FOR YUCATECAN SPECIALTIES: The first **Restaurant Los Almendros** was located deep in the Maya heartland at Ticul. Then a branch opened in Mérida, and now one has been opened in Cancún (tel. 4-0807). Los Almendros specializes in Maya cooking, and the big restaurant on Avenida Bonampak at Calle Saíl is meant to look something like a large Mayan palapa inside. Get in a cab, and for about $1 the driver will take you south on Avenida Tulum, past the Hotel América and toward the airport, and will turn left onto Avenida Bonampak. The restaurant is a few blocks down, on the left-hand side. The menu here has explanations of all the dishes (in English too), and you'll see lime soup; roast venison with radishes, onions, and sour oranges (tzic de venado); and the house specialty, which is grilled pork served with onions, chiles, and beans (poc-chuc). The combinado yucateco is a sampler with small portions of four typically Yucatecan main courses. Wine and beer are served. You can dine at Los Almendros any day of the week, and you may spend 2,500 pesos ($5) per person, or even less.

The **Restaurant Papagayo,** Claveles 31, off Avenida Tulum (no phone), has a lush tropical-garden layout complete with straw-thatched palapa. It's a proper setting for Yucatecan dishes such as lime soup or tikinchik, but the menu goes beyond Yucatecan specialties to more familiar fare. Expect to spend 2,500 to 3,500 pesos ($5 to $7) for a full lunch or dinner; breakfast is served as well. Closed Sunday.

DINNER AND ENTERTAINMENT: A place that was booming on my last visit was **Perico's,** Avenida Yaxchilán 71, at Calle Marañón (tel. 4-3152). Made of sticks to resemble a large Maya house, Perico's has a western decor that includes a few saddles on display here and there. The restaurant is open for dinner only, and features steaks, Cancún seafood, and the more traditional Mexican dishes for very moderate rates. You should be able to choose whatever you like from the menu (except lobster) and still get out for under 5,000 pesos ($10) per person.

A very popular sidewalk restaurant on Avenida Tulum is popular for its food, its ambience, and its clientele—all three. It's **Blackbeard's Taberna.** The food might consist of ceviche, the marinated fish cocktail, followed by a brochette (the specialty) of beef, chicken, shrimp, lobster, or all of the above. Finish with cheesecake, or ice cream topped with a liqueur, accompany your meal with a full carafe of the house wine, and the entire bill for two people might come to 14,000 pesos ($28). You can dine for less, though: say, 5,000 pesos ($10) per person. The decor is rustic Mexican wooden shanty, the clientele mostly international sun-seekers. Open every day.

Across the street from the aforementioned Carrillo's, is **Chocko's & Tere,** at Calle Claveles 13 (tel. 4-1394), a ramshackle, semi-open-air collection of brightly lit dining rooms where the noise level is high, but the fun level is even higher. Something is always going on here—mariachis, a lasso-twirling *charro* (cowboy), or a solo guitarist—to liven up the already lively crowd. The food seems to be of second interest here, and the service is, well, casual. But you can have soup, main course, dessert, and a bottle of beer, tax and tip included, for 4,200 pesos ($8.40). And don't forget all that free entertainment. By the way, the "tip" is a *required* 15%.

If you've enjoyed restaurants of the Carlos Anderson chain in other cities, you can in Cancún too. **Carlos & Charlie's** (no phone) is out in the Zona Hotelera, on the right as you ride out the peninsula. Same upbeat atmosphere, same menu, and price that will put you out about 4,500 to 6,000 pesos ($9 to $12) per person for a full evening.

FOR GERMAN FOOD: For something different, drop in at **Karl's Keller,** in the Plaza Caracol shopping mall on Paseo Kukulcán just west of the convention center (tel. 3-1104). The decor is Bavarian, the air conditioning is arctic, and the menu is in German, English, and Spanish. For starters have Gulaschsuppe (goulash soup, almost a meal in itself) or Bohnensuppe (bean soup), go on to familiar items such as Bratwurst and Wiener Schnitzel, and finish up with Apfelstrudel or Linzertorte, and your bill will come to 6,000 pesos ($12), tax and compulsory 10% service charge included. You can dine quite nicely for just over half that amount if you like. Karl's is open from 8 a.m. to 11 p.m. every day except Sunday, when it's closed.

FOR PIZZA: Is there no place to get a good, inexpensive (under $4) meal in Cancún? There is. At **Pizza Rolandi,** Avenida Cobá 12, between Tulum and Nader (tel. 4-4047), you can get the basic cheese-and-tomato pizza for 1,140 pesos ($2.28), which, with a drink, will satisfy your hunger very pleasantly. The super-special pizza costs 2,750 pesos ($5.50), which isn't bad, and Italian specialties like spaghetti and fettuccine cost about that as well. Italian desserts are offered. Pizza Rolandi is usually crowded, its outdoor patio tables busy with the hungry, thirsty (beer is served), thrifty set. Open daily.

For Breakfast

The popular **Restaurant Pop,** famous in Mérida for a number of years now, has a branch in Cancún at Avenida Tulum 26 (tel. 4-1991), near the corner of Avenida Uxmal and the Hotel Parador. As in Mérida the fare tends to the light, simple, and delicious rather than the elaborate and expensive. Breakfast or a light lunch can be had in the cool comfort of Pop's air-conditioned dining room for 750 to 1,250 pesos ($1.50 to $2.50); a more substantial dinner should be in the range of 2,000 to 3,000 pesos ($4 to $6). Wine and beer are served. Open daily.

Cancún Activities

You've come for the sun and the sea, and Cancún has them in abundance. Locals boast that this resort has over 240 completely sunny days per year. For the most part, the other 125 days are partly sunny, with few days of rain or heavy overcast.

THE BEACHES: Yucatán's native rock is a limestone made up of microscopic star-shaped plankton fossils named disco-aster. When the bedrock breaks down into sand, it yields grains of a brilliant whiteness with polished surfaces. The polish and the whiteness resist heat absorption, so even under the blazing noonday sun, Cancún's "air-conditioned" sand remains cool under foot.

As for the water, it is the lucent blue Caribbean, famed for its coral and multicolor marine life. With the air-conditioned sand, it completes an unbeatable combination.

All beaches in Mexico are public. Strictly speaking, there is no such thing as a private beach from which you (or anyone else) can be excluded. In practice, one can feel self-conscious walking in a bathing suit through a posh hotel lobby on the way to the beach—especially if one is not a guest at the hotel. The hotel has the right to usher you out of the lobby (although this never happens), but not the right to chase you from the "hotel's" beach. Feel free to swim where you like.

When swimming on eastern beaches (those between Punta Cancún and the Club Mediterranée), you must be cautious of deadly undertow and rip tides. These treacherous currents can grab swimmers without warning and rush them out to sea. It's best to swim where the surf breaks well before it reaches the beach; or where there is a vigilant lifeguard; or where signs indicate safe swimming. Sometimes you can recognize a rip tide area because the water is oddly discolored, and waves reach the shore earlier than on other portions of the beach.

If you should be so unlucky as to be swept out to sea, take these measures: First, don't panic. You'll get back to shore if you follow the rules. Second, swim at a normal speed in a direction parallel to the shore. This will get you out of the current. Once outside the current, you can swim into shore. You'll be tired, but you'll make it. If you try to swim directly toward shore against the current, you'll soon be exhausted and unable to continue.

This danger is not nearly so great on north-facing beaches, those between Ciudad Cancún and Punta Cancún.

Having warned you of the danger, here's a tip: the deserted beaches are those farthest south from Punta Cancún. Take a Ruta 1 or Ruta 2 bus south along Paseo Kukulcán, and get off at an undeveloped stretch of the road. Right over the dunes to the east is the beach. But please, please be careful about that undertow.

WATER SPORTS: Cancún has them all, from sailing and sailboarding through scuba-diving and snorkeling to such exotica as jet-skiing and parasailing. Most hotels on Isla Cancún have their own water sports facilities where you can rent all the necessary equipment and sign up for paid lessons.

YACHT EXCURSIONS: Yacht excursions are a favorite pastime here. Modern motor yachts, trimarans, even oldtime sloops take swimmers, sunners, and snorkelers out into the limpid waters, often dropping anchor at Isla Mujeres' Garrafon Beach for lunch and snorkeling around the coral reef. Trips tend to leave at 10 or 11 a.m., last for five hours, include lunch (and sometimes drinks), and cost 7,500 to 15,000 pesos ($15 to $30) per person.

The **Corsario** (tel. 3-0200), an "18th-century pirate sloop," leaves from the marina next to the Hotel El Presidente.

The glass-bottom trimaran **Manta** (tel. 3-1676 or 3-0348) departs the marina next to the Club Caribe Cancún, and several readers have written to recommend it as a fine experience.

The motor yacht **Fiesta Maya** leaves from its dock near the Hotel El Presidente; the boat has a glass-bottom area for watching fish.

The motor yacht **Antares** (tel. 4-1543 or 4-0386) departs from its dock next to the Hotel Casa Maya.

The motor yacht **Tropical** (tel. 3-1488) will take you from the Naval Dock to Isla Mujeres and Garrafón on a cruise from 9 a.m. to 3:15 p.m. daily.

RUINAS EL REY: Cancún has its own Mayan ruins. Though they're unimpressive compared to Tulum, Cobá, or Chichén-Itzá, the Ruinas El Rey are still of interest.

The ruins are about 13 miles from town, at the southern reaches of the Zona Hotelera, almost to Punta Nizuc. Look for the Royal Mayan Beach Club on the left (east), and then the ruins on the right (west). Admission is free daily from 8 a.m. to 5 p.m.; write your name in the register after you pass through the gate.

This was a small ceremonial center and settlement for Maya fishermen built very early in the history of Maya culture, then abandoned, and later resettled near the end of the Postclassic Period, not long before the arrival of the Conquistadores. The platforms of numerous small temples are visible amid the banana plants, papayas, and wildflowers.

ARCHEOLOGICAL MUSEUM: It started out as a fake, more or less—a few bits of Maya flotsam and jetsam meant to entice people to the nearby ruins. But the collection has been expanded now, and though all the truly great stuff is still in greater museums, you can enjoy a visit here.

The Museo Arqueologico de Cancún is right next to the convention center (Centro de Convenciones) near Punta Cancún and the Hotel Krystal. Visit from Tuesday through Saturday from 10 a.m. to 5 p.m.; admission costs 50 pesos (10¢).

BULLFIGHTS: Cancún has its own small bullring near the northern (town) end of Paseo Kukulcán. Any Wednesday at 3:30 p.m.

during the winter tourist season you can witness this Spanish spectacle. There are usually four bulls.

FARTHER AFIELD: Day-long excursions, or perhaps even an overnight stay, are easy using Cancún as a base. The Mayan ruins at Tulum should be your first goal, then perhaps the *caleta* (cove) of Xel-ha, and later to nearby Isla Mujeres. By driving fast or catching the buses right, one can get to Chichén-Itzá, explore the ruins, and return in a day, but it's much better to make a trip of several days and include Mérida and Uxmal on the same trip. If you plan to go south to the island of Cozumel, think of staying on the island at least one night. See upcoming chapters for transportation details and further information on all of these destinations.

Cancún's Nightlife

Ciudad Cancún has hardly been in existence long enough to have developed an indigenous nightlife, although there are a few lively spots that are offshoots of clubs in Mérida or Mexico City. But the real action is in the Zona Turística at the big hotels. Part of the thrill of getting away to the Caribbean is the intrigue of meeting new people either on the beach or in the cool, dark depths of a disco or nightclub.

CLUBS AND DISCOS: All the big hotels have night places, usually both a disco and a supper club with a floor show or at least live music for dancing. Expect to pay a cover charge of about 2,000 pesos ($4) per person in the discos or show bars, or be subjected to a 1,500-peso minimum—since drinks cost 1,000 to 1,400 pesos ($2 to $2.80), this means that you'll actually have to spend a minimum of 2,000 pesos ($4) to cover your "1,500-peso" minimum. Add 15% tax and tip to these prices, and you'll see that a night out in fabulous Cancún is not all that cheap.

Believe it or not, one of the least expensive evenings can be had at the deluxe **Hotel El Presidente,** in the Zona Hotelera. In the lobby bar, groups entertain each night except Wednesday, and no cover or minimum is charged. The music is traditional—mariachis, jarocho, etc.—and changes every half hour. In the hotel's club, called **Bum Bum Cancún,** the thatched roof shivers every night except Monday to the cool jive of salsa music, for dancing, of course.

At the **Hotel Cancún Caribe,** dancers can work out every night of the week except Monday. Look for a two-drink minimum here.

The posh **Camino Real Hotel** hosts a Mexican Music Night each Friday, and lays on as much rhythm as anyone could handle.

The **Lone Star Bar** is next to the Hotel Maria de Lourdes on Avenida Yaxchilán. The cover charge is only about $1, beer is the same, and the music is live country. The Lone Star advertises itself as "Cancún's oldest (1980)"! The bar opens at 9 p.m. every night but Monday, and begins to really go at about 11 p.m.

THE BALLET FOLKLORICO: Dinner-and-a-show here includes a table d'hôte dinner at 7 p.m., followed at 8:30 by a show with more than 30 dancers and musicians. Though hardly equivalent to the extravaganza staged in Mexico City's Palacio de Bellas Artes, you may consider it worth the price of 10,000 pesos ($20). That price covers everything except drinks.

Shows are staged in the Convention Center auditorium (tel. 3-0199) every evening except Sunday.

Chapter IV

ISLA MUJERES: LAID-BACK AND LAZY

THERE ARE TWO VERSIONS of how Isla Mujeres got its name. The more popular one states that pirates used the island as a place to park their women while they were off buccaneering on the Spanish Main. The other account attributes the name to conquistador Francisco Hernández de Córdoba, who was reportedly struck by the large number of female terracotta figurines he found in temples on the island.

Although the more prosaic version is probably correct (aren't they always?), incurable romantics such as myself continue to nurse the forlorn hope that the tale about pirates and their women might have some vestige of authenticity.

Modern Isla Mujeres has happily displayed a healthy immunity toward the latter-day pirate whose prey is American green rather than Spanish gold: There is one moderately priced upscale hotel, and a satisfying number of facilities for budget travelers and even beachcombers.

GET THERE EARLY: In the busy seasons, June to August and December through February, Isla Mujeres can literally fill up with overnight visitors. Making reservations at the island's small hotels does not always go smoothly and reliably, so the best thing you can do is to get to the island as early in the day as possible. You may even have to stay a night in Cancún so that you can arise early for the first ferry. Check-out time in most hotels is 1 or 2 p.m. Plan to arrive no later than that in February, July, and August.

GETTING TO ISLA MUJERES: The island's position at the heart of the Mexican Caribbean's resort area and its location just a few miles from the mainland make it easily accessible.

From Mérida

Buses leave from the bus station several times a day, and you can travel either first or second class depending on the bus. Your destination is Puerto Juárez, from which you take a ferryboat to the island. You can also fly from Mérida to Cancún, and proceed from there (see below).

From Cozumel

AeroCaribe operates daily flights between Cozumel and Isla Mujeres; contact them for schedules and rates at 2-0503 or 2-0928 in Cozumel, 4-1231 in Cancún. If you don't fly, you must take a ferry to the mainland, then a bus to Puerto Juárez, then another ferry to Isla Mujeres (see below, and also in the Cozumel section).

From Cancún

Take a Ruta 8 city bus (80 pesos, 16¢) to Puerto Juárez or Punta Sam to get the boat. Buses can be caught along the Avenida Tulum in Cancún, running about every 15 minutes.

From Puerto Juárez

Puerto Juárez is the dock for the slightly more expensive passenger boats to Isla Mujeres. Boats depart Puerto Juárez at 6:30, 9:30, and 11:30 a.m. and 1:30, 3:30, and 5:30 p.m. on the half-hour trip; one-way fare is 200 pesos (40¢) for a scheduled trip. Boats may run at other than scheduled departure times, but these are *especiales* (special trips), and fares may be considerably higher. Make sure you know the fare before you board.

From Punta Sam

The car ferry to Isla Mujeres accepts passengers as well, and charges only 25 pesos (5¢) per person for the 40-minute ride; cars cost 170 pesos (34¢). To reach Punta Sam, stay on the Ruta 8 bus past Puerto Juárez, all the way to the end of the line at the ferry dock. A taxi from Cancún to the Punta Sam dock costs about 600 pesos ($1.20); make sure the driver understands that he is to take you all the way to the car ferry *(transbordador)* dock, not just to Puerto Juárez.

Note that the car ferries do not run on Monday mornings due to boat maintenance. The first ferry on Monday is at 1:30 p.m., the next at 5:45 p.m. On all other days of the week, departures from Punta Sam are at 8:30 and 11:30 a.m., and 1:30, 5:45, and

8:30 p.m. Departures from Isla Mujeres on the return trip are at 7:15 and 10 a.m., and 12:15, 4:30, 7:30, and 10 p.m.

ORIENTATION: Isla Mujeres is about 5 miles long and 2½ miles wide. At the northern tip is Playa Cocos (Coconut Beach) and the Hotel El Presidente Caribe. Just a few yards south of these is the small town. The ferry docks right at the edge of the town, walking distance from all hotels except (if your luggage is heavy) the Hotel El Presidente.

USEFUL FACTS: The Post Office, telegraph office, and market (Mercado Municipal) are all in a row on Calle Guerrero, an inland street at the north edge of town, which, like most streets in the town, is unmarked by signs.

Where to Stay

Although most hotels on Isla Mujeres are quite inexpensive, there is one modern luxury hotel. Even this place has surprisingly reasonable prices, in keeping with Isla Mujeres's reputation as a low-cost haven in a high-priced area.

THE BIG PLACE: Hotel El Presidente Caribe, Islote El Yunquei, Punta Norte, Isla Mujeres, Q. Roo 77400 (tel. 988/2-0029 or 2-0017, or toll free 800/854-2026 in U.S. except California, and 800/542-6028 in California), has a dramatic situation, perched on its own tiny islet at the northern tip of Isla Mujeres, surrounded by jagged coral and creamy sand splashed by the pellucid waters of the Caribbean. The sound of the surf reaches every one of the 101 guest rooms, all of which have air conditioning and FM radio. Though the hotel is not huge or ultra-fancy, it does have two restaurants and two bars, a swimming pool, and facilities for fishing, scuba-diving, snorkeling, and surfing. Prices for this secluded resort are 19,000 pesos ($38) single, 20,000 pesos ($40) double. A buffet breakfast here costs about 2,500 pesos ($5). This hotel represents exceptionally good value for your vacation dollar.

LESS EXPENSIVE LODGINGS: All of the island's other lodgingplaces are less expensive; most are less than half the price of "the big place." Quality of housekeeping seems to be on a rollercoaster, however: if a hotel fills up, the manager tends to sit back, fire the housekeeping staff, put off repairs, and take it easy. When business drops off, he gets back to work. That's life in these island towns.

The **Hotel Rocas del Caribe**, Avenida Madero 2, Isla Mujeres, Q. Roo 77400 (tel. 988/2-0011), is one of the island's newer small

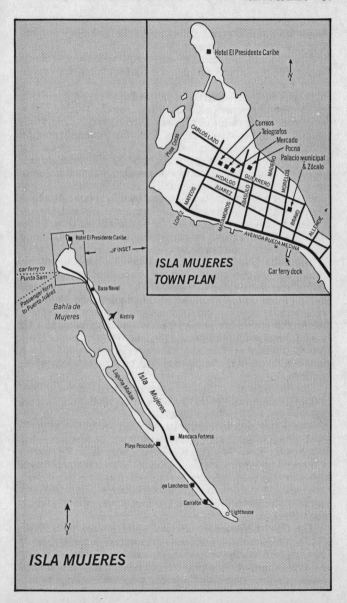

Hotel El Presidente Caribe

Correos
Telegrafos
Mercado
Pocna
Palacio municipal
& Zócalo

CARLOS LAZO

HIDALGO   GUERRERO

JUAREZ   ABASOLO

MATEOS

LOPEZ

MATAMOROS

MADERO

MORELOS

BRAVO

ALLENDE

AVENIDA RUEDA MEDINA

Playa Cocos

ISLA MUJERES
TOWN PLAN

Car ferry dock

Hotel El Presidente Caribe

OF INSET

car ferry to
Punta Sam

Passenger ferry
to Puerto Juárez

Base Naval

Bahía de
Mujeres

Airstrip

Isla Mujeres

Laguna Makax

Mandaca Fortress

Playa Pescador

Playa Lancheros

Garrafón

Lighthouse

N

ISLA MUJERES

hotels, situated right on the eastern open-surf beach. All of the rooms have sea views, a little balcony, a fan, and a private bath. The base price is 8,000 pesos ($16) single, 10,500 ($21) double with fan, about 1,500 pesos ($3) per room more with an air conditioner. The price seems a bit high for what you get in the way of a room, but the location—right on the beach and mere steps from the center of town—is certainly unbeatable.

The **Hotel Rocamar** (tel. 988/2-0101) is perched on the higher ground at the opposite side of town from the ferry dock, and thus has a commanding view of the sea. Everything's done in nautical style here, with every conch shell ever opened in the restaurant going to line the garden walkways; ropes and hawsers are employed as trim; even the bathroom sinks are mounted in Lucite tops, and the Lucite is chock full of small seashells. The sea breezes keep the rooms cool, assisted by ceiling fans. Although definitely among the most well-used rooms on the island, the Rocamar's collection of *quartos* has the breeze and the view. Prices are 8,200 pesos ($16.40) single, 8,600 pesos ($17.20) double. If they're not busy, you can make a deal for a lower price.

The **Hotel Martinez**, Avenida Madero 14, Isla Mujeres, Q. Roo 77400 (tel. 988/2-0154), two blocks from the ferry dock (turn left as you debark, go two blocks, and turn right), has been around for years and years, and satisfied guests keep returning because here the basics are rigidly observed: rooms are spotless, sheets and towels are gleaming white (although perhaps a bit frayed here and there), and little luxuries such as soap are provided. Prices are fair, at 4,500 pesos ($9) single, 4,000 pesos ($8) double per day, ceiling fans (but no air conditioning) included.

Just up Madero from the Martinez is the **Hotel Osorio** (tel. 988/2-0018), which has similar comforts at about the same price: 5,000 pesos ($10) double, with fan.

A relatively new addition to Isla Mujeres's collection of small, basic hotels is the **Hotel Caribe Maya,** Avenida Madero 9, Isla Mujeres, Q. Roo 77400 (tel. 988/2-0190), west of the Restaurant Gomar. The showers are tiled, although a few bits and pieces of furniture (the bedside tables, for instance) may have seen service in some older and now long-gone establishment. The three floors are set up motel style, and rooms rent for 4,500 pesos ($9) single, 5,000 pesos ($10) double.

The **Hotel Berny,** Avenida Juárez and Abasolo (tel. 988/2-0025), is fancier than its prices would suggest—a modern stucco building with handsome red-tile floors and an interior court with a pretty swimming pool. Each room has one queen-size bed and one single bed, plus either a ceiling fan or an air conditioner;

some have a balcony with sea views. The tradition here is to include a continental breakfast in the room prices, which are 6,210 pesos ($12.42) single, 7,475 pesos ($14.95) double, 8,855 pesos ($17.71) triple.

The **Hotel Vistalmar,** Avenida Rueda Medina between Abasolo and Matamoros (tel. 988/2-0096), has a name which means "sea view," and that's exactly what you get from the pleasant veranda. Rooms, with private showers and ceiling fans, are simple but well kept by a resident family, and decently priced at 5,000 pesos ($10) single, 5,400 pesos ($10.80) double. The hotel is just north of the Pemex gas station on Rueda Medina, the waterfront street.

Even more basic than the above choices is the **Hotel Caracol,** just off Avenida Madero 5 (tel. 988/2-0150), which charges 5,000 pesos ($10) single, 5,500 pesos ($11) for its spartan rooms with ceiling fans.

The modest little **Posada San Jorge,** Avenida Juárez 31, near Playa Cocoteros, (tel. 988/2-0052) has decent rooms (and more abuilding), a good location, and excellent prices. For a room with two double beds, fan, and shower, you pay only 4,000 pesos ($8). Can't beat it.

For Beachcombers

Poc-na, at the end of Calle Matamoros (tel. 988/2-0090 or 2-0053) bills itself as "a basic clean place to stay at the lowest price possible," and it's just that. The reception desk just inside the door will rent you a sheet, towel and soap, or blanket, and a canvas bunk or nylon hammock (plus you get your own private locker). The open bunk rooms are arranged around a central palapa-shaded dining area provided with picnic tables and served by a small kitchen. Meals are served cafeteria-style. The location is excellent, only a short walk from the beaches at the northern tip of the island. If you have your own hammock or sleeping bag, the basic charge is 1,300 pesos ($2.60) per person per night. But if you're unequipped, you'll have to rent a mattress to put on top of the rope hammock for 85 pesos (17¢), a sheet, pillow, blanket, and towel for 80 pesos (16¢) each, for a total one-time charge of 405 pesos (81¢). You'll have to put down deposits on all these items, refundable at the end of your stay.

Where to Eat

Dining on Isla Mujeres is not wildly cheap, but it is certainly easier to keep to a budget here than in, say, Cancún or Cozumel. The first thing you must learn is the password: **Avenida Hidalgo.** Going north out of the town's main square, this street is lined with small and inexpensive or moderately priced places to have a meal. With the coming of Cancún's prosperity, Avenida Hidalgo has undergone a facelift and now boasts lots of trees and shrubs. Many houses have rustic gardens in pseudo-Caribbean style. All these decorations were laid out by a landscape architect to make Isla Mujeres "more authentic," and although authenticity may in fact have been driven out, beauty and quaintness have been ushered in. It's a pleasant street.

I will start our culinary excursion in the main square, head north on Avenido Hidalgo, and then afterward mention some places for waterfront dining.

Among Isla Mujeres's most dependable old standbys is the **Restaurant Gomar,** which has two outdoor tables on Avenida Hidalgo and about 16 indoors (no phone). Decor is modern, warm, and nice, with lots of natural wood and the quaint touch of hand-woven tablecloths (protected under glass). In general, prices here are among the highest on the avenida, but this means that meat, fish, or shrimp meals come to about 2,000 to 3,500 pesos ($4 to $7), complete.

The **Restaurant La Peña,** behind (east of) the town square bandstand, near the water tower at Calle Guerrero 5 (no phone), gives you a choice on where to hang out: streetside porch, interior room, or seaside terrace. You get an even greater choice of what to eat, from pizzas (three sizes, many varieties, 600 to 2,900 pesos ($1.20 to $5.80) through seafood to mole poblano. Prices are low to moderate, drinks are served (happy hour from 6 to 7 p.m.). No choice on the music, though. It's rock.

Look for the cozy little **Restaurant El Peregrino,** next to the Hotel Caribe Maya at Madero 8 (tel. 2-0190). The tiny streetside porch has a few tables; the interior is darker but cooler. The draw here is meals at prices lower than the better-known restaurants nearby. Shrimp, for instance, can be had for only 1,200 pesos ($2.40), fish or meat for even less.

Should you be dying of the heat, a few restaurants have air conditioning. You pay for it in meal prices which are 35% to 45% higher than in comparable establishments. For instance, at the **Villa del Mar** or **Martita's** on Avenida Rueda Medina near the ferry dock, a meal that costs 1,500 pesos ($3) at an open-air place will cost 2,200 to 2,500 pesos ($4.40 to $5). On a very hot day, the coolness is well worth it, though.

Of the other restaurants on Hidalgo, most are very similar in price and atmosphere to the **Restaurant La Mano de Dios,** on Hidalgo at the corner of Matamoros. A family operation, one suspects the family beds down for the night right in the dining room after the last dish has been washed. You can have lentil soup—

delicious—and the filet of fish, plus a large fruit salad and a soft drink for a total bill of 1,750 pesos ($3.50), although in the hot weather you might not have the appetite needed to finish it all. Shrimp cocktail, fried bananas, and other such delicacies are offered, along with the regulation chicken tacos, omelets, and breakfast huevos rancheros. Tablecloths are of plastic, the air is moved by ceiling fans, and the whole front of the restaurant is open to the street.

Right next to the plain Hotel Caracol is the fancy restaurant called **Ciro's** (tel. 2-0102), very much like the aforementioned Gomar in decor, and also in price. Various omelets cost 550 pesos ($1.10); turtle, shrimp, or roast meat as an entree will cost about 1,500 pesos ($3); chicken dishes cost a bit less as a rule. At Ciro's, the bonus is air conditioning.

The **Restaurant Estrellita Marinera,** on Hidalgo, always has a collection of café tables enclosed by groups of ardent people-watchers. In the afternoon, it's usually a busy spot as the comida costs a mere 1,000 pesos ($2) and comprises fried fish, rice, frijoles, and salad.

Across the street from the Estrellita Marinera is that essential establishment for fixing your own breakfast and picnics, the **Panadería La Gloria,** filled with fresh bread and sweet rolls.

The **Restaurant Tropicana,** Avenida Rueda Medina at Bravo, directly opposite the car-ferry dock (no phone), has a heavy patronage of local people. You couldn't call its Formica furniture romantic, nor its fluorescent lights, but the prices aren't bad: sopa de pollo, the island favorites of beef, turtle, or chicken, plus dessert and drink, might cost 2,200 pesos ($4.40), twice that for shrimp. Note that the Tropicana is open from 8 a.m. to 10 p.m. daily.

Activities

Isla Mujeres is a sun and sea haven with all the attractions: snorkeling, swimming, fishing, or just plain relaxing. There are two beautiful beaches, one in town called the **Playa Cocos,** to your left as you get off the boat, and **Garrafon National Park,** about five kilometers to your right. Playa Cocos is quite shallow and is better for swimming, while Garrafon beach with its coral reef is excellent for snorkeling.

There are several agencies that offer tours around the island as well as lessons in scuba-diving and deep-sea fishing. Included in this adventure is a visit to the large turtles, and the biological station, swimming and snorkeling at Garrafon beach, and a lunch of fish or shrimp from the day's catch at the little Idios Beach. (**Note:** Make your boating arrangements a day in advance as they like to get an early start at about 8 a.m.) Getting to Garrafon beach on your own is difficult as there are no buses. You can walk (takes 1½ hours), hitch, rent a bicycle or a moped, or take a taxi. While at Garrafon you might like to take a walk to the south end of the island and its lighthouse. Just beyond the lighthouse is a Maya ruin believed to have been an observatory built to the moon goddess Ix-Chel.

The **Fortress of Mundaca** is about four kilometers in the same direction as Garrafon, off about half a kilometer to your left. The fortress was built by the pirate Mundaca Marecheaga who in the early 19th century arrived at Isla Mujeres and proceeded to set up a blissful paradise while making money from selling slaves to Cuba and Belize. The fortress is set in a pretty, shady park, and is a nice trip if you are suffering from too much sun.

Playa Lancheros, south of town a few miles, has shady palapas, a snack stand, and a good sandy beach.

Ask around at the docks, and you'll find a boatman who is willing to ferry you over to **Isla Contoy,** an uninhabited National Park island north of Isla Mujeres where the beaches are very fine, the bird life rich and colorful, and life is blissfully peaceful.

Chapter V

COZUMEL: DIVER'S PARADISE

IN MEXICO'S CARIBBEAN resort area, if Cancún is the jet-set's port of call and Isla Mujeres belongs to the beachcombers, Cozumel, 44 miles south of Cancún, is a little bit of both. More remote than either of the other two resorts, this island (pop. 30,000) becomes more of a world unto itself, a place where people come to get away from the day-tripping atmosphere of Isla Mujeres or the megadevelopment feeling of Cancún, a place to take each day as it comes for a week or more without moving very far from the hotel or the beach. There is actually little reason to leave the island as all the necessaries for a good vacation are here: excellent snorkeling and scuba places, sailing and water sports, fancy hotels and modest hotels, elegant restaurants and taco shops, even a Mayan ruin or two. If, after a while, you do get restless, the ancient Maya city of Tulum and the lagoon of Xel-ha provide convenient and exciting goals for excursions.

Many visitors complain about Cozumel's price structure, which seems high for what you get. But if you're driving at Palancor Reef, it all seems worth it.

GETTING TO COZUMEL: Daily bus service from Mérida via Puerto Juárez and Cancún provides easy access to the towns of Puerto Morelos, the dock for the car ferry to Cozumel, and Playa del Carmen, the dock for the strictly passenger boat to the island. Autobuses del Caribe runs buses that arrive in time to catch departing ferries, and to meet returning ferries.

The Ferryboats

See the sections on Puerto Morelos and Playa del Carmen (Chapter VI) for details on boats to Cozumel.

Flights

Cozumel has an international airport with a surprising number of direct flights from distant cities.

AeroMéxico, downtown in Cozumel at Avenida Rafael Melgar 13 (tel. 987/2-0251 or 2-0422), in the Cine Cozumel building near Calle 4 Norte, has nonstop flights to Houston, Mérida, and Mexico City.

Mexicana, Avenida Rafael Melgar Sur 17 (tel. 987/2-0157 or 2-0263) offers nonstops to Miami, Mérida, and Mexico City. Several other international airlines such as Eastern, American, United, and Continental have flights as well.

AeroCaribe and **AeroCozumel** (tel. 987/2-0928 at Cozumel's airport) both run flights between Cozumel and Cancún at 8 and 10 a.m., noon, and 2, 4, and 6 p.m. A one-way ticket costs 6,385 pesos ($12.77). In addition, AeroCozumel runs a shuttle-type operation between Cozumel and Playa del Carmen.

The minibus from Cozumel's airport into town costs 275 pesos (55¢).

ORIENTATION: Cozumel lies some 12 miles (20 km) out in the Caribbean from Playa del Carmen. The island is roughly 28 miles (45 km) long and 11 miles (18 km) wide. Its only town is San Miguel de Cozumel, usually just called Cozumel.

San Miguel's main waterfront street is called Avenida Rafael Melgar, running along the western shore of the island. Passenger ferries dock right in the center, near the main plaza. Car ferries dock south of town near the hotels Sol Caribe, La Ceiba, and El Presidente.

The town is laid out on a grid, with avenidas running north and south, calles running east and west. The exception is Avenida Juárez, which runs right from the passenger ferry dock through the main square and inland. Juárez divides the town into northern and southern halves.

Heading inland from the dock along Juárez, you'll find that the avenidas you cross are numbered by fives for some reason: "5a Avenida," "10a Avenida," "15a Avenida." If you turn left and head north, you'll discover that calles are numbered even: 2a Norte, 4a Norte, 6a Norte. Turning right from Juárez heads you south, where the streets are numbered odd: 1a Sur (also called Adolfo Salas), 3a Sur, 5a Sur. The scheme is more systematic than it is practical.

The northern part of the island has no paved roads. It's scattered with small Mayan sites, badly ruined, from the age when "Cuzamil" was a land sacred to the moon goddess Ixchel. The sites are best visited by jeep or boat.

North and south of town are many hotels, moderate to expensive in price; many cater to divers. Beyond the hotels to the south is Chancanab National Park, centered on the beautiful lagoon of the same name. Beyond Chancanab is Playa Palancar, and, offshore, the Palancar Reef (*arrecife*). At the southern tip of the island is Punta Celarain, which bears a lighthouse.

The eastern, seaward shore of the island is mostly surf beach, beautiful for walking but dangerous for swimming. There is safe swimming in a few coves.

GETTING AROUND: In the town itself, everything is within walking distance. Though there is limited bus service along Avenida Rafael Melgar from north of town as far south as Palancar, you may find yourself taking taxis in Cozumel. In general, figure about 1,000 pesos ($2) for 15 or 20 minutes of travel. For a day at the beach, finding some like-minded fellow travelers and sharing the cost of a cab is the easy, quick way to go. But for exploring the island, you should consider renting a car or a moped (motorbike).

Car rentals are as expensive here as in other parts of Mexico. See Chapter XIII, "Useful Information," under "Car Rentals" for specifics.

As for motorbikes, it seems as though every shop, garage, restaurant, street cleaner, and mortician in Cozumel is also in the business of renting them. Terms and prices vary from place to place: one renter may only rent by the day or half-day, another may rent you a moped for a minimum three-hour period. One may charge 3,000 pesos ($6) for three hours, most will charge 5,000 to 6,000 pesos ($10 to $12) for a full day (8 a.m. to 5 p.m.); sometimes the rental period is from 12 noon to 12 noon the next day.

As part of your bargaining, carefully inspect the actual moped you'll be renting. Early in the morning, with most of the bikes waiting there to be rented, you can choose one on which all the gizmos are in good shape: horn, light, starter, seat, mirror. Later in the day you'll get the clunker on which everything is broken *and you'll pay the same full price for it*. Rent early.

One final note. Be aware that riding a moped is like sunbathing. No matter how much you cover up, your head, neck, hands, and perhaps legs will be exposed to hours and hours of intense sun. Protect yourself. There's a tendency to forget that riding in the sun all day is like lying on the beach all day.

Here's a price comparison to keep in mind: a couple renting two mopeds for a day will pay 10,000 to 12,000 pesos ($20 to $24).

Car rental for a day may total $40. Hiring a taxi for two hours of chauffeured riding costs about 6,000 pesos ($12).

USEFUL FACTS: The **Post Office** (Correos) is on Avenida Rafael Melgar at Calle 7 Sur, at the southern edge of town.

There's a little **tourist information** booth on Melgar in the main plaza, open at odd hours. They sell the best map of the town and the island, "The Brown Map of Cozumel," for about $1. The SECTUR (Secretaría de Turismo) headquarters is south of the Post Office on Melgar (tel. 2-0357).

There's a long distance **telephone** office on the main plaza.

As for **medical care**, Cozumel has a number of English-speaking American and Mexican doctors in residence. Your hotel or the police can help you contact one.

Cozumel's Hotels

These days Cozumel has a good selection of hotels in all price ranges. In summer there is usually little trouble finding a room. In the high-season months of December, January, February, and March, it's good to call or write ahead for reservations. Prices are higher in those months as well.

THE TOP HOTELS: All of the top hotels are south of town, two near the car ferry dock (2½ miles south of the main square), and one 4 miles south near Chancanab Lagoon. Prices given below are the in-season rates for the winter. You'll pay a surcharge of 15% to 20% if you come for the Christmas and New Year's holiday period. You can expect substantial reductions if you come in summer (mid-April through August), and even greater reductions in the autumn (September to mid-December).

The **Hotel El Presidente Cozumel**, Km 6½, Cozumel, Q. Roo 77600 (tel. 987/2-0322, or toll free 800/472-2427 in U.S., or through Utell), is right on the beach near Chancanab Lagoon, with 189 air-conditioned rooms, two restaurants, two bars, swimming pool and tennis courts, and many facilities for water sports. Staff members are friendly and helpful. The hotel is surrounded by shady palms, and has safe swimming in its own artificial cove. As with other properties in the Presidente chain, prices are quite reasonable for what you get, and represent excellent value. To stay in this modern but unobtrusive hotel in one of the best locations on the island costs 43,700 pesos ($87.40) single, 45,000 pesos ($90) double, $21 for an extra person, in winter.

The **Hotel Sol Caribe Cozumel**, Apdo. 259, Cozumel, Q. Roo 77600 (tel. 987/2-0700, or toll free 800/223-2332 in U.S.), on the

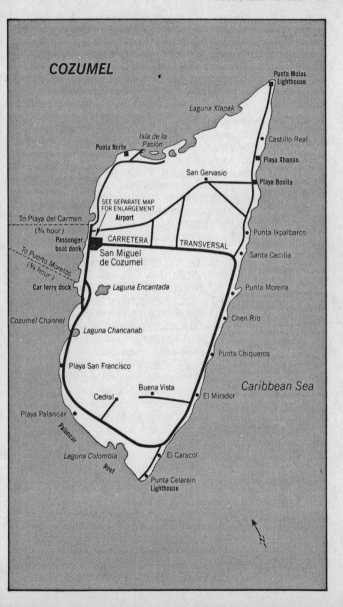

landward side of the road just north of the car ferry dock, is the island's second-largest hotel, with 220 rooms. The entrance is dramatic, beneath a vast thatched canopy, surrounded by tropical greenery, with rocks and replicas of Maya statuary here and there, giving you the impression that you're entering some mysterious Mayan ruin. Lush big-leafed plants and trees are spread throughout the hotel grounds, providing deep shade by the huge swimming pool (which has its own swim-up bar), and to the very edge of the three lighted tennis courts. All rooms have ocean views, air conditioning, a self-service bar, and piped-in music. The hotel's own beach cove, with facilities for water sports, is just across the road. For sustinence, the Sol Caribe provides an upscale restaurant called La Gaviota ("The Seagull"), a coffee shop named La Casa del Pescador, a lobby bar, that bar right in the pool, and a snack bar at the beach. As virtually the entire clientele here is North American, rates are quoted in U.S. dollars: $104 double during the winter season, about 25% less in summer. The Sol Caribe is a Fiesta Americana hotel, operated by Posadas de México, S.A.

Just across from the Sol Caribe, on the beach side of the road, is **La Ceiba Beach Hotel,** Apdo. 284, Cozumel, Q. Roo 77600 (tel. 987/2-0065 or 2-0815, or toll free 800/621-6830 in U.S. except Texas, and 214/669-1991 in Texas). Named for the lofty and majestic tree, sacred to the Mayas, which grows in the tropics, La Ceiba advertises itself as "the intimate resort" and stresses the friendliness of its staff. The 115 rooms have all the comforts, of course, including tubs and showers, air conditioning, color TV, and balconies overlooking the Caribbean. The swimming pool is only steps from the beach. The hotel has its own tennis court, but the emphasis here is on water sports, particularly scuba diving. If that's your passion, be sure to ask about the special dive packages when you call for reservations. These include five or seven nights' lodging, with or without breakfast and dinner each day, unlimited use of tanks during your stay, boat trips to Palancar Reef, a night dive, and a few other treats. Renting a room by the day in winter costs $77 to $89 single, $89 to $100 double, $100 to $112 triple. Room prices are about 18% lower in summer, 40% lower in autumn.

THE UPPER BRACKET: The history of tourism on Cozumel began with a few simple hotels right in town. As the trade developed, fancier hotels were built along the small beaches on the northern shore. Today these hotels are among the older ones on the island, but they've been suitably maintained, and they provide alternatives to the much larger, newer hotels which command the highest prices.

Hotels north of town seem not to be quite so interested in attracting a diving clientele as do those south of town. Rather, these places appeal to vacationers looking for a comfortable room in a smaller hotel with a swimming pool, near the beach. The beaches north of town tend to be tiny little coves surrounded by the jagged coral which makes up Cozumel's bedrock. Here's the rundown, starting with the northernmost hotel and heading south.

The 94-room **Mayan Plaza Hotel,** Apdo. 9, Cozumel, Q. Roo 77600 (tel. 987/2-0072 or 2-0411), near the northern end of the shore road, has tidy, air-conditioned guest rooms, a nice pool, lots of shade trees, and its own tiny beach. If you want a quiet, secluded place away from traffic and the town, this is the place. Rooms rent for 50,700 pesos ($101.43) in winter's high season.

The **Hotel El Cozumeleño,** Apdo. 53, Cozumel, Q. Roo 77600 (tel. 987/2-0050 or 2-0149), is located right on Santa Pilar beach, one of the largest stretches of coral-free sand in the area. The pretty dining room looks out onto the Caribbean, as do all of the 80 air-conditioned guest rooms. There's a very nice palm-shaded swimming pool, with poolside palapa bar. Prices here are quite reasonable for what you get: 43,125 pesos ($86.25) double in winter.

The motel-style **Cabañas del Caribe,** Apdo. 9, Cozumel, Q. Roo 77600 (tel. 987/2-0017 or 2-0072), has 56 rooms facing the Caribbean and Santa Pilar beach, but in many cases the view of

---

A Special Plan

The **Club Cozumel Caribe,** Apdo. 43, Cozumel, Q. Roo 77600 (tel. 987/2-0100, or toll free 800/327-2254 in U.S.), is the largest hotel on Cozumel, with 260 rooms. Many are in the older nine-floor "tower" section, others are more modern junior suites. The hotel operates on a plan whereby you pay one price and receive everything the hotel has to offer: drinks, meals, tennis, water sports, and lodging. You must stay a minimum of three nights, and you may take advantage of special reduced rates for longer stays. The base price in the winter season is $164 for two people, per day. In summer, however, you can get a junior suite, plus meals, drinks, and all other services for a week (seven nights) for $500 double. Call for details of current offerings.

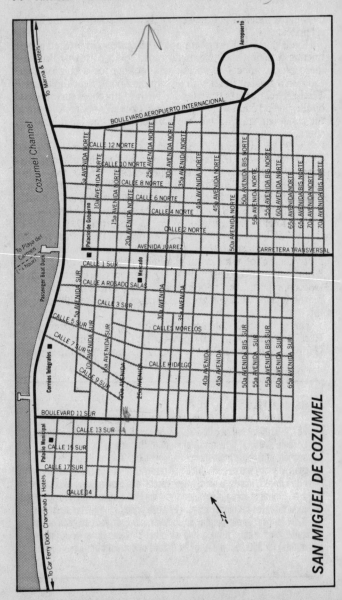

SAN MIGUEL DE COZUMEL

the sea is blocked by palm trees. Rooms have the standard comforts—private bath, air conditioning, etc.—and cost 40,000 pesos ($80) double in winter.

THE MIDDLE RANGE, NORTH OF TOWN: Several hotels north of town have locations that are not quite as choice, rooms that are not so luxurious, and no toll-free reservations numbers, but they do have prices that are refreshingly moderate. Here they are, in order of preference:

The **Hotel Cantarell,** Apdo. 24, Cozumel, Q. Roo 77600 (tel. 987/2-0144), has 100 air-conditioned rooms on four floors, with sea views. The restaurant has a Caribbean view that will make you think you're hanging suspended right above the crystalline waters. The hotel's "beach" is actually a sandy area elevated a few feet above the shore and held in by a retaining wall. It's fine for sunning, and you need only step down from the retaining wall to reach the water. The Cantarell's swimming pool has a palm tree growing right in the middle, from its own tiny "island." The price for a room is eminently reasonable: 20,000 pesos ($40) double in winter.

Similar in price and comforts is the **Hotel Mara,** Apdo. 7, Cozumel, Q. Roo 77600 (tel. 987/2-0300), where each of the 50 rooms, on four floors, has its own balcony where you can watch the sunset. All rooms have an individual air conditioner and private bath, and cost 20,000 pesos ($40) double in winter. The Mara has a nice swimming pool surrounded by lounge chairs for sunning, a restaurant and a bar, a dock for water sports, and a sandy "beach" held up by a retaining wall. It's an excellent place to get value for your money.

The **Hotel Playa Azul,** Apdo. 31, Cozumel, Q. Roo 77600 (tel. 987/2-0033 or 2-0043), facing Playa San Juan, is modern, simple, painted all in white, and lacks a swimming pool, which may account for prices such as these: $46 single, $50 double, $53 triple in the main hotel and in the smaller villas. Suites cost $11 to $14 more per room.

MODERATE PRICES, SOUTH OF TOWN: Because the beaches tend to lie north of town, hostelries to the south cater mostly to the diving set. After all, you don't require a beach if you're going to dive from a boat. However, this does not mean that you must be a diver to enjoy your stay at one of these places. Each one has either a swimming pool, or a tiny cove, or a dock, or all three. You'll be able to swim, sun, and relax at any of these hotels. If you intend to dive, remember to bring proof of your diver's certification.

The **Hotel Barracuda,** Apdo. 163, Cozumel, Q. Roo 77600 (tel. 987/2-0002), is at Avenida Rafael Melgar Prolongación Sur No. 628, about six blocks south of town. It's the closest diver's hotel to town; you can easily walk the distance. Though it has no swimming pool, the Barracuda does have a little man-made cove in which to swim. A room here costs $43 double, breakfast included ($37 double without breakfast), and comes with a sea view, balcony, air conditioning, fan, and refrigerator. The 35-room Barracuda is a favorite with divers, and has been so for years.

The **Galápago Inn,** Apdo. 289, Cozumel, Q. Roo (tel. 987/2-0663, or Aqua-Sub Tours toll free 800/847-5708 in U.S. except Texas, and 713/783-3305 in Texas), is a mile south of the main square. Homey, shady, done in colonial style with white stucco and red brick accents, the inn is usually peopled by divers who have signed up for one of the several money-saving package deals. If you come on your own, you can get a room with balcony, air conditioner, fan, and private bath, plus breakfast and dinner each day, for $91 double. The inn has its own pretty swimming pool, and a bit of beach.

La Perla Beach Hotel, Apdo. 309, Cozumel, Q. Roo 77600 (tel. 987/2-0188 or 2-0819), has 39 nouveau-rustic rooms on three floors overlooking the water, a small beach, and a swimming pool raised above beach level. The atmosphere here is of and for scuba-divers, who pay $56 double (cash) or $66 double (credit card) for an air-conditioned room, continental breakfast included. You're still not all that far from the town here, though you'll probably want to ride rather than walk the distance.

A Private Villa

The **Hotel Villablanca,** Apdo. 230, Cozumel, Q. Roo 77600 (tel. 987/2-0730 or 2-0865), has only 20 rooms, but each one is different—some have Jacuzzis, others are actually junior suites—and the feeling is definitely like staying in a private villa. Columns and statues are placed around the grounds to enhance the effect. For $63 double in winter you get a room, plus use of the tennis court, swimming pool, and the beach dock across the road. There's a restaurant as well.

MODERATE PRICES, RIGHT IN TOWN: Facing the main plaza in San Miguel is the **Meson San Miguel,** Avenida Juárez Z B, Cozumel,

Q. Roo 77600 (tel. 987/2-0233 or 2-0323). Though it has no beachfront, and few rooms with any view of the sea, and no divers' ambience, it does offer 97 very comfortable, air-conditioned rooms with bath for only 18,500 to 21,000 pesos ($37 to $42) double, plus use of the hotel's pretty swimming pool. There's a nice restaurant, and virtually any other restaurant in town is just a few minutes' walk from the hotel's front door.

BUDGET PRICES, IN TOWN: Virtually all of the island's low-priced hostelries are right in the town of San Miguel itself. Some are frequented by the diving crowd, but all welcome any visitor. Prices given below are the normal winter high-season rates, which may go down somewhat in summer, but not by much.

You can hardly do better than the **Hotel Vista del Mar,** on the shoreline promenade called Avenida Rafael Melgar at no. 45 (tel. 987/2-0545). Large rooms here shine with white paint and a joyful decor, which includes, in many rooms, a sea-view wall entirely of glass opening onto a small balcony from which you can gaze at the public beach just across the street, and far out to sea. Each room has its own air conditioner, and prices are set according to the season and whether or not the room has a view: off-season the rooms cost 9,500 pesos ($19) double without the view, 10,500 pesos ($21) with; during high-season months of mid-November to mid-April prices are slightly higher. If you can afford it, try this place first.

Whether or not you will feel "Comfortable as In Your Own Home," as advertised in the brochure, you are certain to admire the **Hotel Elizabeth,** Calle Salas no. 3-A (tel. 987/2-0330), for its cleanliness and the helpfulness of the staff. A minute and manicured garden plot adds a splash of green. You have two choices for accommodations: suites come with kitchen, living room, and bedroom, a refrigerator and all utensils, and cost 10,000 pesos ($20) double; the double rooms (no kitchen) cost 8,000 pesos ($16).

A downtown hotel with great appeal is the **Hotel Mary-Carmen,** 5a Avenida Sur 4 (tel. 987/2-0356 or 2-0581), half a block from the zócalo (main square). Watched over by a conscientious collection of matronly señoras, the hotel specializes in cleanliness and some elegant touches: brocade couches in the lobby, extra decoration in the rooms, screens on the windows, and a mammoth *mamey* tree in the courtyard. The two-story structure harbors 27 rooms priced at 7,600 pesos ($15.20) single or double (with two beds, good for families). All rooms have a beautiful tile bath and also air conditioning.

A hotel on the southern edge of town is the **Hotel Maya Co-**

zumel, Calle 5a Sur no. 4 (tel. 987/2-0011). The upbeat rooms are painted in white and orange and have odd triangular showers. Comfy leather deck chairs add another touch of class. In the rear court is a small swimming pool surrounded by thick lawn and bougainvillea; a small restaurant/bar looks onto the lawn and pool. Rooms come with air conditioning and the price is okay: 10,235 pesos ($20.47) double.

The **Hotel El Marques,** (5a Avenida Sur no. 12 (tel. 987/2-0537), right downtown, has several surprising touches that make it a delight. The rooms have quaint formal-ish touches such as ersatz gold trim and Formica-marble countertops, but the air conditioning is genuine, the baths are kept quite clean, and the staff is attentive. The big surprise is the tiny swimming pool (you won't expect the hotel to have one when you see it) and the ingenious wall-waterfall behind it, next to a minuscule bar. Rates are 10,000 pesos ($20) single, 11,500 pesos ($23) double, less per day if you stay a while. A great place!

Right across the street from the El Marques is a mini-mall of shops, and also the **Hotel Suites Bazar Colonial,** Avenida 5 Sur no. 9, Apdo. 286 (tel. 987/2-0506). Prices at this nice, new hostelry might seem high at 17,000 pesos ($34) double in the junior suites, and 19,000 pesos ($38) double in the master suites, but you get a nicely appointed studio or one-bedroom apartment, with complete kitchenette, for the cost. Pay in cash, get a discount. It's certainly one of the few hotels on the island to have an elevator, which serves its four floors. Rooms are quiet, and air-conditioned.

The **Posada Letty,** Calle 1 Sur at 15a Avenida Sur (tel. 987/2-0257), is hard to find because there's nothing to tell you it's a hotel except for a tiny sign: no lobby, reception desk, potted palms. But the rooms are there, each with louvered wooden shutters on the windows to let in the breeze and ceiling fans to whirl it around. All rooms have a tiled shower and ceiling fan; single travelers pay 3,500 pesos ($7) and two persons pay 4,000 pesos ($8) for any of the eight rooms on two floors. To get to the Letty, walk from the main square up Calle 1 Sur past the Banco del Atlantico until you see the small sign on the right-hand side of the street. The man who runs the Letty works in the little store on the corner just past the pension.

The **Hotel Pepita,** 15a Avenida Sur no. 6 (or no. 120, by a later numbering system), corner of Calle 1 Sur (tel. 987/2-0098), is more like a pension than a hotel. Rooms, some old, some new, some abuilding, have been fixed up with ceiling fans and tile baths and rent for 6,800 pesos ($13.60) single, 7,200 pesos ($14.40) double, 7,500 pesos ($15) triple, but this may include such luxuries as a mammoth bottle of purified water in the room, as well as a small refrigerator to keep it cool. It's very quiet here on the back street, and if your room gets stuffy you can relax in the very beautiful garden terrace to one side of the hotel. For reservations, write to Apdo. Postal 56.

A quiet downtown choice is the **Hotel El Pirata,** 5a Avenida Sur no. 3-A (tel. 987/2-0051), a small place with quite acceptable standard rooms going for 4,500 pesos ($9) single and 5,000 pesos ($10) double with ceiling fan, or 5,500 pesos ($11) single and 6,000 pesos ($12) double with air conditioning. Here you're only two blocks from the ferry dock and a stone's throw from the main square.

The very simple **Hotel Yoli** (or Yoly), Calle 1 Sur no. 164, between the main plaza and 10a Avenida Sur (tel. 987/2-0024), has plain and rather dark rooms, nothing to write home about, but clean. The price, however, is great: 3,500 pesos ($7) double, in expensive Cozumel.

The **Posada Edem,** Calle 2 Norte no. 12 (tel. 987/2-1166), near 5a Avenida Norte and the Sports Page Restaurant, is a newish, modest hostelry where you can get a room with fan, shower, and one bed or two for 4,000 pesos ($8) double.

The **Hotel Aguilar,** 5a Avenida Sur and Calle 3 Sur (tel. 987/2-0307), sounds good when you hear about it: air-conditioned rooms, filtered swimming pool, interior gardens, reasonable rates. The management seems a bit bewildered by the hotel business, but if the gardens are blooming, the air conditioning working, and the pool full, it's well worth the 7,500 pesos ($15) asked for a double room.

Cozumel's Restaurants

Cozumel is well provided with places to dine, but one must be careful in choosing a place because "resort food" is a problem here, as it is in most seaside resorts. Proprietors think that hungry customers will show up whether the food is good or not, and they're not far from wrong. A number of places sometimes rise above this level of thinking, though, and here they are:

Best all-around is a restaurant suitable for breakfast, lunch, dinner, or just a late-night dish of ice cream. The **Restaurant Las Palmeras** (tel. 2-0532) is only a few steps from the zócalo at the corner of Avenidas Juárez and Rafael Melgar, very near the ferry dock. Las Palmeras is open to the four winds, although tables are shaded from the sun. Always busy, service is nonetheless fairly efficient, and prices are moderate. A breakfast of bacon, eggs, and strong coffee will cost 800 pesos ($1.60), a light lunch of enchiladas suizas followed by guayaba con queso (guava paste with a slice of cheese, and crackers—delicious!) will be only about 1,400 pesos ($2.80). Dinner can be light as lunch, or can run to seafood at 1,200 or 1,500 pesos ($2.40 or $3) per plate, or even lobster.

Cozumel, heavily populated with North Americans, finally has its own unabashedly North American restaurant. Called **The Sports Page** (tel. 2-1199), it features a satellite TV antenna on the roof to snag all the stateside network sports action, and displays team pennants and T-shirts on the walls. It's air-conditioned. It serves burgers ($3.70). Its prices are in dollars. It has "all-you-can-eat" nights (shrimp, $9). In short, though Mexican-owned, it is very American. Hours are every day from 10 a.m. to 2 a.m.

Pepe's Grill, (tel. 2-0213) south of the main square on the waterfront drive (Avenida Rafael Melgar), is deluxe: low lights, soft music, solicitous waiters. Tables are open to sea breezes; failing that, ceiling fans move the air. The menu is short and not cheap, with most meat and fish courses costing about 2,500 pesos ($5), although a Mexican combination plate is 2,000 pesos ($4). Despite the prices, it's a very popular place. Open for dinner only, 1 p.m. to 12 midnight.

B.B.Q.'s, on Melgar north of the square between Calles 4 and 6 Norte (tel. 2-1569), is Pepe's place. The specialty is barbecued spare ribs, chicken, and roast beef. The decor and service is beach-bum hideaway, with live country and western dance music accompaniment: old wagon wheels, plants, funky-posh design of wood beams and paraphernalia. There's a view of the bay, and a menu (in English) with prices of 1,100 pesos ($2.20) for chicken or ribs, 2,600 pesos ($5.20) for shrimp kebab.

To escape Cozumel's high prices, escape the town itself. On Avenida Rafael Melgar at the southern outskirts of town, a few steps south of the lighthouse, is the **Restaurant Costa Brava** (no phone). Modest but certainly not plain, the Costa Brava has lots of local decoration, decent service, and fairly good food at exceptionally low prices. Set-price breakfasts, served till 9 a.m., cost 360 to 450 pesos (72¢ to 90¢) and include good coffee with a dash of cinnamon; don't bother with the "orange juice." Lunch or dinner can be bistec or filet of fish, and a three-course repast won't cost more than 2,000 or 2,500 pesos ($4 or $5) unless you have lobster. Wine and beer are served, and the restaurant is open every day from 6:30 a.m. to 11:30 p.m.

FOR PIZZA: When Cozumel has a pizza joint, it's no dive, and so **Pizza Rolandi,** four blocks north of the main square along Avenida Rafael Melgar, is about as elegant a pizzeria as you're likely to run into anywhere. Deck chairs and red-and-white-checkered tablecloths make the interior garden very mod, and candle lamps add romance. The Four Seasons pizza, at 1,600 pesos ($3.20), is eight inches in diameter and serves only one person, but what a serving: it comes topped with black olives, tomatoes, asparagus, cheese, and ham. The pizza margarita costs only 1,100 pesos ($2.20), but others (six kinds) are all priced the same as the Four Seasons. Wine, beer, and mixed drinks are all served. Rolandi is open from noon to midnight daily.

STARVATION-BUDGET RESTAURANTS: Although you may doubt it, there are possibilities for dining on Cozumel that will leave your budget not only intact, but robustly healthy. On Calle 2 Norte, half a block in from the waterfront, is the **Panificadora Cozumel,** excellent for a do-it-yourself breakfast, or for picnic supplies.

Few eateries are cheaper than a Mexican lunchroom, and Cozumel's version is the **Restaurant Los Moros,** 10a Avenida Norte at Avenida Juárez, a block east of the main plaza. Lunch can be soup, Mexican-style bistec or breaded fish filet; with lemonade and a tip, the total comes to 1,300 pesos ($2.60). Though there are fans, it can be hot in here because the kitchen and dining room are one. Open for breakfast, lunch, and dinner, except Monday.

For a quick, healthful pick-me-up on a hot day, drop by the **Fruit and Juice Bar** at the corner of Calle 1 Sur and 5a Avenida Sur, just a few steps from the Hotel El Marqués. The sweet smell of fruit greets you as you enter. Juices, liquados, "the best coffee in town," yogurt, and pastries are served in stark surroundings, at low prices. The señora squeezes fruit, not you.

Touring the Island

The question of tours brings us back to rentals, as there is no good reason to take an organized tour. You can rent a bicycle, motorbike, or car, and the motorized vehicles will take you around the southern part of the island easily in a half day, although it will take all day to cover the 42 miles (70 km) on a bicycle.

Head south along Avenida Melgar out of town, past the Hotel Barracuda. The Hotel La Perla is next, then the Villa Blanca. Remember that no hotel in Mexico "owns" the beach—by law, all beaches are public property, so feel free to use a "hotel" beach. On Cozumel this public ownership is more important than ever, as most of the island is surrounded by coral reefs difficult to walk across (that coral is sharp!) let alone lie on.

About five miles (eight kilometers) south of town you'll come to the big Sol Caribe and La Ceiba hotels, and also the car-ferry dock, for ferries to Puerto Morelos. Go snorkeling out in the water by the Hotel La Ceiba and you might spot a sunken airplane. No, it's not the wreckage of a disaster; it was put there for an underwater movie.

CHANCANAB: A mile past the big hotels is this lagoon, which has long been famous for the color and variety of its sea life. Actually, it became too famous. It was discovered that the intrusion of sightseers was ruining the marine habitat, and that if swimming were not controlled, snorkelers would soon have only one another to look at. So now you must swim in the open sea, not in the lagoon, which is just as well. If you don't have snorkeling gear with you, it's rentable right here.

GOOD BEACHES: Next beach you'll come to, at 10 miles (16 km), is Playa San Francisco, and south of it, Playa Palancar. By Cancún standards they're not much, but on Cozumel they're the best, so plan most of your beach time for here. Food (usually overpriced) and equipment rentals are available.

The underwater wonders of famous Palancar Reef are offshore from Playa Palancar, and you'll need a boat to see them. Numerous vessels on the island operate daily diving and snorkeling tours to Palancar, so the best plan is to shop around and sign up for one of those.

PUNTA CELARAIN: After Playa San Francisco, the drive becomes boring as you plow through the jungle on a straight road for miles. The only distraction is the turnoff (on the left) to Cedral, a tiny market hamlet that is deserted most of the time. Otherwise, all you see is jungle until you're 17½ miles (28 km) from town.

Finally, though, you emerge near the southern reaches of the island on the east coast. The lighthouse you see to the south is at **Punta Celarain,** the island's southernmost tip. The sand track is not suitable for motorbikes, but in a car you can drive to the lighthouse in about 25 minutes.

THE EASTERN SHORE: The road along the east coast of the island is wonderful, with views of the sea and the rocky shore, surf pounding into it, and on the land side are little farms and hamlets. Exotic birds take flight as you approach, and monstrous (but harmless) iguanas skitter off into the undergrowth. Most of the east coast is unsafe for swimming because the surf can create a deadly *undertow, which will have you far out to sea in a matter of minutes.* But at a few places on this coast there are headlands and breakers that create safe swimming areas. At **Chan Río** you can swim, and also at **Punta Morena,** where there is even a small motel and restaurant. **Playa Chiqueros** is also safe, and has a little restaurant.

Halfway up the east coast, the paved road meets the transversal road back to town, 9½ miles (15 km) away.

HEADING ON: Not ready to go back to town yet? For adventure, start out on the sand track that continues north from this junction. Follow this road for 11 very rough and rocky miles (18 km) through the jungle, past little abandoned farms, along the rocky shore to **El Castillo Real,** an unimpressive but authentic Maya ruin in the middle of nowhere. The trip from the paved road to the Castillo takes 1½ hours, and then the same amount of time to return, but the time is spent watching hermit crabs scutter through the sand, watching lizards watch you, and listening to pairs of parrots squawk as they wing overhead. Don't attempt this trip in a large or a low car, or on a motorbike. Best thing to have is a VW Safari.

A scattering of other vestiges from Cozumel's Maya religious past can be found throughout the northern reaches of the island. One of the most popular trips is to **San Gervasio.** A road leads there from the airport, but you'll find it rough going. When it comes to Cozumel's Mayan remains, getting there is most of the fun, and you should do it for the trip, not for the ruins. For real Mayan cities, visit Tulum and Coba, on the mainland.

BACK IN TOWN: The adventure over, spend some time strolling along the Avenida Rafael Melgar admiring the unique black coral found in Cozumel's waters, and made into all sorts of fanciful jewelry.

At night, check out what's playing at the Cine Cozumel, Avenida Rafael Melgar between 2 Norte and 4 Norte. It's probably in Spanish, but when it comes to the light melodrama usually offered here, that's just as well.

Water Sports

Few people come to Cozumel to spend their time on land, even if it's beach land. Like a huge boat moored permanently in the sparkling Caribbean, Cozumel has people jumping from its gunwales day and night (yes! you can go scuba-diving at night!).

SNORKELING AND SCUBA-DIVING: Anyone who can swim can go snorkeling. Rental of the snorkel (breathing pipe), goggles, and flippers should only cost about 1,250 pesos ($2.50) for a half day.

The brilliantly colored tropical fish provide a dazzling show for free.

Various establishments on the island rent scuba gear—tanks, regulator with pressure guage, buoyancy compensator, mask, snorkel, and flippers. Many will also arrange a half-day expedition in a boat complete with lunch for a set price. Sign up the day before, if you're interested.

Sailboards are for rent at several hotels south of town, including the Divers' Inn and the Villa Blanca.

BOAT EXCURSIONS: Another popular Cozumel pastime is the boat excursion, by yourself or as part of a group, with snorkeling or scuba-diving or without. Various types of tours are offered, including a glass-bottom boat tour lasting 1½ hours and costing 3,000 pesos ($6) per person.

Chapter VI

MEXICO'S CARIBBEAN COAST

THE DEVELOPMENT OF resort facilities at Cancún changed the entire aspect of Mexico's Caribbean coast. In times B.C. (Before Cancún), there were only a few small beachfront bungalow hotels, catering to the scuba-diving set, to be found along this coast. The ruined Maya seaport of Tulum was visited occasionally by tourists from Cozumel, but the far more impressive Maya city of Cobá, some 30 miles inland, was peopled only by ghosts and archeologists. Other Maya sites were known only to the local inhabitants, and were otherwise lost in the thick jungle. Some of the country's most heavenly beaches were virtually empty, all year round.

Then came FONATUR, the Mexican government agency charged with developing the country's tourism infrastructure, along with a host of other acronymic agencies, and the Caribbean coast began to change rapidly. Roads and electricity were provided, facilities were built on the better beaches, and one sight (Xel-ha) was declared a national park.

The coast is still undergoing great change, as you'll see by the bulldozers charging through the jungle. And though most of the lodging-places are still very modest, more upscale places are already under construction. Still, if it's comfort you're looking for, you'd better plan—and reserve—ahead to avoid disappointment.

A ramble down the coast from Cancún takes you past beautiful inlets crowded with brilliantly colored tropical fish, along wonderful beaches shaded by coconut palms, to the great Maya cities of Tulum and Cobá, through the farming town of Felipe Carrillo Puerto which figured prominently in the War of the Castes, to beautiful but undeveloped Lago de Bacalar, and finally to Chetumal, booming capital city of the state of Quintana Roo. We'll go the whole distance, north to south.

TRANSPORTATION: Without doubt, the best way to explore the coast is by private car or by tour bus. Even in your own vehicle, you must consider the distances to be covered: from Cancún to Playa del Carmen is about an hour's drive (42 miles), to Tulum and Xel-Ha about two hours' drive (81 miles), and all the way to Chetumal about five hours' drive (242 miles).

If you don't have your own car, transport along the Caribbean coast presents problems. Though there are about a dozen buses a day down the coast (see the introduction to this chapter), you may end up waiting along the sweltering highway for an hour or more only to have a jam-packed bus roar right by you. The difficulty of transport has given rise to a lively practice of hitchhiking. Be prepared to hitch whenever the opportunity presents itself; and if you're driving, why not give rides to hitchers?

Puerto Morelos

Only a short ride (21 miles, 36 km) south of Cancún along Hwy. 307 lies the village of Puerto Morelos. Its reason for being is the car ferry, which departs from a dock here on its voyage to Cozumel, several hours away. So far, Puerto Morelos has not shared measurably in the building boom that has swept this coast, so there are not many recommendable lodging places or restaurants. You need not go without a bed and a meal, however.

WHERE TO STAY AND EAT: The little **Posada Amor** (no phone), on the inland road to the ferry dock (right-hand side as you approach the dock), rents simple rooms with screens on the windows and a common bathroom for 4,500 pesos ($9) double. The rooms are quite plain, but adequate.

The Posada's restaurant is rustic and very amusing: a big thatched hut is decorated with painted wooden masks, craft items, and a motorcycle helmet in each corner. Ask what's cooking, as the "menu" is liable to be limited to one or two items. Prices are reasonable, and an entire meal need cost only 1,500 pesos ($3) or so. No alcohol is served.

As you come into Puerto Morelos from the main highway, you turn right for the Posada Amor and the ferry dock. But if you go well into town and turn left, you'll see the **Cabañas Playa Ojo de Agua** (reservations in Mérida at Calle 65 no. 254-B, Apdo. Postal 709 Yucatán 97000; tel. 992/3-0841 or 1-5150). The Cabañas is very popular with the scuba-diving set, with 21 rooms in little cabañas and bungalows renting for 13,500 pesos ($27). Rooms have fans and good cross-ventilation which, with sea breeze, renders air conditioning unnecessary. There's a restaurant here.

THE CAR FERRY: You won't have trouble finding the car-ferry dock (tel. 988/2-0916, 2-0938, or 2-0849), as it's the largest establishment in town. The ferry schedule does change now and then, so you should call in advance if possible. Note that there is no car ferry service on Monday.

I must mention that the ferries are rarely on schedule. Even so, you must act as though they will be on time, and so you must do this: arrive at the ferry dock any day (except Monday) between 5 and 6 a.m. to buy your ticket for the ferry that will leave (you hope) at 7 a.m. Boarding of vehicles begins at 6 a.m. if all goes according to plan. The journey to Cozumel, not counting the wait on shore, takes between 2½ and 4 hours, depending upon sea and wind. Passenger cars and small campers take precedence over larger vehicles, and so there's not usually a problem getting a ticket and boarding if you're there at the proper time.

The return voyage from Cozumel leaves the car-ferry dock, south of town near the Hotel Sol Caribe, at 12 noon or so, but be there early to buy your ticket and to get in line. (Re-check this schedule as soon as you arrive in Cozumel.)

Fares are 160 pesos (32¢) per person, 830 pesos ($1.66¢) per vehicle—obviously there's a heavy subsidy from the government! Passengers on foot are welcome on the voyage; you are not required to have a car. The voyage from Puerto Morelos to Cozumel is longer than the voyage from Playa del Carmen to Cozumel (45 minutes), but the Puerto Morelos car ferry is a larger, heavier craft, and rarely makes its passengers seasick. On the small boats from Playa del Carmen, seasickness is a problem on any windy day.

ONWARD: Heading south on Hwy. 307 from Puerto Morelos, the village of Muchi is the next landmark. The distance from Puerto Morelos to Playa del Carmen is only 20 miles (32 km) but before you reach the latter town, you'll come to Punta Bete, a few miles north of Playa del Carmen.

Punta Bete

There's no settlement to speak of at Punta Bete, just two hotels aimed at a scuba-diving clientele.

La Posada del Capitan Lafitte (no phone) is at the end of a 1¼-mile-long rough dirt road which heads east from the highway (you'll see a sign). White cement-block bungalows thatched with palm fronds are equipped with beds and rough-and-ready showers. You'll find a swimming pool, dining room, and dive shop. Divers from North America make up virtually the entire clientele here, and pay $84 double in cash (no credit cards accepted) for a bungalow room, breakfast and dinner included. For information, send letters to Apdo. 1463, Succ. "B", Mérida, Yucatán 97000, or call 992/23-0485 or 21-6114; or contact the CVI Group, Box 2664, Evergreen, CO 80439 (tel. 303/674-9615, or toll free 800/538-6802 in U.S.).

About 39 miles (63 km) south of Cancún, and two-thirds of a mile or so south of the turn-off for Capitan Lafitte, is a sign directing you east off the highway, for almost a mile (1½ km) down a rough dirt road to **El Marlin Azul** (no phone), Punta Bete, Q. Roo, the quintessential Caribbean hideaway—the best in the immediate area. The inn has no swimming pool, and it's on a surf beach, but it is surrounded by lots of palm trees and perfect quiet. The price for a room with king-size bed, private bath with hot water, a fan, and a porch, is $75, breakfast and dinner included. For a room with two double beds, three people pay $98, four people pay $121. If you want to get away from it all, this is the place. For more information and reservations, you can contact their office in Mérida, Calle 61 no. 477, Yucatán 97000 (tel. 992/21-7410). By the way, once you've paid, no refunds are given and no cancellations are accepted.

Playa del Carmen

This little Caribbean village came into being because of the passenger boat service to Cozumel, but recently it has developed a tourist trade of its own. Intrepid travelers have discovered that Playa del Carmen's beaches are far better than those on Cozumel, as much of Cozumel's coast is covered by sharp coral or is pounded by dangerous surf.

As of this writing, Playa del Carmen's lodgings consist of several plush and expensive hotels, and a handful of very inexpensive but basic hostelries; there is as yet very little in the way of a comfortable middle ground. But it will come.

WHERE TO STAY AND EAT: The town's most prominent hotels are also its most expensive. Right down by the Cozumel boat dock is the **Hotel Molcas** (reservations in Mérida at Turismo Aviomar;

tel. 992/1-6661 or 1-6620). The very comfortable hotel cascades down the hillside, giving many rooms and the dockside restaurant fine ocean views. The price for a double room is 24,700 pesos ($49.40). You may well get a reduction in price if you try.

On the other (south) side of the boat dock from the Molcos is another lavish place, the **Hotel Playacar** (tel. in Cancún, 988/3-0935), with rooms for $63 double, with air conditioning and a sea view. The Playacar has a deck restaurant overlooking the ferry dock and the beach, the perfect place to while away an hour if you're waiting for the boat. Have a fruit salad, or a plate of enchiladas, or a sandwich and a beer, and it will set you back about 1,500 pesos ($3). Don't eat too much, though. Remember the danger of seasickness!

About the only lodging-place in town in the moderate price range is the **Blue Parrot Inn** (no phone; mail to Apdo. 1258, Cancún, Q. Roo 77500), a short eight blocks north of the ferry dock, on the shore. Built and staffed by Americans, the inn charges $35 double for a room sharing a bath with two other rooms.

Many of the town's inexpensive hostelries are placed along the road that comes into town from Hwy. 307. For instance, right by the highway junction is the **Hotel Maranatha** (no phone), on the left just after you turn from the highway, with double rooms for 8,500 pesos ($17). They tell me that the hot and cold water is always available, as are meals in the little restaurant.

Close in toward the center of town, along the same road, is the **Posada Lily** (no phone), on the right-hand (south) side. Double rooms with shower cost 4,500 pesos ($9). You can walk to the boat dock in 15 or 20 minutes if your luggage is not impossibly heavy.

More or less across the road from the Lily are two more places. The **Posada Marinelly** (no phone) charges 5,000 pesos ($10) for its simple rooms, set back from the road a bit and relatively quiet.

Right next door is the **Hotel Playa del Carmen** (no phone, no sign), with a collection of rooms to rent above a shop. Talk to the shopkeeper and you'll probably be quoted a price identical to that of the Marinelly.

You may be glad to know that Playa del Carmen has many little camping areas down along the water (turn to the left as you come to the center of town). There are also many small, inexpensive restaurants in this same area.

BOATS TO COZUMEL: Passenger boats leave Playa del Carmen's dock for Cozumel three times daily, at 6 a.m., noon, and 6 p.m., on the 45-minute trip. Return trips depart Cozumel at 4 and 9:30

a.m. and 4 p.m. A one-way ticket costs 430 pesos (86¢). Anyone subject to seasickness will be happy to know that there is an alternative method for getting between Playa del Carmen and Cozumel. If it's a windy day, consider flying.

SHUTTLE FLIGHTS TO COZUMEL: AeroCozumel operates an air shuttle service from Playa del Carmen's airstrip at the south edge of town to Cozumel's international airport. The modern twin-engine, eight-seat planes take off about every two hours throughout the day on the ten-minute trip. The price is 2,685 pesos ($5.37) one way. At Cozumel's airport, you will need to pay an additional 280 pesos (56¢) for a minibus ride into town.

It's nice to have this alternative to the ferry ride, which can be noisy, windy, and fraught with the hassles of seasickness.

SOUTH FROM PLAYA DEL CARMEN: Bus transportation from Playa del Carmen south is a chancey thing. In principle, buses meet each boat arriving from Cozumel and whisk passengers north to Cancún, but this may not happen. And to catch a bus south along the highway, you have to walk out to the highway (about 20 minutes) and wait for whatever may come by.

Once in a vehicle, however, you will come to Xcaret, five miles (eight km) south of Playa del Carmen.

Xcaret

As of this writing, Xcaret is someplace magical, a touch of Mayan romance. But the bulldozers have already entered the woods, so it won't last long. Get there soon.

A mile (1½ km) in from the highway brings you to the little **Rancho Xcaret,** a turkey farm which is so authentic with its rail fences and thatched Mayan *na* houses that you'll think its a Yucatecan theme park. But pay the tiny admission charge (50 pesos, 10¢) and walk eastward toward the sea along a path into the bush. Soon you'll pass some tumbledown little Mayan temples overgrown with jungle, and then get a glimpse of the sea.

At the end of the path is a narrow inlet, or *caleta,* bright with sun and flashing with tropical fish. The inlet has already been discovered by snorkelers, who come on foot or in boats, and by one intrepid souvenir seller who has set up shop in a *na.*

On your way back to the rancho, turn right at the Mayan ruins and take a path down a slope into the jungle. Pass several caves on your left, and after a few dozen yards you will see a crystalline pool in a great cave mouth, or grotto, its lightly salted water clear as glass. Though it's not well known to tourists, it's a favorite with local people, who come for a dip and a picnic. It can get busy. Come early or late in the day if you can.

Some 10 miles (16 km) south of Xcaret and a half mile east of the highway is **Pamul,** a safe cove for swimming. Little bungalows with hot-water showers face the beach. You can rent one for 6,000 pesos ($12) double, or camp for much less. Several pet monkeys preside at the simple restaurant-bar, and a sign warns, "They bite." For information in Cancún, contact Sr. Humberto Rosado Loria at Apdo. Postal 1143, Cancún, Q. Roo 77500.

In a very short time you come to Akumal, one of Mexico's newest stars in Caribbean tourism.

Akumal

Of the fledging resorts south of Cancún, Akumal is perhaps the most developed, with moderately priced bungalows scattered among the graceful palms that line the beautiful, soft beach.

Signs point the way in from the highway, and less than a third of a mile toward the sea you will come to the Akumal gateway. The resort complex here consists of three distinct establishments which share the same wonderful, smooth palm-lined beach protected by a breakwater.

The **Hotel-Club Akumal Caribe Villas Maya** (P.O. Box 1976, El Paso, TX 79950; tel. 915/584-3552, or toll free 800/351-1622 outside Texas), rents bungalows easily capable of sleeping two couples or a family. Each is equipped with bath and air conditioner, and costs 20,000 pesos ($40) double.

Las Casitas Akumal (in Cancún at Apdo. Postal 714 Q. Roo 77500; tel. 988/4-1945 or 4-1689) is a collection of villas or bungalows rented by the day, week, or month. Each faces the sea, has two bedrooms, two baths, a living room, fan, and refrigerator, and can accommodate up to five people. A small store and restaurant nearby take care of the food problem, and a diving shop caters to the scuba set. The price for up to five people is 28,000 pesos ($56), or $11.20 per person, daily.

Just 300 yards/meters south of these two places is the **Hotel Akumal Caribe Ina Yana Kin** (tel. in Cancún 988/4-2272), a very nice and modern 116-room, two-story hotel in a palm grove by the beach. Rates for its comfy rooms-with-bath are 21,200 pesos ($42.40) double, 27,00 pesos ($54) triple.

About a half mile south of the Akumal gateway along the highway is the turnoff (east) for **Aventuras Akumal** (tel. in Cancún 988/3-1933 or 3-1002, or toll free 800/826-6842 in U.S.), a luxury hotel, villa, and condominium complex on the beach, opened late in 1985. Set amid nicely landscaped grounds are a little swimming pool, a good stretch of sand, a restaurant and bar, and rooms in quasi-rustic units. Comfort in the rooms is anything but rustic, however, as they boast little pools for bathtubs, a king-size bed or two double beds, and air conditioners. The price is $72 double in winter, less in the warmer months.

After Adventuras Akumal, 3 miles (4 ½ km) south along the highway, comes the beach and camping area at **Chemuyil,** developed by the government as "the most beautiful beach in the world." Though sleepy and deserted in the summer, it's active in winter, with a snack bar, free medical clinic, and an admission fee for cars.

About 1½ miles (2½ km) south of Chemuyil and a quarter mile east of the highway, lies Xcacel, a gorgeous palm-shaded spot where you can pitch your tent or park your van for 250 pesos (50¢) per person per night, including use of changing rooms, toilets, and showers. There's a small restaurant here as well.

After traveling less than 8 miles (13 km) south of Akumal, you come to Xel-ha.

Xel-ha

The Caribbean coast of the Yucatán is carved by the sea into hundreds of small *caletas* (coves) that form the perfect habitat for tropical marine life, both flora and fauna. Many caletas remain undiscovered and pristine along the coast, but one caleta 72 miles (117 km) south of Cancún is enjoyed daily by snorkelers and scuba-divers who come to luxuriate in its warm waters, palm-lined shore, and brilliant fish. Xel-ha (that's *"shell*-hah") is a bit of paradise for swimming, with no threat of undertow or pollution. Being close to the ruins at Tulum makes Xel-ha the best place for a dip when you've finished clambering around the Maya castles. The short 8½-mile hop north from Tulum to Xel-ha is hard to do by bus, but you may have luck hitchhiking. Those who don't have a car and who don't want to chance missing Xel-ha can sign up for a tour from either Cancún or Cozumel: most companies include a trip to Tulum and a swim at Xel-ha in the same journey.

The entrance to Xel-ha is half a mile in from the highway. You'll be asked to pay a 200-peso (40¢) "contribution" to the upkeep and preservation of the site.

Once in the park, you can rent snorkeling equipment, buy a drink or a meal, change clothes, and take showers—facilities for all these are available. When you swim, be careful to observe the "swim here" and "no swimming" signs. *(Hint:* In the swimming areas, the greatest variety of fish are to be seen right near the ropes marking off the "no swimming" areas, and near any groups of rocks.) Xel-ha is an exceptionally beautiful place!

Just south of the Xel-ha turn-off on the west side of the highway, don't miss the Mayan ruins of ancient Xel-ha.

The Maya seaport of Tulum is 8 miles (13 km) south of Xel-ha.

Tulum

At the end of the Classic period in A.D. 900 the Maya civilization began to decline and most of the large ceremonial centers were deserted. The Postclassic Period (A.D. 900 to the Spanish Conquest) in the Yucatán was one of small rival states, Maya in culture but with some imported traditions from the Mexicans. Tulum is one such city-state, built in the 10th century as a fortress city overlooking the Caribbean. Aside from the spectacular setting, Tulum is not otherwise an impressive city. There are no magnificent pyramidal structures as are found in the Classic Maya ruins. The most imposing building in Tulum is the large stone structure on the cliff called the **Castillo** (castle), actually a temple-cum-fortress. At one time this was covered with stucco and painted.

The view from on top of the Castillo is quite grand. From here you get a good view of the city walls, which are constructed of limestone. In front of the Castillo are several palace-like buildings: unrestored stone structures partially covered with stucco. The **Temple of the Frescoes** is directly in front of the Castillo and contains some 13th-century wall paintings, which are quite interesting. They are inside the temple and the lighting is bad, so if you have a flashlight it would be helpful to bring it along. Most of the frescoes are hard to see, but they are distinctly Maya in content, representing the gods Chac (rain god) and Ix Chel (the goddess of the moon and of medicine). On the cornice of this temple is a relief of the head of a god. If you get a slight distance from the building you will see the eyes, nose, mouth, and chin. Notice the remains of the red-painted stucco on this building—at one time all the buildings at Tulum were painted a bright red.

Much of what we know of Tulum at the time of the Spanish Conquest comes from the writings of Diego de Landa, third bishop of Yucatán. He wrote that Tulum was a small city inhabited by about 600 people, who lived in dwellings situated on platforms along the street. The town commanded a strategic point on the Caribbean and thus supervised the trade traffic from Honduras to the Yucatán. Tulum survived about 70 years after the Conquest, when it was finally abandoned.

The ruins are open 8 a.m. to 5 p.m. Admission is 50 pesos (10¢).

WHERE TO STAY AND EAT: It's useful to know that Tulum consists of four distinct areas. First there's the junction of Hwy. 307 and the Tulum access road, where you'll find a small hotel, two restaurants, and a Pemex gas station. Then, less than a mile down the access road, are the ruins of Tulum and a collection of small restaurants, snack shops, and souvenir stands. Past the ruins, the road heads south along a narrow strip of sand to Boca Paila and Punta Allen. Though most of this 60-mile stretch of bad road is uninhabited, you will find a few beachcombers' settlements a few miles south of the ruins. The fourth area is the Mexican village of Tulum, right on Hwy. 307 about 1½ miles (2 km) south of the Hwy. 307–Tulum access road junction. There's nothing much in the way of services in Tulum village. Let's look at what the first three areas have to offer, in order.

Tulum Junction

Right at the junction of Hwy. 307 and the Tulum access road is the aptly named **Motel El Crucero,** which has rooms for rent plus a small restaurant. The rooms, though very basic, come with ceiling fans, hot and cold water, and cost 3,000 pesos ($6) double. In the thatched restaurant, rough-and-ready simple meals are yours for 1,500 to 1,800 pesos ($3 to $3.60). Beer is served, and a counter at one side of the restaurant serves as a tiny "convenience store."

Across the street from El Crucero is the **Restaurant El Faisan y El Venado,** with similar meals and prices.

Tulum Ruins

In at the entrance to the ruins are small soft-drink stands and eateries serving up things at resort prices. Not much you can do about it, though, if you're hungry. The **Centro Chac-Mool**—it's that modern palapa on the beach north of the ruins—gives more, but charges more as well.

Boca Paila

Down the road past the ruins are some lodgings (no phones) that might be good for the intrepid traveler. Hitchhiking is the only transport. The paved road ends 3 miles (4½ km) south of the ruins. Here's where you'll see the **Cabañas Chac-Mool,** a thatched-hut-and-campsite establishment. Though you can rent a very basic thatched-hut cabaña with bedding for an expensive 5,000 pesos ($10), you may find that you need mosquito netting. In effect, this is a place to come if you already have the camping gear you'll need.

The **Cabañas Los Arrecifes,** south of the Chac-Mool, about 3½ miles (5½ km) south of Tulum, are about the nicest on this stretch of beach, though still quite simple. A room set back from the beach, without a sea view and without a private bath, costs 4,500 pesos ($9) double; one right on the beach with bath goes for 7,500 pesos ($15) double. The ambience here is very laid-back.

The **Cabañas Tulum,** four miles (six km) south of the Tulum ruins, are little thatched bungalows facing a heavenly stretch of ocean beach (deadly surf). Each bungalow comes with well-used cold-water shower, two equally well-used beds, screens on the windows, rickety table, one electric light, and a veranda good for hanging a hammock. The cost is 4,000 ($8) double per night. The electricity is on from 5 to 10 p.m. only, so bring candles or a flashlight. A small restaurant serves three meals a day at fairly low prices; beer and soft drinks are on sale. Bring your own towels, soap, and blankets.

About a mile south of the turnoff to Tulum, on Hwy. 307, is the road to Cobá, another fascinating Maya city. Less than a mile past the Cobá road is Tulum village, with little to offer the tourist. If you're driving, turn right when you see the signs to Cobá, and continue on that road for 30 miles (50 km).

Cobá

The Yucatán is rich in breathtaking Mayan cities, but in its time, fewer were grander than Cobá. Linked to important cities many miles distant by excellent, straight roads through the jungle, Cobá itself covered numerous square miles on the shores of two Yucatecan lakes.

Today the city's principal monuments are on display again, but unless you take a tour or rent a car, they're difficult to reach.

Pay the 50-peso (10¢) admission fee at the little entrance shack, and stroll into the ruins. Keep your bearings as it's very easy to get lost on the maze of dirt roads in the jungle.

The Grupo Cobá boasts a large, impressive pyramid just in the entry gate to the right. Were you to go straight, you'd pass near the badly ruined *juego de pelota* (ball court).

Straight in from the entry gate, walk for 10 or 15 minutes to a fork in the road. The left fork leads to Nohoch Mul group, which contains El Castillo, the highest pyramid in the Yucatán (higher than the great El Castillo at Chichén-Itzá and the Pyramid of the Magician at Umal). The right fork (more or less straight on) goes to the Conjunto Las Pinturas. Here, the main attraction is the Pyramid of the Painted Lintel, a small structure with traces of the original bright colors above the door. You can climb up to get a close look.

Throughout the area, intricately carved stelae stand by pathways, or lie forlornly in the jungle underbrush.

It can be hot here deep in the jungle. You'd be well advised to visit Cobá in the morning, or after the heat of the day has passed.

WHERE TO STAY AND EAT: Staying at Cobá entails a choice between rags or riches. The very nice **Villa Arqueológica Cobá** (tel. in Cancún 988/4-2574), a Club Med operation, is here, right at lakeside, a five-minute walk from the ruins. The hotel has a French polish because of the Club Med affiliation and, as you might expect, the restaurant is top-notch, with full meals for about 4,600 pesos ($9.20). Comfortable rooms have private bath and air conditioning, and cost 9,000 pesos ($18) single, 13,200 pesos ($26.40) double, tax included. Besides rooms, the hotel has a library of books on Mesoamerican archeology (with books in French, English, and Spanish), and a swimming pool. You can make reservations in Mexico City at Hoteles Villa Arqueológicas, Avenida Masaryk 183, México, DF 11570 (tel. 905/203-3886).

Then there's the **Hotel Isabel** (no phone), a five-minute walk from the ruins back along the road to the highway. At the Isabel you can rent a bed for 1,900 pesos ($3.80), and I mean *a bed*. There's no bath, no washbasin, no running water, no linens, no blankets, no privacy, no screens; just a place to lie down and sleep. The place will no doubt get fancier in years to come, but right now it's pretty darn basic.

El Bocadito (no phone) is a restaurant and lodging near the Isabel with a handful of rooms priced at 3,000 pesos ($6) double. For this you get modern construction, washbasin and shower, and use of an electric lantern. There are only a handful of these rooms, and they may well be full unless you arrive to claim one early in the day. Don't expect anything fancy, but the proprietors do their best.

Felipe Carrillo Puerto

From the Cobá turnoff, the main highway (no. 307) heads southwest through Tulum village. About 14 miles (23 km) south of the village are the ruins of **Chunyaxche,** on the left-hand side (look for the little restaurant and camping area called "El Caminero"). The ruins aren't very exciting, but the price is right: admission is free after you sign the register. In exploring Chunyaxche, I was virtually eaten alive by mosquitos in the beautiful jungle. You may have better luck, though.

After Chunyaxche, the highway passes 45 miles (72 km) of jungle-bordered road with few distractions. Then comes an oasis of sorts.

Felipe Carrillo Puerto (pop. 15,000) is the only oasis in the jungle along the road to Ciudad Chetumal, and has this offer: several banks (off the zócalo), gas stations, a market, a small ice plant, a bus terminal, the intersection with the road back to Mérida, and a presentable handful of modest hotels and restaurants to serve the traveler's needs. Carrillo Puerto is the turning point for those making a "short circuit" of the Yucatán peninsula, as Hwy. 184 heads west from here to Ticul, Uxmal, Campeche, and Mérida. It is quite possible you may have to spend the night here, and very probable that you will arrive in town hungry.

As you spend your hour or your overnight in Carrillo Puerto, recall its strange history: this was where the rebels in the War of the Castes took their stand, guided by the "Talking Crosses." Some remnants of that town—Chan Santa Cruz—and that time are still extant. Look for signs in town pointing the way. For the full story, refer to Chapter I, "Yucatán's Fascinating History."

WHERE TO STAY: The highway goes right through the town, becoming Avenida Benita Juárez in town. Coming from the north, you will pass a traffic circle with a bust of the great Juárez. The town market is here.

Turn right (west) at the traffic circle, and you will immediately see, on the left-hand side of the road, the **Hotel La Colina** (no phone). Plain rooms, the only type to be found in town, rent for 2,500 pesos ($5) double. Watch out for the street noise when you choose a room.

Head south from the traffic circle to get to the other hotels and restaurants in town.

A few blocks south of the traffic circle, on the left-hand side of the road, just past the Restaurant Zona Maya is the small **Hotel San Ignacio**, a simple place with an interior court (for parking), and clean if very bare rooms. Prices are 1,500 pesos ($3) single, 2,000 pesos ($4) double, 1,300 pesos ($4.60) triple, with private bath and ceiling fan. Get to bed early—this town wakes with the dawn.

The street that crosses Avenida Juárez at the Hotel San Ignacio is Calle 67. Turn right onto it, go up past the banks (Banobras,

Banamex, and Banrural), and you will see the main square. Turn right just before the square for the **Hotel Chan Santa Cruz** (tel. 983/4-0170), located more or less behind the bank buildings. The plain rooms here, grouped around a courtyard in older buildings, cost 2,600 pesos ($5.20) double with fan, 4,200 pesos ($8.40) double with air conditioning.

On the main square, diagonal to the church, is an old Caribbean-style building—look for the wooden gallery on the second story. This houses the **Hotel Esquivel,** an odd collection of rooms, many with added-on showers, all neat and well kept if basic. Ceiling fans keep you cool; in some cases, double-knit sheets and pillowslips keep you hot. The lamp tables are sections of Mayan columns from temples. Original oil paintings decorate some walls. As for prices, the Esquivel is similar to the other places in town: 2,200 pesos ($4.40) double, for a room with a fan. Parking in the rear.

WHERE TO EAT: Starting from the traffic circle again, and heading south, the **Restaurant El Faisan y El Venado** is on the left-hand side. This is one of the townfolks' favorites, with a modern airy dining room equipped with ceiling fans, and even a small air-conditioned section (used mostly for private parties). Chances are that many tables will be filled at mealtimes, and people will happily be chowing down from the standard Mexican menu for only about 1,500 pesos ($3) all in.

Just down the street a few steps are two more dining choices, one of them air-conditioned. With a Pemex gas station on your right, the **Restaurant 24 Horas** will be on your left. Similar to El Faisan y El Venado, and priced about the same, the 24 Horas has long hours—24 of them, in fact—to recommend it, plus decent food at moderate prices. Also, it has a breathtaking Mayan glyph picture stone gracing the wall of its dining room. Be sure to take a look. This is the place to come for breakfast especially, as it'll be the only place in town open early. Scrambled eggs, ham, instant coffee, and watermelon slices will cost 850 pesos ($1.70). Beef entrees are priced about 2,100 pesos ($2.20). For cheaper fare, you can wait until the little café across the street opens up.

The aforementioned restaurant is not bad, although it tends to fill up in the evening with beer drinkers rather than diners. For a nice dinner, the pillars of local society go to the place right next door, the **Restaurant Zona Maya.** Open for lunch and dinner only, the Zona Maya is wonderfully air-conditioned, be-Muzak'd, and supplied with provisions. A good hamburger or sandwich, with a soft dirnk, will cost 975 pesos ($1.95); a pizza big enough for two people will be 1,950 pesos ($3.90); a plate of roast chicken with french fries, 1,075 pesos ($2.15). Decor (as though it mattered, with that heavenly air conditioning) is a leopard skin, some crossed machetes, and a bug zapper. And double-knit tablecloths. Felipe Carrillo Puerto, it has been noted by this observer, is a town dedicated to the creative use of double-knit synthetic fabrics. By the way, beer—and wine!—are served, and the beer-only crowd is kept at bay by a sign that says "We reserve —strictly—the right of admission."

Lago de Bacalar

From Carrillo Puerto to Chetumal is another 2½ hours' ride. About 64 miles (100 km) past Carrillo Puerto you'll sight the limpid waters of Lake Bacalar, a crystal-clear body of water fed by swamps and streams. It's a heavenly place to swim, and the perfect place for a resort, but so far progress in building facilities has been painfully slow. If you're in your own car, take a detour through the village of Bacalar and down along the lakeshore drive. You'll pass the **Hotel Laguna,** which has been under construction for a decade, and will probably be that way for another decade. Rooms here (there are only a few complete) are overpriced at 7,600 pesos ($15.20) for two, but this is all there is. Past the Laguna a way is a small, extremely primitive camping area on the shore.

As you approach the end of the lake, Hwy. 307 intersects Hwy. 186. Turn right, and you're headed west to Escárcega, Palenque, and Villahermosa; turn left, and you'll be going toward Chetumal. The turnoff to Belize is on the road *before* you enter Chetumal, but you may need to stop in the town for a meal or a bed.

Chetumal

Quintana Roo became a state only in 1974, and Chetumal (pop. 50,000) is the capital of the new state. While Quintana Roo was still a territory, it was a free-trade zone to encourage trade and immigration, and as the free-trade regulation is still in effect, much of the town is given over to small shops selling a strange assortment of imported junk and treasures at pretty inflated prices. The old part of town, down by the river (Río Hondo), preserves a Caribbean atmosphere with its wooden buildings (and sticky heat), but the newer parts are modern (and rather raw) Mexican. Lots of noise and heat, so your best plan would be not to stay—vacant rooms are difficult to find—but if you must, here are some hints.

WHERE TO STAY: The **Hotel Continental Caribe** (tel. 983/2-1100), across the street from the bus station entrance, at Avenida Héroes 71, is a luxury establishment with central air conditioning, a series of swimming pools in the courtyard, a restaurant large as a basketball court (and cold as a cave), and prices to match: 12,500 pesos ($25) single, 14,000 pesos ($28) double. It rents a lot of rooms at those prices, because Chetumal is booming and rooms are scarce—particularly comfortable, air-conditioned rooms.

Down the hill from the bus station on Avenida Héroes, 1½ blocks in toward the center of town, is the Continental Caribe's competition. The **Hotel El Presidente** (tel. 983/2-0542 or 2-0544) has similar central air, pool, and restaurant, and is presently attempting to swipe the Continental's business by charging 11,500 pesos ($23) single, 13,000 pesos ($26) double.

Still farther down along Avenida Héroes at the corner of Avenida Obregón, four longish blocks from the bus station, is the **Hotel Jacaranda** (tel. 983/2-1155), a modernish two-story hostelry undistinguished except for its prices, which are a pleasure to relate: 2,300 to 3,400 pesos ($4.60 to $6.80) single, 3,600 to 4,900 pesos ($7.20 to $9.80) double, the higher prices being for rooms with that blessed air conditioning. Many similarly priced hotels are right nearby.

Behind the Central Bus Station is the **Hotel Real Azteca,** Calle Belize 186 (tel. 983/2-0666. Walk out the front door of the bus station, turn left and walk past the market (on your left), turn left again (so the large CFE plant is on your right), and go down a block to the Calle Belize. Turn right, and the hotel is on the left-hand side of the street. It's all air-conditioned, and costs 4,200 pesos ($8.40) single, 5,450 pesos ($10.90) double.

WHERE TO EAT: As for places to dine, there are many little market eateries (and indeed the produce-filled market itself) right next door to the bus station. Across the street from the station, the **Hotel Continental Caribe's** immense restaurant puts out a mammoth breakfast buffet until 11 a.m. for 2,400 pesos ($4.80).

Two blocks down the hill on Avenida Héroes is the **Restaurant Grijalva,** just past the Hotel El Presidente on the left-hand side of the street. Three señoras bustle about, one hands you an impossibly inclusive menu, and then chirps ¡*No hay!* ("We don't have it!") to most of your selections. Nevertheless, they always have the makings for enchiladas or quesadillas, and the charge will be only 460 to 750 pesos (92¢ to $1.50). Chicken and fish dinners cost twice that figure.

The **Restaurant Baalbek,** in the middle of the block past 9a

Calle (or Calle Plutarco Elias), demonstrates by its name that some of the immigrants were Lebanese—not unusual in the Yucatán. Prices are a bit high here, but the bills must pay for the wrought-iron café furniture out front and the tablecloths inside. A big refrigerator keeps the food fresh until it's served. A plate of eggs or a fruit salad costs only 440 pesos (88¢), but heartier fare— fried chicken, grilled meat, fish—is in the 1,400- to 1,800-pesos ($2.80 to $3.60) bracket. Tacos and enchiladas are in between.

All the way down by the Río Hondo, in the old Caribbean section of town, is the incongruously modern **Restaurant Chetumal,** on Calle 5 de Mayo a block northwest of Avenida Héroes, on the riverbank. Open to cooling sea breezes from the Bay of Chetumal, it's a fine place for a refreshing salad of chicken or fruit for 525 to 1,000 pesos ($1.05 to $2), or a big Mexican combination plate for 1,500 pesos ($3). Look around at the quaint wooden buildings nearby.

TRANSPORTATION FROM CHETUMAL: Lots of bus service, a few flights.

By Bus

From the bus station in Chetumal you can get a seat to Tulum, Playa del Carmen, or Puerto Juárez to the north; Villahermosa, Veracruz, and Mexico City to the west; or to Belize City in the country to the south, once called British Honduras but (since 1973) officially named Belize.

Twelve direct first-class buses a day go to Cancún via Tulum, Playa del Carmen, and Puerto Morelos. With changes en route, four first-class buses a day go to Mexico City, seven a day go to Villahermosa.

Second-class bus service includes routes daily to Tulum and the coast (two buses), Mérida (four buses), Campeche (two buses), Villahermosa (four buses), San Andres Tuxtla, Veracruz, and Mexico City (one bus).

To Belize, a bus runs daily, departing at 4 p.m. and making the run through Corozal, Orange Walk, and roadside villages to Belize City. If you're coming from Puerto Juárez, get an early bus (before 10 a.m.) in order to make this connection.

By Air

One daily flight by AeroMéxico links Chetumal with Mérida, and thus with Mexico's major cities.

Leaving Chetumal

From Chetumal you can make the long, hot trip due west to Escárcega and Palenque; you can cut diagonally across the peninsula to Mérida; you can retrace your steps to Cancún; or you can go on south to Belize and even Guatemala.

Chapter VII

CHICHÉN-ITZÁ: THE MAYA CAPITAL

THE FABLED PYRAMIDS and temples of Chichén-Itzá are Yucatán's best-known ancient monuments. You can't really say you've seen Yucatán until you've gazed at towering El Castillo, sighted the sun from the Maya observatory called El Caracol, or shivered on the brink of the gaping cenote that served as the sacrificial well. Luckily for travelers on a budget, Chichén-Itzá is well and frequently served by buses, as it's on the main highway (no. 180) between Mérida and Cancún. Also, being on the main highway, Chichén-Itzá has a decent selection of hotels in all price ranges.

HOW TO SEE CHICHÉN-ITZÁ: I strongly urge you to spend the night here. No matter what the time of year, it will be hot in the middle of the day, and instead of clambering up pyramids you should be taking a siesta after lunch, in a cool hotel room. If you come on a day-trip, you'll arrive just in time to hike the pyramids in the heat of the day. You'll have to rush through this marvelous ancient city in order to catch another bus, which will take you away just as the once-fierce sun is softening to a benevolent gold and burnishing the temples.

Here's the plan: drive a rental car or get a bus from Mérida or Cancún in the morning, find your hotel room, then head for the ruins. After lunch, take that siesta, then return to the ruins for a few more hours. The next morning, get to the ruins early, before the intense heat. When the heat of the day approaches, head for your next destination. This may involve paying the admission fee more than once, but the fee is minimal, the experience maximal!

Note that it's possible (but not probable) that your chosen hotel at Chichén-Itzá might be booked up. If you want to make a reservation, be advised that it is difficult to reach Chichén by phone; however, most hotels have a means by which you can make reservations in Mérida. Read the hotel descriptions for details.

An attractive, and money-saving, alternative to staying at Chichén is to stay in the sleepy town of Valladolid (that's "Bye-ah-doh-*leet*"), 25 miles (40 km) east of the ruins. You can get an early bus from Cancún, spend the day at the ruins, then trundle back to Valladolid in a half hour. In recent years Valladolid has acquired some nice, simple, modern hotels (see below), and since they're a distance from the ruins, prices are very reasonable and crowds are not a problem.

ORIENTATION: Highway 180 used to plough right through the midst of the archeological zone, but has now been re-routed to pass completely around the zone to the north. Coming from Cancún, you must bear left at the fork where the old highway and the new bypass divide. Bearing left will take you to the Villa Arqueológica, Hotel Hacienda Chichén, and Hotel Mayaland, in that order, before coming to a dead end at the entrance to the zone.

Chichén-Itzá's little airstrip is on the bypass to the north of the zone.

The village of Pisté is on the highway about a 15-minute walk (1 mile) west of the archeological zone. Moderately-priced and inexpensive hotels and restaurants are in the village proper, or on the road between the village and the zone.

Hotels and Restaurants at Chichén-Itzá

WHERE TO STAY: The best place to stay, in my opinion, is right next to the archeological zone. The hotels here are the most efficient and charming, and they're within walking distance to the ruins. But there are alternatives, many cheaper, both to the west of the zone in Pisté, and to the east of the zone, out in the country and, as discussed below, in Valladolid.

Top Hotels Near the Ruins

The **Hotel Hacienda Chichén** is a short walk from the ruins, and guests stay in the bungalows built for those excavating the ruins some years ago. There's a fine pool—which, by the way, is open also to those who drop in for the 2,000-peso ($4) lunch—and all is quite plush. Rates are 12,500 pesos ($25) single, 14,300 pesos ($28.60) double. Each cottage is named for an early archeologist working at Chichén. You can make reservations for the Hacienda by contacting the Mérida Travel Service, in the Hotel Casa del Balam at Calle 60 no. 488, corner of Calle 57 (Apdo. Postal 407, Mérida, Yucatán; tel. 922/21-9212). *Note:* as of this writing, the Hacienda Chichén is closed, but it may again be open by the time you arrive. Call for the latest details, or ask your travel agent to do so.

The **Hotel Mayaland,** sister hotel to the Hacienda Chichén and very close to it, is perhaps the most genteel and sumptuous of Chichén-Itzá hotels. Built positively to reek of jungle adventure, it boasts such subtle touches as a front doorway that frames perfectly El Caracol (the observatory) as you walk from the lobby outside. It has a swimming pool and restaurant-bar, of course, and very attractive rooms for 14,300 pesos ($28.60) double. Make reservations as at the Hacienda Chichén.

The **Hotel Villa Arqueológica** (tel. 985/6-2830) is part of the Club Méditerranée operation, as you might guess by a glance at the lavishness of the layout: tennis courts, a pool, and garden-like grounds. On my last inspection tour I was quoted rates of 9,775 pesos ($19.55) for one person, 10,925 pesos ($21.85) for two—a very reasonable price for what you get. Meals are more expensive here than at the nearby Hacienda Chichén or at the Hotel Misión. For reservations in Mexico City, contact the Club Méditerranée office at Liebnitz 34, or telephone 514-4995 or 511-1284.

Moderately Priced Hotels in Pisté

The **Hotel Misión Chichén-Itzá** (tel. Pisté 4) is a fancy establishment. With two floors of rooms, a pretty pool, a shopping arcade, and a restaurant-bar, the Misión is the "compleat" place to stay: double rooms cost 11,660 pesos ($23.32). Meal plans are available, or you can drop in for breakfast, lunch, or dinner. For reservations in Mexico City, go to Florencia 15-A in the Pink Zone, or call 533-5953 or 553-3560.

Less than a mile west of the ruins, near Pisté, is the **Pirámide Inn** (tel. Pisté 5), with large rooms equipped with king-size beds, air conditioning, wall hangings of local handicrafts, plus the bonuses of a pool and absolutely gorgeous landscaped gardens and grounds. A number of people on the staff speak English. For all this comfort one pays 6,555 pesos ($13.11) single, 7,705 pesos ($15.41) double. Besides the 42 rooms, the Pirámide has ten bungalow suites, priced higher, and there's a trailer park on the other side of the highway. You can make reservations in Mérida by contacting the Pirámide's sister hotel there, the Principe Maya

Airport Inn, Avenida Aviación km. 4.5, Apdo. Postal 433 (tel.
992/4-0411).

Rock Bottom in Pisté

The budget choice here, next to the Pyrámide Inn, is the very
basic **Posada Novelo** (phone the Pirámide Inn), with adequate if
bare rooms, all with a shower for 2,200 pesos ($4.40) for single,
2,600 pesos ($5.20) double.

Out in the Country

A good place to stay overnight is the **Hotel Dolores Alba**, 1½
miles (2.4 km) past the ruins on the road going east to Cancún. (If
you go to Chichén-Itzá by bus from Mérida, ask for a ticket on a
bus that is going *past* the ruins—to Valladolid or Puerto Juárez—
and then ask the bus driver to stop at the Dolores Alba; he will be
glad to do so. Or take a taxi from the ruins to the hotel.) The 12
rooms are kept clean and neat, and several of them have been
equipped with air conditioners to help the ceiling fans. Besides
the motel-style rooms, which are older, you'll find two modern,
air-conditioned rooms and a separate cottage that sleeps four in
two bedroms. Prices are 3,000 pesos ($6) single, 9,500 pesos ($9)
double, 5,500 pesos ($11) triple, and 6,500 pesos ($13) for four
(in the cottage). All rooms have a shower, of course, and there's
a pretty little swimming pool besides. Good meals are available
here at decent prices, but you should realize that when it comes to
dining you have little choice—the nearest alternative restaurant,
or tienda to buy your own supplies, is several miles away. For
your trips to the ruins, the Dolores Alba provides free transportation to guests without cars. By the way, this hotel is run by the
same family that runs the Dolores Alba in Mérida (tel. 992/21-
3745) at Calle 63 no. 464. Either hotel will help you to make reservations at the other one.

WHERE TO EAT: Choices are limited here, but you won't go hungry, and you may even have a memorable meal. If not, the con-
viviality of fellow adventurers at dinner makes up for uninspired
fare.

Best Bets

The acknowledged leader in the culinary arts is the French-
style dining room at the **Villa Arqueológica.** Mexican and continental specialties share the menu here, and a full dinner with
wine will cost about 5,000 to 8,000 pesos ($10 to $16).

After the Villa, the place to dine is the **Hotel Mayaland.** Food
here is much simpler, but still presentable and filling. Plan to

spend about 4,000 pesos ($8) for lunch, 6,000 pesos ($12) for a table d'hôte evening repast.

Eateries in Pisté

Actually, these days Pisté's restaurants are pushing their prices up and standardizing their fare so that there is little difference among them. Expect to find your silverware encased in a plastic bag, and mood music (old Swingle Singers records, etc.) pulsing in the background—whether you like it or not. In any of the restaurants—El Carrusel, La Fiesta, or the Poxil—they'll try to sell you an entire lunch of four or five courses, and will balk at à la carte orders. The cost will be about 1,700 pesos ($3.40); that's a bit high, considering that the Hotel Misión, also in Pisté and very posh, charges only 1,950 pesos ($3.90) for lunch. About the cheapest of the town's restaurants are the Nicte-Ha and the Parador Maya. The Restaurant Xaybe, across from the Hotel Misión, is air-conditioned and rather fancy.

Hotels and Restaurants at Valladolid

Although it remained untouched by tourism for centuries, Valladolid is no newcomer to Yucatán. It was founded in 1543 near the site of a Maya religious center called Zací. The Franciscans built an impressive monastery here, called the **Convento de San Bernardino de Siena** (1552), and the town can boast of half a dozen colonial churches and two cenotes.

The main square is called the **Parque Francisco Cantón Rosado,** and when you find your way there, you'll be just a few steps from a variety of acceptable hotels and restaurants.

WHERE TO STAY: Walking around the main square, here's what you'll find: El Parroquía de San Servasio (the parish church) on the south, the Palacio Municipal (Town Hall) on the west (with a little tourism information desk out front, open from 9 a.m. to noon daily).

Near El Parroquía, at the southwest corner of the square, is the **Hotel San Clemente** (tel. 985/6-2208 or 6-2065), a modern, colonial-style building covered in white stucco. The 64 rooms, each with air conditioning, ceiling fan, and tidy bath, are located on two floors around a central garden quadrangle complete with swimming pool (which may or may not have water in it). Rates, compared to those at Chichén or Cancún, are very low: 3,300 pesos ($6.60) double, all included.

On the west side of the square is the **Hotel María de la Luz** (tel. 985/6-2070), which is well known for its breezy restaurant overlooking the square. A daily set-price lunch is featured for only 600 pesos ($1.20), beverage included. The food is hearty rather than delicate, but filling. A heaping fruit salad and a cold soft drink costs less than 500 pesos ($1). The rooms at the Luz are similar to those of the aforementioned hotel in accoutrements, although they're a bit more worn, and cost 3,000 pesos ($6) double. The swimming pool at the Luz is definitely not crystal clear.

The north side of the square holds the **Hotel El Mesón del Marqués,** a nice old colonial building at Calle 39 no. 203 (tel. 985/6-2073). Signs in English advertise the restaurant (very tidy) and gift shop. Most of the rooms are in a modern addition, however, and come with air conditioning for 4,370 pesos ($8.74) single, 4,974 pesos ($9.94) double, 6,124 pesos ($12.24) triple, 7,274 pesos ($14.54) for four people. The addition is behind the pretty tree-shaded courtyard, and therefore away from street noise. There's a nice little swimming pool here, and even a small zoo!

My favorite hotel in Valladolid is not on the main square proper, but just a block off it. It's the **Hotel Don Luis,** Calle 39 no. 191, at Calle 38 (tel. 985/6-2024). From the north side of the square (which is Calle 39) go east (that's away from the Hotel Maria de la Luz) one block, and the Hotel Don Luis is on the left-hand side: you'll spot the sign. Despite its being on a busy street, the Don Luis's rooms are quiet, big, and air-conditioned. All are doubles, many with two double beds. A thoughtful touch is that the washbasin is located *outside* the bathroom, so one can wash while another showers. The swimming pool in the courtyard is attractive and very clean, and prices are good: 2,484 pesos ($4.96) single, 3,266 pesos ($6.53) for a double room with fan, or 3,266 pesos ($6.53) single, 3,864 pesos ($7.72) for a double with air conditioning; an extra person in a room pays 750 pesos ($1.50).

WHERE TO EAT: The hotel restaurants are not bad here. I especially like the one at the aforementioned Hotel María de la Luz, because you can watch the activity in the plaza as you dine.

But for a real Valladolid adventure, and the lowest prices of all, take a stroll through the **Bazar Municipal,** that little arcade of shops beside the Hotel El Mesón del Marqués. The little cookshops here open at mealtimes, and their family-owners set out tables and chairs in the courtyard. Local farmers and traders in town on business come to chow down. You won't find a printed menu often, let alone one in English. But a quick look around at nearby tables will tell you what's cooking, and a discreet point of a finger will order it. Ask the price as you order, for the record, so you won't be charged something exorbitant when it's too late.

My favorite cookshops here are the **Doñ Mary** and **El Amigo Panfilo.** A three-course meal of soup, enchiladas, and dessert in either one should cost no more than 750 pesos ($1.50).

What to See at Chichén-Itzá

This Mayan city was absorbed by the Toltecs in A.D. 987, when, as legend has it, a man named Kukulcán, who was the same as Quetzalcóatl from the Toltec capital of Tula, arrived from the west "for the redemption of his people." Here he built a magnificent metropolis combining the Maya Puuc style with Toltec motifs of the feathered serpent, warriors, eagles, and jaguars.

TOURING THE RUINS: The archeological zone at Chichén is open from 6 a.m. to 6 p.m. daily. Admission costs 100 pesos (20¢), less on Sunday and holidays. There are actually two parts of Chichén-Itzá: the northern zone, which is distinctly Toltec; and southern zone, which is of an early period with mostly Puuc architecture. A day is needed to see all the ruins here, preferably from 6 or 7 a.m. to 1 p.m., and 3 or 4 p.m. to 6 p.m.

Before marching off to El Castillo, however, it's important that you understand the basics of the Maya system for measuring time. Without such an understanding, El Castillo is merely an impressive pile of rock. With an understanding, it's a marvelous and complex celestial sundial, which has kept perfectly accurate time for centuries.

The Mayan Sense of Time

The amazingly exact and intricate Maya calendar system begins with the year 3113 B.C., before Maya culture even existed. From that date, the Mayas could measure time—and their life cycle—to a point 90,000,000 years in the future! Needless to say, they haven't felt the need for the whole system yet. For now, just note that they conceived of world history as a series of cycles moving within cycles.

The Solar Year: The Mayan solar year was very precisely measured, and consisted of 365.24 days. Within that solar year there were 18 "months" of 20 days each (total: 360 days) plus a special 5-day period.

The Ceremonial Year: A ceremonial calendar, completely different from the solar calendar, ran its "annual" cycle at the same time. But this was not a crude system like our Gregorian calendar, which has saints' days, some fixed feast days, and some moveable feasts. The Maya ceremonial calendar "interlaced" exactly with the solar calendar. Each date of the solar calendar had a name, and each date of the ceremonial calendar also had a name; so every single day in Maya history has two names, which were always quoted together.

The ceremonial calendar was a very complex and ingenious system with 13 "months" of 20 days, but running within that cycle of 260 days was another of 20 "weeks" of 13 days!

The Double Cycle: After 52 solar years and 73 ceremonial "years," during which each day had its unique, unduplicated double name, these calendars ended their respective cycles simultaneously on the very same day, and a brand-new, identical double cycle began. Thus, in the longer scheme of things, a day would be identified by the name of the 52-year cycle, the name of the solar day, and the name of the ceremonial day.

Mystic Numbers: As you can see, several numbers were of great significance to the system. The number 20 was perhaps most important, as calendar calculations were done with a number system with base 20. There were 20 "suns" (days) to a "month", 20 years to a *katun,* and 20 katuns (20 × 20, or 400 years) to a *baktun.*

The number 52 was of tremendous importance, for it signified, literally, the "end of time," the end of the double cycle of solar and ceremonial calendars. At the beginning of a new cycle, temples were rebuilt for the "new age," which is why so many Maya temples and pyramids hold within them the structures of earlier, smaller temples and pyramids.

The Mayas, obviously, were obsessed by time. (You'd have to be, to deal with such a system!) Time for them was not "progress," but the Wheel of Fate, spinning endlessly, determining one's destiny by the combinations of attributes given to days in the solar and ceremonial calendars. The rains came on schedule, the corn was planted on schedule, and the celestial bodies moved in their great dance under the watchful eye of Maya astronomers and astrologers.

It's no wonder that Chichén's most impressive structure, El Castillo, is in fact an enormous "time machine," and that this imperial city included a huge and impressive astronomical observatory.

El Castillo

Begin with the beautiful 75-foot **El Castillo** pyramid, built with the calendar in mind: there is a total of 364 stairs plus platform, which makes 365 (days of the year), 52 panels on each side which represent the 52-year cycle of the Maya calendars, and nine terraces on each side of the stairways, a total of 18 terraces to represent the 18-month Maya solar calendar. If this isn't proof enough of the mathematical precision of this temple, come for the spring equinox (March 21), and when the sun goes down you'll see the seven stairs of the northern stairway plus the serpent head carving at the base touched with the last rays of the fading sun; within a 34-minute period the "serpent" formed by this play of light and shadow appears to descend into the earth as the sun leaves each stair, going from the top to the bottom, ending with the serpent head. To the Maya this is a fertility symbol: the golden sun has entered the earth: time to plant the corn.

El Castillo, also called the Pyramid of Kukulcán, was built over an earlier structure of Toltec design. A narrow stairway, entered at the western edge of the north staircase, leads into the structure, where there is a sacrificial altar-throne encrusted with jade, and a chac-mool figure. The stairway is open at odd and irregular hours, is claustrophobic, usually crowded, very humid and uncomfortable. Plan your visit for early in the day, if possible. By the way, you can indeed reach the top of the pyramid via the interior staircase.

Main Ball Court (Juego de Pelota)

Northwest of El Castillo is Chichén's main ball court, the largest and best-preserved anywhere. This is only one of nine ball courts built in this city.

The game was played with a hard rubbery ball. Players on two teams tried to knock the ball through one or the other of the two stone rings placed high on either wall, using only their elbows, knees, and hips (no hands). The losing players, so it is said, paid for defeat with their lives.

The game must have been an exciting event, heightened by the marvelous acoustics of the ball court. Have someone walk to the North Temple at the far end, and speak or clap hands. You'll hear the sound quite clearly at the opposite end, about 450 feet away.

The North Temple has sculptured pillars, and more sculptures inside. For a look at the teams after a game, walk along the bas-reliefs on each wall. Two opposing teams are facing the center. At the midpoint in the wall, Death accepts the sacrifice of one team's captain, who has been decapitated by the captain of the other team, who wields an obsidian knife.

Temple of Jaguars (Tigres): Near the southeastern corner of the main ball court is a small temple with serpent columns and carved panels showing jaguars *(tigres)*. Up the flight of steps and inside the temple, a mural chronicling a battle between Mayas and Toltecs was found. The Toltecs, with the feathered serpents, are attacking a Maya village of thatched houses, or *nas*.

Tzompantli (Temple of Skulls)

When a sacrificial victim's head was cut off (some unlucky ball player, for instance), it was stuck on a pole and displayed here, in a tidy row with others. Just in case the skull population dropped, the architects have provided rows of skulls carved into the platform. Also carved into the stone are pictures of eagles tearing hearts from human victims. The word *Tzompantli* is not Mayan, but came from central Mexico with the Toltecs.

Platform of the Eagles

Next to the Tzompantli, this small platform has reliefs showing eagles and jaguars clutching human hearts in their talons and claws.

Platform of Venus

East of the Tzompantli and north of El Castillo, near the road to the Sacred Cenote, is the Platform of Venus. Don't look for beauty, for the planet Venus, in Maya-Toltec lore, is thought to have been represented by a feathered monster, or a feathered serpent with a human head in its mouth, not a luscious lady. A chac-mool figure was discovered "buried" within the structure, which is why it is sometimes called the Tomb of Chac-Mool.

The Sacred Cenote

Follow the dirt road that heads north from the Platform of Venus, and after five minutes you'll come to the great natural well that may have given Chichén-Itzá (The Well of the Itzáes) its name. By now you must have heard the sacrificial virgin lore. It seems that the priests herded a rather different breed of person to death in the watery depths here. Anatomical research done in the earlier part of this century by Ernest A. Hooten suggests that children and adults, male and female, were used as sacrificial victims. Judging from Hooten's evidence, the victims may have been outcasts: diseased, feebleminded, or generally disliked.

Whatever the worth of the sacrificial victims, the worth of other presents to the rain god Chac was very considerable. Edward Thompson, American consul in Mérida and a Harvard professor, bought the hacienda of Chichén in the beginning of this century, explored the bottom of the cenote with dredges and divers, and brought up a fortune in gold and jade. Most of these he spirited out of the country and lodged in Harvard's Peabody Museum of Archeology and Ethnology. Later excavations, in the 1960s, brought up more treasure. It appears, from studies of the objects recovered, that offerings were brought from throughout Yucatán, and even farther away.

Temple of the Warriors

One of the most impressive structures at Chichén, the Temple of the Warriors (Templo de los Guerreros), also called the Group of the Thousand Columns, is due east of El Castillo. Climb up the steep stairs at the front to reach a figure of chac-mool, and several impressive columns carved in relief to look like enormous feathered serpents. The building gets its name from the carvings of warriors marching along its walls. Other motifs, as you may have guessed by now, include feathered serpents, jaguars, and eagles.

South of the temple was a square building called by archeologists the market (mercado). Its central court, surrounded by a colonnade, may well have been just that.

Beyond the temple and the market, in the jungle, are mounds of rubble that have yet to be uncovered, excavated, analyzed, or reconstructed.

The main Mérida–Cancún highway used to cut straight through the ruins of Chichén, and though it has now been diverted, you can still see the great swath it cut. South and west of the old highway's path are more impressive ruined buildings. On the way to these buildings is a shady little stand selling cold drinks.

Tomb of the High Priest

Past the refreshment stand, to the right of the path, is the Tomb of the High Priest (Tumba del Gran Sacerdote), which stood atop a natural limestone cave in which skeletons and offerings were found, giving the temple its name.

Next building along, on your right, is the House of Metates (Casa de los Metates), named after the concave corn-grinding stones used until recently by the Mayas.

Past it is the Temple of the Stag (Templo del Venado), fairly tall though ruined. The relief of a stag which gave the temple its name is long gone.

Chichán-chob (Little Holes), the next temple, has a roof comb with little holes, three masks of rain-god Chac, three rooms, and a good view of the surrounding structures. It's one of the older buildings at Chichén, built in the Puuc style during the Late Classic Period.

El Caracol

Construction of the Observatory (El Caracol), a complex building with a circular tower, was carried out over quite a long period of time. No doubt the additions and modifications reflected the Mayas' increasing knowledge of celestial movements, and their need for ever more exact measurements. Through slits in the tower's walls, Mayan astronomers could observe the cardinal directions and the approach of the all-important spring and autumn equinoxes, and the summer solstice. The temple's name, which means "snail," comes from a spiral staircase within the structure.

On the east side of El Caracol, a path leads north into the bush to the Cenote Xtoloc, another natural limestone well. The Sacred Cenote of Chichén was reserved for sacrifices; its water was not used for drinking (good thing!). The city's daily water supply came from Xtoloc.

Temple of Panels

Just to the south of El Caracol are the ruins of a steambath (Temazcalli), and the Templo de los Tableros, named for the carved panels on top. This was once covered by a much larger structure, only traces of which remain.

Edifice of the Nuns

If you've visited the Puuc sites of Kabah, Sayil, Labná, and Xlapak, the Nunnery here (Edificio de las Monjas) will remind you at once of the "palaces" at the other sites. It is enormous, and was built in the Late Classic Period. Like so many other Mayan buildings, a new edifice was built right over an older one. Suspecting that this was so, an archeologist named Le Plongeon, working earlier in this century, put dynamite in between the two and blew part of the newer building to smithereens, thereby revealing part of the old. You can still see the results of Le Plongeon's delicate exploratory methods.

On the eastern side of the Nunnery is an annex (Anexo Este) in highly ornate Chenes style, with, as usual, lots of Chac masks and serpents.

The Church

Next to the annex is one of the oldest buildings at Chichén, ridiculously named The Church (La Iglesia). Masks of Chac decorate two upper storeys. Look closely and you'll see among the crowd of Chacs an armadillo, a crab, a snail, and a tortoise. These represent the Mayan gods called *bacab*, whose job it was to hold up the sky.

Akab Dzib

The Temple of Obscure Writing (Akab Dzib) is due east of the Edifice of the Nuns along a path into the bush. Above a door in one of the rooms are some Mayan glyphs, which gave the temple its name. In other rooms, traces of red hand-prints are still visible. The earliest part of this building is very old, and may well be the oldest at Chichén. It was reconstructed and expanded over the centuries.

Old Chichén

For a look at more of Chichén's oldest buildings, constructed well before the Toltecs arrived, follow signs from the Nunnery southwest into the bush to Old Chichén (Chichén Viejo), about half a mile away. Be prepared for this trek with long trousers, insect repellant, and a local guide. The attractions here are the Temple of the First Inscriptions (Templo de los Inscripciones Iniciales), with the oldest inscriptions discovered at Chichén, and the restored Temple of the Lintels (Templo de los Dinteles), a fine Puuc building.

GRUTAS DE BALANKANCHÉ: Spelunkers take note: the **Grutas** (caves) **de Balankanché** are 2 ¾ miles (4 ½ km) from Chichén-Itzá on the road to Cancún. You can see them with a guide only. Guides begin their tours at 9, 10, and 11 a.m. and 2, 3, and 4 p.m. (Sunday at 8, 9, 10, and 11 a.m. only). Admission costs 20 pesos (4¢).

Getting down into the caves takes some doing as you will probably end up taking a taxi to the caves, and having it wait for your return. The entire excursion takes about two hours. Check at the main entrance to the Chichén ruins for current tour hours at the caves, which may or may not prove to be fully accurate. The Chichén entrance is also the place to ask about hiring guides, should you want one.

The natural caves became wartime hideaways after the Toltec invasion of Yucatán. You can still see traces of carving and incense-burning, as well as an underground stream that served as the sanctuary's water supply.

THE ROAD TO MÉRIDA: Next stop on our circuit of Yucatán is its colonial capital and commercial metropolis. The 75-mile (120-km) trip from Chichén-Itzá to Mérida will take between 1½ and 2 hours.

Along the way, tiny Maya hamlets with thatched houses (called *na)* dot the highway. Sometimes the frames of sticks are covered in mud plaster and whitewashed. The women take pride in wearing the traditional white *huipil,* which always has embroidery around the neckline, and several inches of lacy slip showing at the hem.

This is henequen country, and just east of Mérida you'll pass a big Cordemex plant that gathers in the leaves from the surrounding fields. Tied in bundles, the leaves form huge piles by the plant, waiting to have the sisal fibers extracted and made into rope and cloth. Henequen has been the principal industry of Yucatán for centuries, and the vast henequen haciendas were owned by absentee landlords and worked by peasants who were little better than slaves. The great haciendas have been split up in recent years, but the hacienda complexes—house, smokestack, factory, chapel, workers' houses, gateway, narrow-gauge railways—still stand along the road. In every direction stretch the numberless stone-walled fields where the spiny henequen plants grow, taking years to reach maturity.

Chapter VIII

MÉRIDA: THE COLONIAL CAPITAL

YUCATÁN'S CHARMING CAPITAL city (pop. 500,000) has been the hub of peninsular life since the Spanish founded it in the mid-1500s on the ruins of the defeated Mayan town of Tiho. Little remains of Tiho, but a great deal remains of the Spaniards' colonial town. There's lots to see and do, many fine places to dine, and many good hotels in which to stay. You'll like it here.

You're liable to hear North American accents on Mérida's streets in January and February, July and August, for that's when most foreign visitors come. If you visit in the summer months, be advised that the weather can be intensely hot and humid. Consider taking a hotel room with air conditioning. If you don't, make absolutely sure the fan in your room works well. You're going to need it.

Also be advised that brief showers wash down Mérida's streets in late May, June, and July, during the rainy season. You may have to duck under cover any day until mid-October, but the rains are most frequent in the first two or three months.

GETTING TO AND FROM MÉRIDA: Unless you have a private car, it's simple: arrive by air or by bus.

Arriving (and Departing) by Air

Mérida enjoys nonstop air connections with the following cities (flights per day): Cancún (two), Chetumal (one), Cozumel (two), Havana (three flights per week), Houston (two flights per week), Mexico City (eight or nine per day), Miami (two), Veracruz (four per week), and Villahermosa (one per day).

Flying into Mérida's modern airport, you'll find yourself on the southwestern outskirts of town, where Hwy. 180 enters the city.

Taxis between the airport and downtown hotels cost about

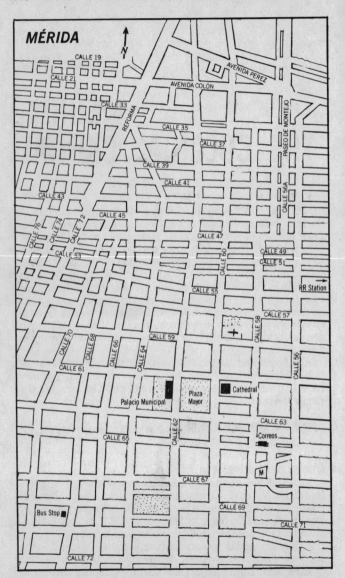

1,500 pesos ($3). The "Transporte Terrestre" minibuses charge 720 pesos ($1.44) per person for the ride downtown, so if you're traveling in a group, take a cab as it'll work out to be cheaper.

City bus no. 79 ("Aviación") operates between the center and the airport. This is the cheapest way to go, of course, with a one-way ticket costing only 40 pesos (8¢), though the buses are not all that frequent. Other city buses run along the Avenida de los Itzáes, just out of the airport precincts, heading for downtown.

You can make reservations and buy air tickets from one of the many travel agencies in Mérida.

The two national carriers have offices downtown as well: **Aero-México** is at Avenida Paseo de Montejo no. 460 (tel. 27-9000) and at Calle 60 no. 499-A (tel. 24-4786 or 24-4692). At the airport, phone them at 24-8554 or 24-8576. **Mexicana** is at Calle 58 no. 500 (tel. 24-6623) and Calle 56-A no. 493, at Paseo de Montejo (tel. 24-7421 or 23-0508). At the airport, their number is 23-8602 or 23-6986.

Arriving (and Departing) by Bus

Mérida's main bus station (BUS), run by the Unión de Camioneros de Yucatán, is on Calle 69 between Calles 68 and 70, about six blocks southwest of the Plaza Mayor. The ADO line runs from here, as do Unión de Camioneros buses. The station has a travel agency with tours to the ruins, a newsstand, a bank, and various stalls selling souvenirs and snacks.

Coming from the west (Cancún, Chichén-Itzá, Valladolid), your bus may make a stop at the old bus station on Calle 50 between 65 and 67. If you're headed for the Plaza Mayor, you might as well get off here. It's six blocks to the plaza from here as well.

As for departures, buses to Uxmal depart at 6, 7, and 9 a.m., and 12 noon, 3, and 5 p.m.; return trips are at 8:30 and 11:30 a.m., and 2:30, 5:30, and 7:30 p.m.

Going via Mayapán, catch a bus to Oxcutzcab, which will take you through Kanasin and Acanceh, to Ruinas de Mayapán, and then through the villages of Mayapán, Mama, etc. Be sure to tell the driver you want to get off at the ruinas, or he'll assume you want to go to the village, several kilometers farther on.

For Chichén-Itzá there are buses at 6:30 and 8:30 a.m. and 4:30 p.m. If you're planning to go out and back in a day (something I don't recommend if you enjoy seeing impressive ruins), take the 8:30 a.m. bus and reserve a seat on the 3 p.m. bus returning from Chichén. A one-way ticket on the 2- to 2½-hour trip costs 731 pesos ($1.46), by the way; a round-trip ticket is precisely twice as much.

To Cancún and Puerto Juárez (the dock for boats to Isla Mujeres), there are buses almost every hour on the hour throughout the day, from 7 a.m. to just past midnight. The trip takes about five hours and costs 1,970 pesos ($4).

For buses north to Progreso, you must go to a special bus terminal at Calle 62 no. 524, between Calles 65 and 67. Buses leave every five or ten minutes or so throughout the day on the 45-minute trip.

There are buses to Campeche from the main bus station about every 30 minutes or so throughout the day on the three- or four-hour trip (the duration depends partly on which route you pick, the short way via Hwy. 180, or the longer route past Uxmal and Kabah via Hwy. 261).

About 18 ADO buses per day head out to Villahermosa via the Palenque junction, a trip of about 11 or 12 hours.

Seven buses a day make the long grind all the way to Mexico City.

Arriving (and Departing) By Train

Just in case you arrive by train, you should know that the station is about eight blocks northeast of the Plaza Mayor on Calle 55 between Calles 48 and 46.

ORIENTATION: As with most colonial Mexican cities, Mérida's streets were laid out in a grid. Even-numbered streets run north-south, odd-numbered streets run east-west. In the last few decades, the city has expanded well beyond the grid, and several grand boulevards have been added on the outskirts to ease traffic flow.

A word of warning about street numbers: What with unnumbered dwellings and -A, -B, and -C additions, these progress agonizingly slowly. Example: I wanted to get from 504 to 615D on Calle 59 and did—after walking 12 blocks! Otherwise, the street grid is fairly easy to find your way in.

Plaza Mayor

The center of town is the very pretty Plaza Mayor, sometimes called the Plaza Principal, the main square, with its shapely, shady trees, plus benches, vendors, and a social life all its own. Around the plaza are the massive cathedral, the Palacio de Gobierno (state government headquarters), the Palacio Municipal, and the Casa de Montejo, a mansion built by the founder of Mérida and now occupied by a bank. Within a few blocks of the Plaza Mayor are several smaller plazas, each next to a church; the University of Yucatán; and the sprawling market district.

Paseo de Montejo

Mérida's most fashionable address, however, is over seven blocks northwest of the Plaza Mayor. It's the Paseo de Montejo, a wide tree-lined boulevard laid out during the 19th century and lined with houses and mansions built by politicos and henequen barons. The Paseo, which extends northward for over a dozen blocks, is home to Yucatán's anthropological museum, several upscale hotels and auto dealerships, and the American Consulate.

GETTING AROUND: Most of the time, you'll walk, because many of the most attractive sites are within a handful of blocks from the Plaza Mayor.

Taxis are usually easy to find in the center of town. A short ride, perhaps between the Plaza Mayor and the bus station or the Paseo de Montejo, might cost 600 pesos ($1.20) or 700 pesos ($1.40).

Another way to tour the town is in a horse-drawn carriage. Look for a rank of them near the cathedral, then haggle for a good price. An hour's tour might cost 2,000 pesos ($4) to 2,500 pesos ($5).

City buses are the cheapest of all, charging only 40 pesos (8¢) for a ride. You might conceivably take one to the large, shady Parque Centenario on the western outskirts. Look for the bus of the same name ("Centenario") on Calle 64.

As for rental cars, you may well want one of these for your explorations of Mayapán, Uxmal, Kabah, etc. You don't really need one to get around Mérida, or to Chichén-Itzá or Cancún. The bad news is that rental cars are very expensive these days in Yucatán, averaging out to $50 or $60 per day for a VW Beetle. The good news is that you can often haggle for a lower price. You should, in any case, shop around among the local agencies for a good price. I have not had the same rash of complaints about the little local businesses in Mérida that I've had about many other cities.

Keep these tips in mind as you scour the city for a rental car deal: Kilometers and insurance are the most expensive charges, daily rental and fuel are the least. Don't be impressed by a very low daily charge, unless it includes unlimited kilometrage. In every single case, get the absolutely final figure for a rental before you decide; if you can't get kilometers included, estimate the distance you'll travel by adding up the highway mileages, then add 15% for wrong turns and detours. Keep in mind that you can often get lower rates if you rent for more than a day or two, and if you promise to pay at the end of the rental in cash dollars (you'll need a credit card at first for the paperwork, though). For more information on car rental, see Chapter XIII, "Useful Information," under "Car Rentals."

Here are some of the local agencies that seem to be good. Please write and tell me about your car rental experiences, both good and bad:

México Rent-A-Car, Calle 60 no. 495, between 59 and 57 (tel. 992/21-7840), across from the Parque de la Madre, in the garage entrance of the Hotel del Parque, is a small, dependably friendly firm with prices a good deal lower than the big international firms.

Rentadora "Lol-tún," Calle 62 no. 483-A, between 61 and 59 (tel. 992/23-3637), is operated by two brothers, José Alberto and Victor González Loeza, who readily adjust their prices according to demand. I was quoted a flat price of $72 for two days' rental, unlimited kilometers, tax, and insurance all included.

Budget Rent-A-Car, (Prolongación no. 497), (tel. 992/27-8755), on the northern reaches of the Paseo de Montejo, and at the airport, also offers an unlimited mileage rate which works out to about $51 per day, all included except gas.

You might also try **Volkswagen Rent,** Calle 60 no. 486-F, between 57 and 55 (tel. 992/21-8128), which tends to be competitive with (usually slightly higher than) Lol-tún.

TOURIST INFORMATION: The most convenient source is the office operated by the Estado de Yucatán (tel. 24-9290 or 24-9389), in the hulking edifice known as the Teatro Peón Contreras, on Calle 60 between 57 and 59, open Monday through Friday from 9 a.m. to 9 p.m., Saturday from 9 a.m. to 4 p.m., Sunday from 9 a.m. to 12 noon.

You can also try the Palacio Municipal, on the western side of the Plaza Mayor (opposite side from the cathedral), which has a tourism office open daily from 8 a.m. to 8 p.m., Sunday from 11 a.m. to 5 p.m.

The Secretaría de Turismo (SECTUR) building (tel. 24-9431 or 24-9542), where not much seems to be happening, is at the corner of Calles 54 and 61.

USEFUL FACTS: The information below will help answer your questions concerning the location of various services in Mérida.

Banks: Banamex, in the Palacio Montejo on the Plaza Mayor, has its own casa de cambio which usually provides a better rate of exchange than the banks. Other banks are located on and off Calle 65 between Calles 62 and 60.

Consulates: The **U.S. Consulate** is at Paseo de Montejo no. 453, corner of Avenida Colón (tel. 992/25-5011 or 25-5409), next to the Holiday Inn. Hours are 8 a.m. to 1 p.m. and 2 to 5:30 p.m., Monday through Friday; closed on Mexican and American holidays. The telephone number of a duty officer is posted at the entrance. The **British Vice-Consulate** is at Calle 53 no. 489, corner of Calle 58 (tel. 992/21-6799). Open in principle from 9:30 a.m. to 1 p.m., you may find no one. The vice-consul fields questions about travel to Belize as well as British matters. The **Canadian Consulate** is at Calle 62 no. 309-D-19 (tel. 992/25-6299). The **Alliance Française** has a branch at Calle 56 no. 476 (tel. 992/21-6013).

Medical Care: If Montezuma's Revenge has got you, see the introduction to this book for tips. If it gets serious, ask your hotel to call a doctor after you've got an estimate of his fee. The city's Hospital O'Horan (tel. 992/23-8711) is on Avenida de los Itzáes at Calle 59A, north of the Parque Centenario.

Post Office: Mérida's main post office is at the corner of Calles 65 and 56, in the midst of the market. It is open from 8 a.m. to 7 p.m. Monday through Friday, Saturday from 9 a.m. to 1 p.m.; closed Sunday.

Telephones: Long-distance casetas are at the airport, the bus station, at Calles 59 and 62, and Calles 59 and 64, on Calle 60 between 55 and 53 in "El Calendario Maya," and at the intersection of Avenidas Reforma and Colón in a farmacia. Remember that international calls are extremely expensive, but at least from a caseta you won't pay a hotel's gross "service charge."

Mérida's Hotels

The hotel situation in Mérida is wonderful: wide selection, many styles, and prices range from an amazing backpackers' special at $3 double, to the Holiday Inn's very moderate $46 double.

So low are the prices, and such are the attractions of this city, that it is possible some of Mérida's hotels might not be able to accommodate you in the busy months of February, July, and August unless you reserve in advance. To be certain of getting exactly the room you want, particularly in the better hotels, call in advance.

THE TOP HOTELS: Mérida's best places to stay are new, modern, efficient, pleasant, and moderately priced.

The **Holiday Inn Mérida,** Avenida Colón 498, between Calle 60 and the Paseo de Montejo (tel. 992/25-6877, 212/683-0060 in New York, or toll free 800/465-4329 in U.S.), is a lavish low-rise layout right next to the American Consulate. Somewhat imposing at first because of its blockhouse style, the hotel becomes a sympathetic and human-scale place when you walk inside. If you check into one of the 214 rooms, each with individual climate controls, color television, AM/FM radio, servi-bar refrigerator, and purified water, have your bathing suit handy, for the hotel has a nice swimming pool complete with swim-up bar. Other assets include a pair of tennis courts, two restaurants, several bars, and a nightclub. The price for a room is 23,000 pesos ($46), single or double. Though the Holiday Inn is at a prestigious address, you'll find yourself taking taxis often to reach the main plaza, the colonial monuments, and the shopping streets.

In terms of price and style, you can't do better than the **Hotel Los Aluxes,** Calle 60 no. 444, at Calle 49 (tel. 992/24-2199, or toll free 800/221-6509 in U.S. except New York, and 800/522-0457 in New York). Pronounced "ah-*loo*-shes," the name refers to the magical elves who acted as guardian angels to the ancient Mayas. This modern 109-room hotel is Mérida's newest, and offers you a patio café with thatch-shaded tables, a coffeeshop, a posh restaurant, a swimming pool and sundeck on the mezzanine level, and a staff ready to please. Air-conditioned rooms are priced at 11,500 pesos ($23) single or double, 12,650 pesos ($25.30) triple, all included. The hotel has its own parking lot.

MODERN ROOMS AT MODERATE PRICES: Very moderately priced, the following hotels offer modern accommodations, swimming pools, air conditioning, and all the other comforts and pleasures of mid-range hotels.

Near the Plaza Major

The **Hotel Mérida Misión,** Calle 60 no. 491, Mérida, Yucatán 97000, corner of Calle 57 (tel. 992-23-9500), is actually a large modern addition grafted onto a gracious older hotel. The location, right across the street from the university and the Teatro Peón Contreras, and only two short blocks from the Plaza Mayor, is excellent. Enter the hotel's cool lobby from the noisy street, and you enter an oasis complete with bubbling fountain, high ceilings, and a nice little swimming pool. Though the public rooms are colonial in style, the 150 air-conditioned guest rooms are modern, and priced at 12,650 pesos ($25.30) single, 13,800 pesos ($27.60) double, 16,100 pesos ($32.20) triple, 20,700 pesos ($41.40) for a suite.

The **Hotel María del Carmen,** Apdo. 411, Calle 63 no. 550, Mérida, Yucatán 97000, between 68 and 70, three blocks west of the Plaza Mayor (tel. 992/23-9133), has 93 air-conditioned rooms on four floors, and a nice swimming pool, all for 13,000 pesos

($26) single, 14,000 pesos ($28) double. Children can share their parents' room for no extra charge.

The **Hotel Castellano,** Calle 57 no. 513, two blocks west of the Plaza Mayor (tel. 992/23-0100), has been patronized by North American visitors for decades. Though construction is modern, inspiration is colonial, and furnishings are complete: television, air conditioning, and radio are found in each room. The hotel has a swimming pool, restaurant and bar, a parking lot (you pay a bit extra for this), and a nightclub. The location is fairly convenient to the square.

Small but sleek, the **Hotel del Gobernador,** Calle 59 no. 535, Mérida, Yucatán 97000, at the corner of Calle 66 (tel. 992/23-7133), qualifies as being among Mérida's most modern mid-range hotels. Each of the 43 rooms and 16 junior suites has air conditioning, telephone, and radio, with prices of 8,600 pesos ($17.20) single, 10,350 pesos ($20.70) double, 1,500 pesos ($3) for each extra person. If you have more than two people in your party, you're liable to want a junior suite for only a few dollars more; these have two double beds each. You'll enjoy use of a small swimming pool here, a cafeteria, bar, and parking lot.

Another good choice is the **Hotel Panamericana,** Calle 59 no. 455, between 52 and 54 (tel. 992/23-9111 or 23-9444). The Panamericana has a secret: you enter an ornate 19th-century doorway to register at the front desk. Then you pass through a classic Spanish atrium with its fancy stone and woodwork, and head for a modern annex which holds the up-to-date guest rooms, the restaurant, and the swimming pool. The old building is quite charming, the new one quite efficient. For one of the 90 rooms with bath, air conditioning, television (with satellite programming), and perhaps a five-city view, you pay 11,500 pesos ($23) single or double; 12 junior suites cost about 2,500 pesos ($5) more per room, six suites yet another 1,500 pesos ($3).

Along Paseo de Montejo

The thoroughly modern **Hotel Conquistador,** Calle 56-A no. 458, Mérida, Yucatán 97000 (tel. 992/26-2155), is on the Paseo de Montejo (that's Calle 56-A) at Calle 35. Rising nine stories over the boulevard, it holds 64 guest rooms, 20 junior suites, and five full suites, each with telephone and television; standard rooms are priced at 11,500 ($23) single, 13,225 pesos ($26.45) double. A small interior swimming pool is provided for your enjoyment, along with a solarium, a restaurant, a cafeteria, and a lobby bar. Though the hotel itself is modern, it stands amid a bevy of dowager colonial mansions from Mérida's gilded age.

Two hotels along the Paseo de Montejo are operated by the

company named Hoteles Montejo, Apdo. 961, Mérida, Yucatán, 97000 (tel. 992/24-6046 or 24-7644). Both are modern, built several decades ago and maintained to keep them comfortable. The **Hotel Montejo Palace,** Paseo de Montejo no. 483-C, is the more expensive of the two, with air-conditioned rooms priced at 11,000 pesos ($22) single, 11,500 pesos ($23) double, 12,000 pesos ($24) triple. The **Hotel Paseo de Montejo,** across the boulevard at no. 482, quotes prices about $5 or $6 lower.

BUDGET ROOMS: Mérida's line-up of hotels is a budget traveler's dream-come-true. From the very expensive to the very low-priced, from the modern to the romantically old-fashioned, everyone can find a place that suits. Most hotels offer at least a few air-conditioned rooms (and current weather reports will tell you whether or not you'll need this), and a few of the places in the budget line-up even have swimming pools!

Modern, with Colonial Touches

As in many Mexican towns, the hotel lineup in Mérida includes numerous establishments which are basically modern in amenities and construction, but colonial in inspiration and decor. Mérida has quite a few of these, in a nice range of prices. Expect a serviceable and comfortable if not particularly charming room, and a fairly central location, in any of these places.

At the corner of Calles 59 and 60, a mere half-block northeast of the Plaza Mayor, is the 43-room **Hotel Caribe** (tel. 992/21-9232), with three floors arranged around a quiet central courtyard. The restaurant's tables are set out in a portico surrounding the court; on the top floor is a small but quite serviceable swimming pool, a sundeck, and a vantage point for views of the cathedral and the town. Most of the rooms here have an air conditioner, television, phone, ceiling fan, and a modern tile bathroom, usually with a walk-in shower. Attached to the hotel is a sidewalk cafe with wrought-iron tables set out in the shady Parque Cepeda Peraza. Prices for a room with ceiling fan are 4,600 pesos ($9.20) single, 5,520 pesos ($11.04) double, 6,440 pesos ($12.88) triple; with air conditioning, you pay 5,060 ($10.12) single, 5,980 ($11.96) double, 6,900 ($13.80) triple. Suites cost about 2,000 pesos ($4) more per room.

The **Hotel Janeiro,** Calle 57 no. 435, between Calles 48 and 50, about seven blocks from the Plaza Mayor (tel. 992/23-3602), is owned by the same family as the Dolores Alba (see below). Since buying the Janeiro, they've spruced up the rooms and added a nice little swimming pool and patio tables for breakfast or snacks.

Rooms come with ceiling fan for 3,320 pesos ($6.64) single, 4,000 pesos ($8) double; with air conditioning and TV for 4,400 ($8.80) single, 5,300 ($10.60) double. They have parking places for a few cars.

Only a block and a half north of the Plaza Mayor is the small **Hotel del Parque,** Calle 60 no. 495, at Calle 59 (tel. 992/24-7844). The hotel entrance and restaurant are quite colonial, but the 21 rooms are actually in the modern structure next door. Although the rooms are quite small, they're bright with floral wallpaper, tiled baths, and ceiling fans. The hotel has its own large enclosed parking lot. Figure to pay 3,000 pesos ($6) single, 3,565 pesos ($7.13) double here.

Colonial Inns

A few of Mérida's lodging places have an authentic colonial ambience, somewhat faded, it's true, but still charming.

The **Hotel Dolores Alba,** Calle 63 no. 464 between Calles 52 and 54 (tel. 992/21-3745), is an old Mérida house converted to receive guests. Twenty rooms here come with air conditioning, ceiling fans and showers, plus decorations of local crafts. A big open court and another court with a nice clean swimming pool give a sense of space. You'll pay 3,000 pesos ($6) single, 4,500 pesos ($9) double, 5,500 pesos ($11) triple for a room with a fan. Air conditioning costs a bit more. The Dolores Alba is run by the Sanchez family, who also have the Hotel Janeiro, and the Hotel Dolores Alba at Chichén-Itzá. Make reservations at one hotel for space at the other hotel, if you like.

Once a Private Mansion

I'm very fond of the hotel **Posada Toledo,** Calle 58 no. 487 at the corner of Calle 57 (tel. 992/23-2256), once a private mansion but now run as an inn with 19 rooms and a rooftop deck, good for sitting and viewing the city in the cool of the evening. The place seems to be a cross between a garden and a museum with antique furnishings and lots of verdure. Rates are 6,000 pesos ($12) single and 7,000 pesos ($14) double with ceiling fan, 6,500 pesos ($13) single and 7,500 pesos ($15) double with air conditioning.

The **Casa Bowen,** Calle 66 no. 521-B, near Calle 65 (tel. 992/21-8112), is actually two buildings. The original old building, with small, bare rooms around a courtyard, has been supplemented with a big new addition next door. Rooms come with tile showers, and ceiling fans for 3,000 to 3,500 pesos ($6 to $7). Rooms in the old building are cheaper, but well used. The location is good, though.

You're sure to notice the crumbling façade of the **Gran Hotel,** overlooking the Parque Cepeda Peraza at Calle 60 no. 496, between 59 and 61, a half-block north of the Plaza Mayor (tel. 992/ 24-7622). It has obviously seen better days, but those in search of faded splendor will like its fancy woodwork, wrought-iron balustrades, and marble staircases. Everyone likes its prime location, and some go for its restaurant. Room prices, with private bath and ceiling fan, are 3,150 pesos ($6.30) single, 3,800 pesos ($7.60) double.

ROCK-BOTTOM PRICES: The aforementioned hotels offer excellent value for money, but if your budget is even slimmer, consider the following ones, which offer suitable if spartan accommodations for unbeatable prices.

The **Hotel Peninsular,** Calle 58 no. 519, between 65 and 67 (tel. 992/23-6996 or 23-6902), is right in the heart of the market district less than three blocks southeast of the Plaza Mayor. In such a busy district, you'll be surprised to find this warren of tidy, quiet little rooms at the end of the long entrance corridor. There's even a small restaurant. Prices are 2,160 pesos ($4.31) single, 2,600 ($5.20) double with ceiling fan; 2,900 ($5.80) single, 3,500 ($7) double with air conditioning.

Four blocks northeast of the Plaza Mayor is the **Hotel Mucuy,** Calle 56 no. 481, between Calles 56 and 58 (tel. 992/21-1037). The hotel is named for a small dove said to bring good luck to places where it alights, and you should have good luck, as many alight here. The two floors of rooms, all with window screens, tile shower, and ceiling fan, are lined up on one side of a garden with fine grass and bougainvillea; you can park your car within the hotel gates for free. The owners are Sr. Alfredo and Sra. Ofelia Comin, who live on the premises. Señora Comin speaks English. Rates are 2,400 pesos ($4.80) single, 3,000 pesos ($6) double, 3,600 pesos ($7.20) for three persons. A laundry sink and clothesline are available for guests' use. The roses and bougainvillea seem to be in bloom all summer here.

Near the Bus Station

The **Hotel Posada del Angel,** Calle 67 no. 535, between Calles 66 and 68, Mérida, Yucatán 97000 (tel. 922/23-2754), is a mere

1½ blocks from Mérida's main bus station, and thus a good choice for late arrivals. It's a tidy, modern white place with red tile accents and semicircular windows, two floors, and 26 rooms. The few rooms on the front are very noisy due to the bus thrumming, but most rooms are in the back. Make sure yours is. Prices are 2,865 pesos ($5.73) single, 3,450 pesos ($6.90) double, for a room with bath and fan. There's free parking if you've come by car, not bus.

Right across the street from the aforementioned place is the **Casa Becil,** Calle 67 no. 550-C, between 66 and 68, Mérida, Yucatán 97000 (tel. 992/21-2957), a homey casa de huespedes where you pretty much live with a pleasant family. Most of the 12 rooms are around a tiny court in back where it's quiet. They're plain, but suitable, and go for 2,200 pesos ($4.40) for one bed (one or two people), 2,500 pesos ($5) for a room with two beds.

Mérida's Restaurants

Although Mérida cannot approach such cosmopolitan centers as Mexico City and Guadalajara in terms of diversity of restaurants, it has a comfortable number of good places to dine. Continental cuisine, Mexican specialties, American favorites, even Middle Eastern and French dishes are available.

You should make a point of trying some of the special dishes of Yucatán during your stay in Mérida. I'll give you a few suggestions, but first you must know how things are seasoned and prepared.

SEASONINGS, SAUCES, AND SURPRISES: The hot pepper of Yucatán, called *chile habanero,* is among the hottest in all Mexico, and if you tangle with one, you won't soon forget it. But you needn't worry, as dishes are not heavily doused in habanero, although it is used. Often it lurks in a fiery sauce served on the side.

A popular sauce is *achiote,* made of sour orange juice, salt, onion relish, habanero peppers, and cilantro (fresh coriander leaf). There's also *pipián,* a sauce made with pumpkin or sunflower seeds; and escabeche, a thick, mildly piquant concoction reminiscent of a stew, though the word means "pickle."

Yucatecan Specialties

Huevos motuleños: Said to have originated in the Yucatecan town of Motul, these breakfast eggs come atop a tortilla, garnished with beans, peas, ham, sausage, and grated cheese.

Sopa de lima: This lime soup is tangy and flavorful, made with chicken stock.

Cochinita pibil: Try suckling pig wrapped in banana leaves and baked in a barbecue pit (if it's authentic), flavored with achiote. Look also for the similar pollo pibil, made with chicken.

Papadzules: Tortillas are stuffed with hard boiled eggs and seeds (cucumber or sunflower) in a tomato sauce.

Pavo relleno negro: Pavo means turkey, and Yucatán was the original home (along with New England) of this marvelous bird. Stuffed turkey, Yucatán-style, is filled with chopped pork and beef and cooked in a rich, dark sauce.

Poc-chuc: This translates into slices of pork with onion in a tangy sauce of sour oranges or limes.

Venado: Venison (deer), a popular dish, is served numerous ways, perhaps as pipián de venado, steamed in banana leaves and served with a sauce of ground squash seeds.

Queso relleno: Called "stuffed cheese," this dish is made with a mild yellow cheese stuffed with minced meat and spices.

Beer: As for drinks, Yucatecan beers such as Carta Clara and Montejo (lager) and León Negro (dark) are delicious, but harder and harder to find as the gigantic brewing companies from central Mexico move in and crowd the market.

Liquor: *Xtabentún (*shtah-ben-*toon)* is the local high-octane firewater, traditionally made by fermenting honey, then flavoring the brew with anise. Today the xtabentún you buy in the market may have a lot of grain neutral spirits in it instead of fermented honey. Think of the drink as Yucatecan ouzo or pastis. It comes *seco* (dry), or *crema* (sweet).

THE BEST PLACES: Here are my favorite dining places in Mérida.

Mexican

A place to try if you're feeling romantic is the **Restaurante Portico del Peregrino,** Calle 57 no. 501 (tel. 21-6844), right next door to the ever-popular Pop and across the street from the university. The restaurant aims to recapture the 19th century in Mexico, and does this rather well. You enter through a little garden court—a good place to take a bench seat and wait for laggers in your party —then through a cross-topped gateway into another little courtyard set with tables and shaded by vines and trees. If the weather is too warm for outdoor dining, escape to the air-conditioned bliss of the two enclosed dining rooms, which are well stocked with antique beveled mirrors and elegant sideboards. Table settings are done with white cloths and decent glassware. For less than 3,500 pesos ($7) you can have soup, fish filet, a brochette of beef, or pollo pibil, plus rum-raisin ice cream for dessert. The Peregrino is open for lunch and dinner, noon to 3 p.m. and 6 to 11 p.m., every day of the week.

French

Those in the mood for French cuisine will want to try the **Yannig Restaurante,** Calle 62 no. 480, between 57 and 59 (tel. 21-8468). Chef Yannig Oliviéro was trained in France, and serves up the old favorites and some of his own creations: onion or garlic soup, Roquefort salads and crêpes, pâté maison, beef with unripe pepper sauce, fish amandine, coq au vin, pêche Melba. The bright, cheery, cozy little restaurant is a pleasant change from the normal fluorescent lighting. Plan to spend 2,000 pesos ($4) for a light meal, 4,500 pesos ($9) for a feast with wine. Only dinner is served, Monday through Saturday from 5 to 11:30 p.m., Sunday from 1 to 10:30 p.m.

Yucatecan

As Yucatecan cuisine spreads throughout Mexico, the fame of poc-chuc pork goes with it. The dish, a delectable concoction of grilled pork, tomatoes, onions, *cilantro* (fresh coriander leaves), and salt, was created in Mérida at **Los Almendros,** Calle 50 no. 493, between Calles 57 and 59, facing the Plaza de Mejorada (tel. 21-2851). Actually, the first Los Almendros is deep in the Maya hinterland, at Ticul, but the branch in Mérida has become the favorite spot to sample local delicacies. Start with venison broth (sopa Mestiza), then have poc-chuc, pollo pibil, or pavo relleno negro (baked turkey with a black stuffing of ground pork, roasted peppers, and Yucatecan spices). You'll find lots of similarly exotic and delicious entrees, all for about 900 to 1,050 pesos ($1.80 to $2.10) with descriptions in English! The daily special plate, always a good bargain, costs about 1,250 pesos ($2.50) and constitutes a full meal. Over the years, I've been alternately delighted and mildly disappointed at Los Almendros. You must try it, though.

Lebanese

In Yucatán? A Middle Eastern restaurant? Why? Because 19th-century Mexico, and particularly Yucatán, had a significant population of Ottoman traders, mostly from the sultan's province of Lebanon. The **Restaurant Cedro del Libano,** Calle 59 no. 529, between Calles 64 and 66 (tel. 23-7531), is a simple but tidy place with experienced waiters and a menu that lists berenjena con tijini (eggplant with tahini), labne (yogurt), labin (like buttermilk), tabouli, kibi, and alambre de kafta (ground meat grilled on skewers). I had the fatta Cedro del Libano, which turned out to be chicken topped with chick peas, yogurt, and sliced almonds. Meat dishes cost about 1,400 to 1,500 pesos ($2.80 to $3), and a full meal can be had for 2,500 pesos ($5) or so. Hours are 11:30 a.m. to 11:30 p.m. every day.

Vegetarian

Any Mexican town of considerable size has a vegetarian restaurant, and Mérida is no exception. Here it's the **Restaurante Vegetariano La Guaya**, Calle 60 no. 472, between 55 and 53, just a few steps north of the Parque Santa Lucia (tel. 23-2144). Enter to find a little patio café in a courtyard, combined with a bookstore featuring health-related titles. Lots of different salads are offered here, as well as a Hindu dish of oats, wheat, and fish, named Kama Sutra! The daily set-price meal costs 900 pesos ($1.80). Come any day for lunch or dinner.

FULL SERVICE, LOW PRICES: Probably the most popular meeting place in town is the **Café-Restaurant Express,** facing the park at Calles 59 and 60 (tel. 21-3738). Here, hordes of townspeople—mainly men—sit and ogle the hours away, totally devoid of atmosphere, with all attention focused on the sidewalk or at least a newspaper. The menu is vast—lengua a la Mexicana (Mexican-style tongue), pollo pibil (the chef wraps and marinates the chicken in banana leaves before cooking), huachinango milanesa (red snapper). Top off whatever you choose with pasta de guayaba con queso (guava paste with cheese). Or simply while away some time here with coffee, good and strong. Plan to spend 800 pesos ($1.60) for breakfast, about 1,250 pesos ($2.50) for the set-price lunch, and 2,600 pesos ($5.20) for dinner. Open 6 a.m. to 1 a.m. every day.

I used to recommend a number of restaurants on Calle 62 just north of the main plaza, but in recent years the traffic noise and fumes (particularly from the buses) have become overwhelming. Nowadays one is much better off dining right on the plaza, at the **Restaurant Nicte-Ha,** for instance, at Calle 61 no. 500 (tel. 23-0784). Although very plain, the Nicte-Ha is pretty quiet and pollution free, and prices are low: tacos, hamburgers, even carne asada and chicken dishes cost 750 to 1,300 pesos ($1.50 to $2.60).

Soon after your arrival in Mérida you'll discover **El Meson** (tel. 21-9232), the tiny place just to the left of the Hotel Caribe's entrance. Wrought-iron tables are set out in the shady Parque Cepeda Peraza (alias Parque Hidalgo), and they're often full. The food is usually pretty good; I especially enjoy the sopa de verduras (vegetable soup), and prices are great: the set-price meal, usually served right into the evening hours, is only 1,050 pesos ($2.10). El Meson is open for three meals a day, every day.

For a light lunch, try **Pop,** on Calle 57 between Calles 60 and 62, next to the university (tel. 21-6844). The little place is air-conditioned, clean, bright, and modern, and seems to be where the gilded youth of Mérida have their afternoon snack. Apple pie, Bavarian fudge cake, the best hamburgers in town, and the air-conditioning are the attractions. Prices are okay: 400 to 500 pesos (80¢ to $1) for a hamburger, 500 pesos ($1) for a fruit salad with ice cream. "Pop," by the way, is the first month of the 18-month Maya calendar.

A Plaza Café

For after-dinner ice cream or Mexican pastries and cakes, the **Dulcería y Sorbetería Colón** sets out bent-wire café tables and chairs in the portico on the Plaza Mayor (Calle 61 side). Besides serving dessert at budget prices—320 pesos (64¢) for ice cream, 100 to 150 pesos (20¢ to 30¢) for cake—it provides the best vantage point for people-watching in the late afternoon or evening. Try some of their exotic tropical fruit ice creams such as coconut or papaya. Open 8 a.m. to midnight daily. Try to pick a time of day when auto traffic (with its noise and smelly fumes) is not so heavy in the square.

For Breakfast

A good breakfast choice, particularly if the day is already hot, is the aforementioned **Pop,** which is air-conditioned and has set breakfasts priced at 400 pesos (80¢) for a continental breakfast, 520 pesos ($1.04) with two eggs, and 620 pesos ($1.24) with two eggs plus bacon or ham.

To make your own breakfast, feast your eyes (and later your appetite) on pastries and sweet rolls from the **Panificadora Montejo,** at the corner of Calles 62 and 63, which is the southwest corner of the main plaza. It's hard not to overeat with your eyes as you choose from a dozen or more delectable breakfast treats.

With a hot drink a suitable light breakfast can be thrown together for about 150 pesos (83¢).

For those (like me) who simply cannot start a day without fresh orange juice, here's good news. Juice bars with the name of **Jugos California** or **Jugos Florida** have sprouted up all over Mérida. Three of these thirst-quenching establishments are on or just off the main plaza: one on Calle 62 near Calle 61, one on the Calle 63 side of the plaza, and another just across the corner from it on Calle 62! Demand is brisk, and prices are not high for what you get: a tall ice-cream-soda glass of juice squeezed right before your eyes for 200 to 450 pesos (40¢ to 90¢).

STARVATION-BUDGET FOOD: Cafetería Erik's, Calle 62 no. 499A (no phone), just off the main plaza, among the various other Erik's restaurants in town belonging to the chain, has the reputation for the best tortas—fried sandwiches stuffed with ham and cheese, turkey, roast pork—for 350 to 675 pesos (70¢ to $1.35) apiece. A few of these are very filling. A pleasant wood-paneled place with tablecloths, it features smooth jazz in the background.

El Louvre, Calle 62 no. 499 (tel. 21-3271), right next door to Erik's off the main plaza at Calles 61 and 62, is rather inaptly named unless you consider it a gallery of people. Open 24 hours a day, this big open place probably feeds everybody who comes to Mérida at one time or another—chicle workers, laborers from the henequen fields, planters, and townspeople. Prices are low: sandwiches for 300 to 425 pesos (60¢ to 85¢), eggs motulenos (Yucatán style on a fried tortilla with fried beans and chopped ham) for 475 pesos (95¢), lots of combination plates, and a daily set-price lunch for a mere 700 pesos ($1.40). Calle 62 between the main plaza and Calle 57 is a riot of such small, rock-bottom food shops offering everything from chalupas to chow mein. Starvation-budgeteers are sure to find things to fit the appetite and the wallet all along the street.

Where the Students Eat

Mérida is the home of the Yucatán's university, and thus of student throngs deep into plain living and high thinking. Living plainly does not mean badly, however, for the humble torta (sandwich) always provides tasty and nutritious fare at a rock-bottom price. The mecca for this time- and budget-saver is **Las Mil Tortas,** on Calle 62 between Calles 57 and 55 (no phone). Very small, this shop-of-a-thousand-sandwiches sports a long list of sandwiches priced from 200 to 320 pesos (40¢ to 76¢). The few small tables are often filled with the student crowd, but you can get your tortas and *refresco* (soft drink) to go, all for less than 500 pesos ($1). By the way, Las Mil Tortas is branching out now, and you may see similar shops in other parts of the city. There's one on Calle 56 near Calle 57, around the corner from the Hotel Mucuy.

What to See and Do

Mérida is pretty, congenial, friendly, and in summer it's also very, very hot. Just before the coming of the muggy, rainy months (June through September), Mérida can get up to 108° F (42° C). You'd do well to arise early, snatch a quick breakfast, and do your walking well before the noonday sun does its worst. Then have lunch, and a siesta, and issue forth in the evening, refreshed and ready for the next round.

If you're lucky enough to be visiting in January or February, you'll be able to spend most of the day outdoors without discomfort.

Start your explorations of old Mérida at the city's focal point, the Plaza Mayor.

PLAZA MAYOR: This beautiful town square, now shaded by topiary laurel trees, began its history as the Plaza de Armas, a training field for Montejo's troops. Later called the Plaza Mayor, it was renamed the Plaza de la Constitución in 1812, then the Plaza de la Independencia in 1812. Other common names for it include Plaza Grande, Plaza Principal, and even (sometimes) zócalo.

The city was laid out by the conquering Montejos on the classic Spanish colonial plan. Surrounding the plaza were the cathedral, the archbishop's palace, the governor's palace, and the mansions of notables. Let's examine each in turn.

The Cathedral

On the east side of the plaza, the cathedral was under construction from 1561 to 1598. It looks like a fortress, as do many other early churches in Yucatán. That was actually their function in part for several centuries, as the Mayas did not take kindly to European domination. Much of the stone in the cathedral's walls came from the ruined buildings of Maya Tiho.

Inside, decoration is sparse and simple, the most notable feature being a picture over a side door of Ah Kukum Tutul Xiú visiting the Montejo camp. To the left of the main altar is a smaller shrine with a curious burnt cross, recovered from the church in the town of Ichmul, which burned down. The figure was carved by a local artist in the 1500s from a miraculous tree which burned but did not char. The figure burned, though, along with the church, and broke out in blisters as it did. The local people named it Cristo de las Ampollas (Christ of the Blisters).

Also take a look in the side chapel (open 8 to 11 a.m. and 4:30 to 7 p.m.), which has a life-size diorama of the Last Supper. The Mexican Jesus is covered with prayer crosses brought by supplicants asking for intercession.

The archbishop's palace and a seminary once stood to the right (south) of the cathedral. The palace was torn down during the Mexican Revolution (1915); part of the seminary remains, but is now used for shops.

Palacio de Gobierno

On the north side of the plaza, this site was first occupied by a mansion built for the colonial administrators; the present building dates from 1892.

Between 8 a.m. and 8 p.m. (Sundays 9 to 5) you can visit the palace and view the large murals painted mostly between 1971 and 1973. Scenes from Mayan and Mexican history abound, the painting over the stairway combining the Mayan spirit with ears of sacred corn, the "sunbeams of the gods." Nearby is a painting of the mustached benevolent dictator Lázaro Cárdenas, who in 1938 expropriated 17 foreign oil companies and was hailed as a new Mexican liberator.

Palacio Municipal

Facing the cathedral across the plaza from the west side is the Palacio Municipal, or City Hall, with its familiar clock tower. It started out as the cabildo, the colonial town hall and lock-up, in 1542. It had to be rebuilt in the 1730s, and rebuilt again in the 1850s, when it took on its present romantic aspect.

Palacio Montejo

Also called the Casa de Montejo, it was begun in 1549 by Francisco Montejo "El Mozo," and was occupied by Montejo descendants until the 1970s. It now houses a bank branch (Banamex), which means you can get a look at parts of the palace just by wandering in during banking hours (9 a.m. to 1:30 p.m., Monday through Friday). Note the arms of the Spanish kings and of the Montejo family on the Plateresque façade, along with figures of the Conquistadores standing on the heads of "barbarians" overcome by their exploits. Look closely and you'll find the bust of Francisco Montejo the Elder, his wife, and his daughter.

THE MARKET DISTRICT: Mérida's bustling market district is just a few blocks southeast of the Plaza Mayor, roughly the area bounded by Calles 63 to 69, and 62 to 54. The market proper is right next to the post office, at the corner of Calles 56 and 65. Wade into the clamor and activity, browsing for leather goods, hammocks, Panama hats, Mayan embroidered dresses, men's formal guayabera shirts, and handcraft items of all kinds. A few tips and pointers might be helpful.

Buying hammocks

The supremely comfortable Yucatecan fine-mesh hammocks (hamacas) are made of string from several materials. Silk is wonderful, but extremely expensive, and only for truly serious hammock-sleepers. Nylon is long-lasting. Cotton is attractive, fairly strong and inexpensive, but it wears out sooner than nylon. There are several grades of cotton string used in hammocks.

What will probably serve your needs best is a cotton hammock of good quality string. Here's how to find it: First, look at the string itself. Is it fine and tightly spun? Are the end loops well made and tight? Grasp the hammock at the point where the body and the end strings meet, and hold your hand level with the top of your head. The body should touch the floor; if not, the hammock is too short for you. Next, open the hammock and look at the weave. Are the strings soiled? Are there many mistakes in the pattern of the weave? Then, decide on size. Keep in mind that any of these hammocks is going to look big when you stretch it open, but many will seem small when you actually lie in them, so you want a hammock as big as you can afford.

Hammocks are sold as *sencillo* (single, 50 pairs of end strings, about $5), *doble* (double, 100 pairs of end strings, about $8 to $10), *matrimonial* (larger than double, 150 pairs of end strings, about $12 to $15). The biggest hammock of all is called *una hamaca de quatro cajas,* or sometimes *matrimonial especial,* and it is simply enormous, with 175 pairs of end strings; if you can find one, it'll cost you about $16 to $18. Buy the biggest hammock you think you can afford. You'll be glad you did. The bigger ones take up no more room, and are so much more comfortable, even for just one person.

Where should you buy your hammock? Street vendors will approach you at every turn. "Hamacas, Señor, Señorita?" Their prices will be low, but so may be their quality. Buy from these guys if you're willing to take the time and go through all the steps listed above. Otherwise, booths in the market will have a larger selection to choose from, at only slightly higher prices.

For years I've been recommending the store called **La Poblana, S.A.,** Calle 65 no. 492, between 60 and 62 (tel. 21-6503), with no complaints. Sr. William Razu C., the owner, is usually on the job and ready to whip out dozens of hammocks for your inspection. Prices are marked, and bargaining is not encouraged. If you've spent some time in the market for hammocks, and you seem to know what you're talking about, Sr. Razu may usher you upstairs to a room wall-to-wall with hammocks, where you can give your prospective purchase a test-run. La Poblana sells ropes and mosquito nets for hammocks as well, and also Mayan women's dresses and men's guayaberas.

Panama hats

Another very popular item is this soft, pliable hat made from fibers of the palm and *jipijapa* plants in several towns along Hwy. 180 in the neighboring state of Campeche. If you travel through the town of Becal, for instance, you'll see a sculpture in the main square composed of several enormous concrete hats tipped up against one another. It's a fitting monument to a townfolk who have made their wealth (such as it is) weaving the pliant fibers into handsome headgear while sitting in humid limestone grottoes and caves. The caves provide just the right atmosphere for shaping the fibers. Stop and ask for a demonstration, and any citizen will be glad to oblige.

There's no need to journey all the way to Becal, however, as Mérida has the hats in abundance. Just the thing to shade you from the fierce Yucatecan sun, the hats can be rolled up and carried in a suitcase for the trip home. They retain their shape quite well.

Jipi hats come in three grades, judged by the quality (pliability and fineness) of the fibers and closeness of the weave. The coarser, more open weave of fairly large fibers will be sold for a few dollars (or by street vendors in Cancún and Cozumel for up to $10!). The middle grade, a fairly fine, close weave of good fibers, should cost about $10 in a responsible shop. The finest weave, truly a beautiful hat, can cost twice this much. For most people, the middle grade is fine.

A tried and true *sombrería* is **La Casa de los Jipis,** Calle 56 no. 526, near Calle 65 (no phone), where a phlegmatic señora will show you the three grades of hats, grumping the while. Find your size, more or less, and the señora will tie a ribbon around the hat for final adjustment. If you'd like to see how the hats are blocked, wander into the shady depths of the rear of the store.

Crafts Museums and Shops

For a look at the best of Yucatán's crafts and handwork, drop by the **Museo Regional de Artesanías,** Calle 59 between 50 and 48, open for free from Tuesday through Saturday, 8 a.m. to 8 p.m., Sunday till 2 p.m., closed Monday. Another place to examine crafts is at **La Casa de la Cultura,** Calle 63 no. 513, between 64 and 66, a beautiful restored monastery with exhibits of crafts, and a shop where you can buy them. There are also two galleries here with changing exhibits, plus a bookstore, a bulletin board listing cultural events, and an inexpensive cafeteria.

EXPLORING CALLE 60: Many of Mérida's old churches and little parks are located along Calle 60 north of the Plaza Mayor. Plan a stroll along this street, perhaps continuing to the Paseo de Montejo and its Museo Regional de Antropología.

Parque Cepeda Peraza

As you leave the Plaza Mayor, you'll pass the site of the Seminario de San Ildefonso, an early hospital, on your right. You then come to the little Parque Cepeda Peraza (also called the Parque Hidalgo), named for the 19-century General Manuel Cepeda Peraza. Part of Montejo's original plan for the city, the parque borders the church called **La Iglesia de Jesus,** or El Tercer Orden (the Third Order), built by the Jesuit order in 1618. The entire city block in which the church stands was part of the Jesuit establishment, and the early schools started by these worthies ended up being the Universidad de Yucatán. The Biblioteca (library) Cepeda Peraza, founded by the general in 1867, is beside the church.

Down Calle 59 a few steps past the park and the church is the former **Convento de la Mejorada,** a late-1600s work of the Franciscans.

Parque de la Madre

This park is sometimes called the Parque Morelos. By its statue shall you know it, this little park with its modern madonna and child. The statue is a copy of the work by Lenoir that stands in the Luxembourg Gardens in Paris.

Teatro Peón Contreras

Designed by Italian architect Enrico Deserti in the beginning of the present century, the enormous yellow building holds the state Tourist Information Office (facing the park). The main entrance, with its Carrara marble staircase and frescoed dome, is closed most of the time, unfortunately.

Universidad de Yucatán

On the west side of Calle 60, at the corner of Calle 57, is the university, founded in the 19th century by Felipe Carrillo Puerto with the help of the aforementioned General Cepeda Peraza. Wander in, ask directions to the **fresco** (1961) by Manuel Lizama, and the painting will tell you the whole story of the founding.

Heading north on Calle 60, the Hotel Mérida Misión is on your left, the Hotel Casa del Balam on your right. Soon you'll come to the Parque Santa Lucia.

Parque Santa Lucia

Facing the park is the ancient **Iglesia de Santa Lucia** (1575). The plaza itself, surrounded by an arcade on the north and west sides, used to be the place at which visitors first alighted in Mérida from their stagecoaches. The plaza is floodlit at night, and on Thursday there are concerts of local music at 9 p.m. On Sunday afternoons, the plaza fills up with vendors and browsers during the weekly Antiques and Crafts Bazaar.

To reach the Paseo de Montejo, walk up Calle 60 to Calle 47, turn right, and the Paseo is two blocks away.

PASEO DE MONTEJO: Most guidebooks compare the Paseo to Paris's Champs-Élysées, but you'll see at once that they're pretty different. Even so, it is a broad, tree-lined thoroughfare lined with imposing banks, hotels, and a number of the old 19th-century mansions put up by henequen barons, generals, and other Yucatecan potentates.

Museo Regional de Antropologia

Most impressive mansion of all is that occupied by the local anthropology museum, at the corner of Calle 43. The **Palacio Cantón** (1909–1911) was designed by Enrico Deserti, the architect who designed the Teatro Peón Contreras, and built during the last years of the Porfiriato as the home of General Francisco Cantón Rosado (1833–1917). The general got to enjoy his palace for only six years, until his death. After this short occupancy the imposing edifice began a new career as a school, then as the official residence of Yucatán's governor, before becoming first the archeological museum, and now the Regional Museum of Anthropology.

Don't neglect to admire the building itself as you walk around. It's the only Paseo mansion that you'll get to visit. Note especially a great luxury of the time: the little art deco elevator.

The museum is open from 8 a.m. to 8 p.m. Tuesday through Saturday, to 2 p.m. on Sunday, closed Monday. Entry costs 40 pesos (8¢).

On the right as you enter is a room for changing shows. After that are the permanent exhibits, with captions in Spanish only. Starting with fossil mastodon teeth, the exhibits take you down through the ages of Yucatán's history, giving special attention to the daily life of its inhabitants. You'll see how the Mayas tied boards to babys' skulls in order to reshape the heads, giving them the slanting forehead that was then a mark of great beauty, and how they filed teeth to sharpen them, or drilled teeth to implant jewels. Enlarged photos show the archeological sites. The one of Mayapán, for instance, clearly shows the city's ancient walls. Even if you know little Spanish, the museum provides a good background for your Mayan explorations.

Monumento a la Patria

Continue your stroll along the Paseo, and you'll walk by the **Parque de las Americas,** planted with trees and shrubs from throughout the New World, to the grandiose Monumento a la Patria (Monument to the Fatherland), done by Rómulo Rozo in the 1950s in neo-Mayan style.

PARQUE CENTENARIO: Due west of the Plaza Mayor along Calle 61 or 65, lies the large Parque Centenario, bordered by the Avenida de los Itzáes, which leads to the airport and Campeche. The parque is a fine place for an afternoon stroll, especially with children. There's a small zoo with Yucatecan animals; the deer, for instance, are quite graceful and nimble.

A DAY-TRIP TO PROGRESO: Want to zoom out to Progreso for a day? There's a good beach, not touristy but very Mexican, a fantastically long *muelle* ("mu-*wey*-yeh," or pier) that shoots out into the bay to reach water deep enough for ocean-going ships, and a few seafood restaurants (nothing great, though).

To get there, go to the special Progreso bus station on Calle 62 at no. 524, between Calles 65 and 67. Buses leave every five or ten minutes during the day, starting at 5 a.m. The trip takes 45 minutes.

Once in Progreso, Calle 19 runs along the beach. The bus station is about four blocks south of this street. The beach seems endless, and is crowded with coconut palms (and on weekends, with Mexican families). The **Restaurant Carabela,** Calle 69 no. 146, on the seashore Avenida Malecon, will serve you a fish platter for 1,450 pesos ($2.90), shrimp for just a bit more.

MÉRIDA NIGHTLIFE: There are band concerts every Sunday at 9 p.m. in the Plaza Mayor. Every Thursday in **Santa Lucía Park,** on the corner of Calles 60 and 55, you can hear some festive music and serenades by different mariachis. They begin at 9 p.m. and stop when their enthusiasm turns to thirst.

Take a stroll past the **Jardín de los Compositores** (Garden of Composers), behind the Palacio Municipal, to see what's happening. This is the venue for many concerts, movies, and general happenings. Another good place to check is the **Teatro Peón Contreras** at Calles 60 and 57. Ask at the Tourist Information Office right in the building about current shows. They often have Yucatán's own ballet folklorico in performance, but usually on Sunday mornings at 11 rather than at night.

Hotel bars, lounges and discos depend largely upon the crowd of customers presently staying at each hotel. Most of Mérida's downtown hotels are filled with tour groups whose members, after an exhausting day, seek to rest rather than rock.

For a cross-cultural experience, you might want to try the club named **Tulipanes,** Calle 42 no. 462-A (tel. 27-2009 or 27-0967), which has a restaurant, bar and disco. Every evening from 8:30 to 10 they put on a floor show inspired, however remotely, by Mayan customs, ancient and modern. Cover charge is 3,000 pesos ($6); the restaurant menu tends toward Yucatecan specialties such as pollo pibil, venison steaks, and chuleta Yucateca (pork chops with achiote).

Chapter IX

UXMAL AND THE PUUC CITIES

THOUGH IT IS NOT quite as famous as Chichén-Itzá, Uxmal is equally impressive, and perhaps even more dramatic. And when you consider that Uxmal, 50 miles (80 km) south of Mérida, is only one of a half-dozen impressive archeological sites in the Puuc (hill country) region, you've got an attraction of major proportions.

You can and should spend more than a day in touring the region. Secure a reservation at one of the excellent hotels right at Uxmal to use as your base. Though it's possible to visit Uxmal itself in a day, try to spend at least two days (one night), or even three (two nights) before heading back to Mérida, or onward to Campeche, or across the peninsula to the Caribbean coast.

Want the full rundown? First there's Mayapán, the ancient **Maya** capital city, badly ruined now but in a lush setting. It's thrilling to consider yourself walking among the ruins of the great Maya capital. Then there's Uxmal, with several of the most beautiful and awe-inspiring buildings ever constructed by man. Then 17 miles (27 km) southeast of Uxmal is Kabah, with a unique palace, several other grand buildings, and a decorative style very different from that at Uxmal. From Kabah it's only a few miles to Sayil, with its immense palace reminiscent of Minoan structures. Xlapak ("Shla-*pahk*") is almost walking distance (through the jungle) from Sayil, and Labná just a bit farther east. A short drive east from Labná brings you to the caves of Loltún. Backtrack to the main road (Hwy. 261) and you can head southwest to spend the night in Campeche.

Those with only a little time and/or money will have to limit themselves to seeing Uxmal on a day-trip by bus (see above, Chapter VIII, "Getting To and From Mérida," for details). The ideal but more expensive way to tour the ruined cities south of Mérida is to rent a car, plan to stay the night in a hotel at Uxmal, and allow two full days for sightseeing before hitting Campeche or returning to Mérida, or driving on toward Tulum and Cancún. How interested are you in Mayan archeology? If you enjoy it as much as I do, then find some friends to share expenses, rent a car in Mérida, and enjoy yourself.

Another way to do it is to ignore Mayapán, get an early start in your rental car, and head south on Hwy. 261 directly to Uxmal. Spend the morning there, and the afternoon at Kabah, Sayil, Xlapak, and Labná, and then head on to find an inexpensive hotel in Campeche, or return to Mérida. This tour would be about 275 miles (445 km) round trip.

Here, then, is a stone-by-stone description of the ruined Maya cities south of Mérida, starting with Mayapán and the old pottery-making town of Ticul.

Mayapán

Founded by the semi-legendary Quetzalcóatl (Kukulcán in Maya) in about 1007, Mayapán ranked in importance with Chichén-Itzá and Uxmal. It was a vast city, and for almost two centuries it was the capital of a Maya confederation of city-states that included Chichén and Uxmal. But before the year 1200 the rulers of Mayapán put an end to the confederation by attacking and conquering Chichén, and by forcing the rulers of Uxmal to live as vassals in Mayapán. For almost 250 years Mayapán was the center of power in Yucatán.

You can take a village bus to the Ruinas de Mayapán (not to be confused with the village of Mayapán (see above, Chapter VIII, "Getting To and From Mérida," for details). But the easiest way is to drive. Ask directions frequently—it's very easy to take wrong turns or to get onto unmarked roads by mistake.

Head out of Mérida toward Kanasin and **Acanceh** ("Ah-kahn-*keh*"), about 12 miles (20 km).

This is not as easy as it sounds, as signs are few and sometimes wrong. Here are some hints: Get to Calle 65 in the Mérida *colonia* (suburb) named Miraflores, on the eastern edge of the city. Head east on 65, bear right at its end, then take an easy left at a big intersection. Follow the wide, divided highway complete with speed bumps, cross Mérida's *circunvalación* (ring road)—you'll see signs to Cancún (left) and Campeche (right)—and continue straight on. Soon you'll enter Kanasin. Watch for signs that say *desviación* (detour) as you approach the town. As in many Yucatán towns, you're being redirected to follow a one-way street through the urban area. Go through the market, pass the church on your right, the main square on your left, and continue straight out of town.

The next village you come to, at Km 10, is San Antonio Tehuitz, an old henequen hacienda. At Km 13 is Tepich, another hacienda village, with those funny little henequen-cart tracks crisscrossing the main road. After Tepich comes Petectunich, and finally Acanceh.

In **Acanceh** there's a partially restored pyramid to the left of the church, overlooking the main square, and several others tucked away in back yards. Should you need sustenance, Acanceh's market, complete with little loncherías, is just to the right of the church.

Turn right in the main square (around that statue of a smiling deer) and head for Tecoh (5½ miles, 9 km) and Telchaquillo (6¾ miles, 11 km). This route takes you past several old Yucatecan haciendas, each complete with its big house, chapel, factory with smokestack, and workers' houses. Shortly after the village of Telchaquillo, a sign on the right-hand side of the road will point to the entrance of the ruins, on the right.

A hundred yards in from the road, after passing the guards' hut, are the remains of **Mayapán.** The main pyramid is ruined but still lofty and impressive. Next to it is a large cenote (natural limestone cavern, used as a well), now full of trees, bushes, and banana plants. A small temple with columns and a fine high-relief mask of Tlaloc, the hook-nosed rain god, are beside the cenote. Other small temples, including El Caracol, with its circular tower, are in the nearby jungle, reached by paths.

These piles of stones, though impressive, give one no idea of what the walled city of Mayapán must have been like in its heyday. Supplied with water from 20 cenotes, it had over 3,000 buildings in its enclosed boundaries of several square miles. Today, all is covered in dense, limitless jungle.

Sr. Fausto Uc Flores, the guard, or his wife, Sra. Magdalena, whom you may meet as you enter the ruins, will sell you the requisite admission ticket for 40 pesos (8¢) and help you with any bits of information you may need.

Heading onward, continue along the main road to Tekit (5 miles, 8 km), turn right and go to Mama (4⅓ miles, 7 km), turn right again for Chapab (8 miles, 13 km), and finally you'll reach Ticul (6¼ miles, 10 km), the largest town in the region.

Ticul

You can have an excellent lunch here, or get a soft drink, or change some money, or pick up snacks in the market, or even stay the night in modest comfort, if necessary.

This sprawling town actually has only 20,000 inhabitants, many of whom make their living embroidering huipiles (the Mayan women's costume), weaving straw hats, and shaping pottery. Workshops and stores throughout the town, and especially in the market area, feature these items.

The main street is Calle 23, also sometimes called the Calle Principal. It's where you'll find the market, a hotel, and Ticul's best-known restaurant.

WHERE TO STAY AND EAT: The nicest hotel in town is actually a motel on the outskirts. The **Hotel-Motel Cerro Inn** is just at the edge of town, 1¼ miles (2 km) from the market, on the highway to Muna and Mérida (no phone). Its nine rooms, dark but cool, with showers and fans, face a shady grove and a nice palapa restaurant. Prices are 2,500 pesos ($5) for a double bed (single or double), 6,000 pesos ($6) for two beds. This place doesn't look so great as you enter, but it's not bad at all.

Right downtown, mere steps from the market, is the little **Hotel San Miguel,** Calle 28 no. 195, at the intersection with Calle 23 (no phone). The 20 very simple rooms here with shower and fan, arranged along a corridor in what can only be called Mexican cell-block fashion, cost 1,300 pesos ($2.60) double in a double bed, 1,600 pesos ($3.20) double in twin beds.

The **Hotel Sierra,** on the main square (no phone), charges about a dollar more than the San Miguel for its tidy rooms.

The restaurant called **Los Almendros** is on Calle 23 not far from the market (tel. 2-0021). Set in the courtyard of a big old Andalusian-style house, this is the original of the chain with branches now in Mérida and Cancún. The specialties are Mayan, such as papadzules (the stuffed tortillas) and poc-chuc. The illustrated menu in English explains the dishes in detail, so you're not in for a mystery meal. Stop in any day for lunch or dinner, and your bill will come to about 1,500 or 1,900 pesos ($3 or $3.80).

Just off the Plaza Principal is the **Restaurant Los Delfines,** Calle 26 no. 195, between 21 and 23 (tel. 2-0070). Miguel Angel Cachon Lara and his wife, Aída, proprietors of the place, will serve you a comida corrida for a mere 800 pesos ($1.60) or so, à la carte main course items for slightly more. Liquor is served, and the restaurant is open long hours, from 8 a.m. to 11 p.m. daily.

Right near the market there's a cantina called "Bar 'Tu Hermana'" (Your Sister). I can't recommend it, but as a veiled insult or the punch-line to a ribald joke, it's unbeatable!

WHAT TO DO: Ticul's annual festival, complete with bullfights, dancing, and carnival games, is held during the first few days of April.

Besides the pottery shops, Ticul offers a look at some impressive caves, those called **Yaxnic** (yash-*neek),* on the grounds of the old Hacienda Yotolín, within the city limits. Virtually undeveloped, the caves full of colored stalactites and stalagmites are visited by means of a perilous descent in a basket let down on a rope.

ONWARD: It's 14 miles (22 km) from Ticul to Muna. At Muna, turn left and head south on Hwy. 180 to Uxmal, 10 miles (16 km) away. Buses depart Ticul for Muna almost hourly during the day. At Muna, change to a bus heading south to Uxmal.

Uxmal

Prepare yourself for one of the highlights of your Yucatán vacation, for the ruins of Uxmal are truly breathtaking.

If you've decided to come directly from Mérida on Hwys. 180 and 261, you get a bonus: the chance to tour a real Yucatecan hacienda, **Yaxcopoil.** This unpronounceable Maya name designates a fascinating old hacienda on the road between Mérida and Uxmal. It's difficult to reach by bus, but if you're driving, look for it on the right side of the road 21 miles (33 km) south of Mérida, 10 miles (16 km) south of Uman, on Hwy. 261. Take a half hour to tour the house, factory, outbuildings, and museum. You'll see that such haciendas were the administrative, commercial, and social centers of vast private domains, almost little principalities, carved out of the Yucatecan jungle.

When you leave Yaxcopoil, you still have 28 miles (45 km) to drive to reach Uxmal.

Although the ruins of Uxmal are visible from the highway, the impressiveness of this site will not strike you until you enter the archeological zone and walk around. Coming from the north along Hwy. 261, you'll pass four hotels before you reach the ruins proper, three of them moderately priced and one quite cheap. Here's what to expect.

WHERE TO STAY AND EAT: Unlike Chichén-Itzá, which has several classes of hotels from which to choose, Uxmal has mostly one class: comfortable and moderately priced. Each of these hotels is willing to offer you room-with-meals plans, and you should look into them. Buying your dinner and breakfast—and perhaps even lunch—with your room in a package will ultimately save you money, because there's nowhere to eat but at the three hotels.

Buying the meals separately adds up to more than buying the package. For savings, pack a box lunch in Mérida and bring it along.

My favorite of the hotels here is the oldest one, the **Hotel Hacienda Uxmal,** Uxmal, Yucatán 97840 (tel. 4-7142; for reservations, contact Mérida Travel Service in the Hotel Casa del Balam in Mérida, Calle 60 no. 488, tel. 992/21-9212). Right on the highway across from the ruins, the Hacienda Uxmal was built as the headquarters for the archeological staff years ago. Rooms are large and airy, with equally large bathrooms, screens on the windows, ceiling fans, and blocky, substantial furniture. The rambling building groups many rooms around a central garden courtyard complete with fine swimming pool and bar. A dining room and gift shop fill out the spare rooms. Singles cost 15,075 pesos ($30.15); doubles are 16,400 pesos ($32.20); huge triple rooms are 17,700 pesos ($35.40). For dinner and breakfast, add 8,200 pesos ($16.40) per person to these prices. You should definitely take the meal package here, as dinner alone costs almost as much as the entire meal plan if you buy it separately. In effect, you get a full breakfast for no extra charge when you take the meal plan. It's a five-minute walk to the ruins from the hotel. Check-out time is 2 p.m., so you can spend the morning at the ruins and take a cooling dip (you'll need it!) before you check out and head out on the road again.

Even closer to the ruins is the **Villa Arqueológica** (no phone) —the hotel driveway starts at the ruins parking lot. A Club Med operation, the Villa Arqueológica has a swimming pool, tennis court, library, audio-visual show on the ruins in English, French, and Spanish, and 40 air-conditioned rooms that are fully modern. The layout is posh and tasteful—it's the "designer" version of the Hacienda Uxmal. Room prices here are 8,625 pesos ($17.25) single, 10,810 pesos ($21.62) double; meals are à la carte only.

Farther out, north of the ruins 1¼ miles (2 km) on the highway is the **Hotel Misión Uxmal** (no phone), a new and modern 40-room hotel that you can't help but notice as you drive. Same services here: restaurant, bar, pool, etc. The comfortable, air-conditioned rooms sell for 11,660 pesos ($23.30) double.

Now there is an exception to the high-priced places near Uxmal, but only if you have strong legs and a sun hat, or a car. The **Rancho Uxmal** (no phone), on Hwy. 261 north of the ruins 2¼ miles (3½ km), is a modest little place with a thatched-roof restaurant, a few primitive camping spots, and four comfy rooms with showers and fans. If the rooms were in Mérida they'd rent for much less, but as they're here in a high-rent district near the ruins, they go for 4,500 pesos ($9) double. Camping is very cheap: 500 pesos ($1) per person, with electrical hookup and use of a shower. In the restaurant, most main-course plates cost less than 900 pesos ($1.80). It should take you about 30 minutes to walk to the ruins from here, but remember—that sun gets awfully hot.

Unidad Uxmal

There is now a new service center at the ruins, called the Unidad Uxmal. Within the modern complex are toilets, a first-aid station, a small museum, shops (for publications, photo supplies, and craftwork), and a cafeteria. This is the most convenient place to get a snack or light lunch for about 1,000 pesos ($2).

Otherwise, the Hacienda Uxmal has a little lunchroom and bar called the **Posada Uxmal, Café-Bar Nicte-Ha,** in a building right across the highway from the turnoff to the ruins. A ham-and-cheese sandwich costs about 750 pesos ($1.50), a fruit salad only slightly less. This is a lot for what you get, but it's less to spend than the 3,000 pesos ($6) or so you'd spend on the set-price full lunch in the hotel. The café-bar is open from 12:30 p.m. to 7 p.m.

SEEING THE RUINS: The ruins of Uxmal are open from 8 a.m. to 5 p.m. every day. Admission is 50 pesos (10¢); on Sunday and holidays admission is 30 pesos (6¢).

It can give you quite a thrill to ponder what Uxmal must have been like in its heyday: great lords and ladies clad in white embroidered robes and feathered headdresses moving here and there; market day, when the common people would come from their thatched huts and gather nearby in a tumultuous scene of barter and brouhaha. Uxmal flourished in the Late Classical Period, about A.D. 600 to 900, and then became subject to the Xiú princes (who may have come from the Valley of Mexico) after the year 1000. Four and a half centuries later, the Xiú conquered Mayapán (1440s). The conquistadores moved in shortly after, ending forever the glories of Mayan cultural independence.

A 45-minute sound-and-light show is staged each evening, in Spanish for 300 pesos (60¢) at 7 p.m., and in English for 800 pesos ($1.60) at 9 p.m. The special sound-and-light bus from Mérida only stays for the Spanish show. If you came on this bus for the show, you've got to find your own ride back to Mérida.

The Pyramid of the Magician

As you enter the ruins, note first of all the *chultún* (cistern) just inside the fence to the right, the ticket booth being to your left. Besides the natural underground cisterns (such as cenotes) formed in the porous limestone, these chultúnes were the principal source of water for Maya civilization. You'll see more of them at Sayil and at sites near it.

After buying your ticket and walking a few steps farther, you'll be confronted with Uxmal's dominant building, the Pyramid of the Magician. Legend has it that a mystical dwarf who had hatched from an egg built this pyramid in one night, which is where it gets its name. Actually, there are several temples underneath the one you see. It was common practice for the Maya to build new structures atop old ones, even before the old structures were ruined.

The pyramid is unique because of its oval shape, its height and steepness (wait till you see the steps on the other side!), and its odd doorway. The doorway is on the opposite (west) side near the top, and is actually a remnant of the fourth temple built on this site (what you see today is the fifth). In contrast to the clean, simple style of the rest of the pyramid, the doorway is in Chenes style, with elaborate decoration featuring stylized masks of the rain god Chac. In fact, the doorway is a huge Chac mask, with the door as mouth.

The View from the Top

It's a tiring and even dangerous climb, but what a view! You're now in an ideal position to survey the rest of Uxmal. Next to the Pyramid of the Magician, to the west, is the Nunnery Quadrangle, so called because it resembles a monastery or convent. To the left (south) of the Nunnery is the ruined ball court, and south of that are several large complexes. The biggest building, with a 320-foot-long façade, is called the Governor's Palace. Near it is the small House of the Turtles. Behind the Governor's Palace is the Great Pyramid, only partly restored, and beyond that the Dovecote, a palace with a lacy roofcomb that looks as though it'd be a perfect apartment complex for pigeons.

These are the main structures you'll notice from atop the Pyramid of the Magician, but there are others. For instance, the small ruined pyramid directly south is called the Pyramid of the Old Woman, which may be the oldest building at Uxmal. Due west of the pyramid is the Cemetery Complex, a temple with roofcomb that's pretty ruined. There's also a Northern Group, mostly covered with jungle and in ruins.

Uxmal is special among Maya sites because of the broad terraces or platforms constructed to support the building complexes —look closely and you'll see that the Governor's Palace is not on a hill or rise, but on a huge square terrace, as is the Nunnery Quadrangle.

Now that you've got your breath, prepare for the climb down. If you came up the east side, try going down the west.

The Nunnery

No nuns lived here. It's more likely this was a military academy or a training school for princes, who may have lived in the 70-odd rooms. The buildings were constructed at different times: the northern one was first, then the southern one, then east, then west. The western building has the most richly decorated façade, with interesting motifs of intertwined snakes. Masks of the rain god Chac, with his hooked nose, are everywhere. The richness of the geometric patterns on the façades is one of the outstanding features of Uxmal.

As you head toward the archway out of the quadrangle to the south, notice that above each doorway in the south building is a motif showing a Maya cottage, or *na,* looking just like you see them today. All of this wonderful decoration has been restored, of course—it didn't look this good when the archeologists discovered it.

The Ball Court

The ball court is ruined, and not so impressive. Keep it in mind, and compare it to the magnificent restored court at Chichén-Itzá.

The Turtle House

Up on the terrace south of the ball court is a little temple decorated with colonnade motif on the façade, and a border of turtles. It's small, but simple and harmonious—one of the gems of Uxmal.

The Governor's Palace

This is Uxmal's masterwork, an imposing edifice with a huge mural façade richly decorated in mosaic designs of the Puuc style. "Puuc" means "hilly country" and Uxmal has many examples of this rich decoration. The Puuc hills, which you passed over coming from Mérida, are the Mayan "Alps," a staggering 350 feet high! Mayan towns near the hills favored this style of geometric patterns and masks of Chac, giving the style its name.

The Governor's Palace may have been just that: the administrative center of the Xiú principality, which included the region around Uxmal. The Xiú rulers later conquered the emperors at Mayapán, and became supreme in the region. The fall of Mayapán allowed Yucatán to split up into smaller principalities. It was just great for the conquistadores, who arrived less than a century after the fall of Mayapán and mopped up the principalities one by one. The great princes of Xiú, as it turns out, did the Maya people no favor by breaking up the hegemony of Mayapán.

Before you leave the Governor's Palace, note the elaborate stylized headdress patterned in stone over the central doorway.

The Great Pyramid

A massive structure partially restored, it has interesting motifs of birds, probably macaws, on its façade, as well as a huge mask —the Uxmalians went in for masks in a big way. The view from the top is wonderful.

The Dovecote

It wasn't built to house doves, but it could well do the job in its lacy roofcomb. The building is remarkable in that roofcombs weren't a common feature of temples in the Puuc hills, although you will see one (of a very different style) on El Mirador at Sayil if you visit that site.

LEAVING UXMAL: South and west of Uxmal are several other Maya cities well worth your exploration. Though the scale of these smaller cities is not as grand as that of Uxmal or Chichén-Itzá, each has its gems of Maya architecture. You will not be spending your time looking at the same old pyramids and temples. Rather, the great façade of masks on the Codz Poop at Kabah, the enormous palace at Sayil, the fantastic caverns of Loltún may be among the highpoints of your trip.

Transportation to these sights is not easy. Though buses do run occasionally along the road south from Uxmal to Kabah, it is difficult to reach the other sites without a private car.

If you're off to Kabah, head southwest on Hwy. 261 to Santa Elena (8⅔ miles, 14 km) then south to Kabah (8 miles, 13 km).

Kabah

The ancient city of Kabah sits astride the highway, but you turn left into the parking lot. Buy your ticket from 8 a.m. to 5 p.m. daily for 40 pesos (8¢), the same to park your car.

The most outstanding building at Kabah is the one you notice first: that huge palace up on a terrace. It's called the Palace of Masks, or **Codz Poop** ("rolled-up mat") from a motif in its decoration. Its outstanding feature is the façade, completely covered in masks of the hook-nosed rain god Chac. All those eyes, hooked noses, and grimacing mouths, used as a repeated pattern on a huge façade, have an incredible effect. There's nothing like this façade in all of Maya architecture.

Once you've seen the Palace of Masks, you've seen the best of Kabah. But you should take a quick look at the other buildings, and follow the paths into the jungle, for a look at the **Tercera Casa** (Third House), or "Las Columnas." This temple has fine colonnaded façades on both front and, even better, back.

Across the highway, you'll pass a conical mound (on your right) that was once the **Great Temple**, or Teocalli. Past it is a great arch. This triumphal arch was much wider at one time, and may have been a monumental gate into the city. For all their architectural achievements, the Maya never discovered the principle of the true arch made of many small fitted stones and a keystone. Instead, they used this corbelled arch, which is simply two flat stones leaned at an angle against one another. Compare this ruined arch to the one at Labná (below), which is in much better shape.

Sayil

About three miles (just under five km) south of Kabah is the turnoff (left, east) to Sayil, Xlapak, Labná, Loltún, and Oxkutzcab. Drive along 2½ miles (4 km) and find the ruins of Sayil, just off the side of the road. The ruins are open from 8 a.m. to 5 p.m., and the admission cost is 40 pesos (8¢), half price on Sunday and holidays.

Sayil is famous for **El Palacio,** the tremendous 100-room palace that is a masterpiece of Mayan architecture. The rows and rows of columns and colonettes give the building a Minoan appearance. There are some nice decorative details, but for the most part El Palacio impresses one by its grandeur and simplicity.

Off in the jungle past El Palacio is **El Mirador,** a small temple with a slotted roofcomb, an odd structure. Beyond El Mirador, a crude stele has a phallic idol carved on it, with greatly exaggerated proportions. The Maya didn't normally go in for this sort of thing, and this crude sculpture may well be unique.

Climb to the top of El Palacio if the heat is not too intense. The breeze up here is cooling, and the view of the Puuc hills delightful. Sometimes it's difficult to tell which are hills and which are unrestored pyramids, as little temples and galleries peep out at unlikely places from the jungle foliage. That large circular basin on the ground below the palace is a catch basin for a chultún (cistern). This region has no natural cenotes (wells) to catch rainwater, so the natives had to make their own.

Xlapak

Back on the road, it's just under 3½ miles (5½ km) to Xlapak ("Shla-*pahk*"), a small site with one building. The Palace at Xlapak bears the inevitable rain god masks. If you do this tour of the ruins in the summer rainy season, it may be at this point that Chac responds to your earnest pleas for a break from the heat. When I was there, Chac let loose a downpour. It soaked through. Cool, though.

Labná

Labná is only about 1¾ miles (3 km) past Xlapak, open 8 a.m. to 5 p.m. Admission is 40 pesos (8¢). The first thing you should look at here is the monumental arch. Good old Chac takes his place on the corners of one façade, and stylized Mayan huts are fashioned in stone above the doorways. El Mirador, or **El Castillo** as it is also called, stands near the arch, with its roofcomb towering above it.

The **Palacio** at Labná is much like the one at Sayil: huge, restrained, monumental. It's not in quite as good shape as that at Sayil, but still impressive. In the decoration, find the enormous mask of Chac over a doorway, and also the highly stylized serpent's mouth, out of which pops a human head.

Loltún

About 18½ miles (30 km) past Labná on the way to Oxkutzcab (that's "Ohsh-kootz-*kahb*") are the caverns of Loltún, on the left-hand side of the road.

No sign marks the entrance to the caves, so look for a tidy fence with a small park behind it, entered by a gravel drive. Wander in, and someone will fetch a guide. If they tell you that you've missed the last tour of the day, offer to pay a substantial tip (a few dollars) and you will get your tour.

You will have to pay a small admission fee—about 50 pesos (10¢)—and also tip the guide at the end of the hour-long tour; I'd suggest a dollar or two if the tour has been a good one.

The caves are fascinating. Not only were they the home of ancient Mayas, but they were used as a refuge and fortress during the War of the Castes (1847–1901). You can examine statuary, wall carvings and paintings, chultúnes (cisterns), and other signs of Maya habitation. Besides the Mayan artifacts, you'll be impressed by the sheer grandeur and beauty of the caverns themselves.

HEADING NORTH, SOUTH, EAST, WEST: From Loltún, you can drive the few miles to Oxkutzcab, and from there north on Hwy. 184 to Ticul, Muna, and Mérida (62 miles, 100 km). Or you can head back past Sayil, then south on Hwy. 261 to Campeche. Those intrepid souls out to do a circuit of the northern peninsula can strike out southeast toward Tekax, Tzucacab, and Polguc on Hwy. 184. After about 124 miles (200 km) you'll arrive in the town of Felipe Carrillo Puerto, where there are restaurants, hotels, banks, and gas stations. Carrillo Puerto thus serves as your jumping-off point for the tour north to Tulum, Xel-ha, Cozumel, and Cancún. See Chapter VI for more information.

THE ROAD TO CAMPECHE: Highway 261 heads south for several miles, then passes beneath a lofty arch which marks the boundary between the states of Yucatán and Campeche. You then pass through Bolonchén de Rejón (*bolonchén* means "nine wells").

Grutas de Xtacumbilxuna

Just under two miles (three km) south of Bolonchén you'll notice a sign on the side of the road pointing west to the Grutas de Xtacumbilxuna (though the sign spells it "Xtacumbinxunan"). Another sign says that these "Caves of the Hidden Girl" are 300 meters along the dirt track, and yet a third says they're 500 meters. In fact, the parking area is a half mile (.8 km) west of the highway, only a ten-minute walk.

Legend has it that a Mayan girl, to escape an unhappy love affair, hid herself in these vast limestone caverns. It wouldn't be hard to do, as you'll see if you sign the guest register and follow the guide down for the 30- or 45-minute tour in Spanish (tip the guide at the end).

But if she did hide down here, the girl left no trace. Unlike the fascinating caves at Loltún, filled with traces of Mayan occupation, these have only the standard bestiary of limestone shapes: a dog, an eagle, a penguin, madonna and child, snake, and so on, the fruit of the guide's imagination. The caves are open whenever the guide is around, which is most of the time.

Chenes Ruins

At Hopelchén there's a turn-off for Dzibalchén, near which you can see several unspoiled, unexcavated, all but undiscovered ruined cities in the Chenes style. You've got to be an explorer for these **Chenes ruins.** It's good if you have some food and water. Head for Dzibalchén, 25½ miles (41 km) from Hopelchén, then begin asking for the way to Hochob, San Pedro, Dzehkabtun, El Tabasqueño, and Dzibilnocac.

From Hopelchén, Hwy. 261 heads west, and after 26 miles (42

km) you'll find yourself at the turn-off for the ruined city of Edzná, 12½ miles (20 km) farther along to the south.

Edzná

At one time, a network of Mayan canals crisscrossed this entire area, making intensive cultivation possible, and no doubt contributing to Edzná's wealth as a ceremonial center. But today what you'll see at this "House of Wry Faces" (that's what *edzná* means) is a unique pyramid of five levels with a fine temple, complete with roof-comb, on top.

The buildings at Edzná were mostly in the Chenes, or "well country" style, so named because of the many wells found in the region.

Back on Hwy. 261, it's about 8¾ miles (14 km) to the intersection with Hwy. 180, and then another 19¼ miles (31 km) to the very center of Campeche.

Chapter X

CAMPECHE: PIRATES' PRIZE

CAPITAL OF THE STATE of the same name, Campeche (pop. 121,000) started life in 1517 as a military camp for the invading Spaniards under Francisco de Córdoba, but the town really came to life as a municipality after its founding by Francisco de Montejo as Salamanca de Campeche in 1531.

Being right on the shore, having no bay with headlands, or outlying islands, to protect it, Campeche was prey to constant attack by Caribbean pirates. The townspeople, fed up with these depredations by the late 1600s, poured money into construction of fortifications so massive that it was not worth the pirates' while to assault them. The city's system of *baluartes* (bulwarks, or ramparts) is still visible. Many of its strong points now serve as museums, libraries, and other public buildings. So the citizens of Campeche are still getting a return on their investment after almost three centuries!

Before the creation of Cancún, when most traffic into Yucatán came by road from Villahermosa and Ciudad del Carmen, Campeche benefited by being the last rest-stop on the drive to Mérida. But since the opening of the airport at Cancún, and the finishing of Hwy. 261 (which bypasses Campeche), tourist trade to Campeche has declined considerably. The city's economy now depends on its traditional source of wealth—harvesting fish, shrimp, and other crustaceans from the teeming waters of the gulf—and on its new bonanza, oil.

Though it is slightly out of the way, Campeche is a very pleasant coastal town with a smooth, leisurely pace, and many well-preserved colonial streets and buildings. You won't regret a night spent here.

ORIENTATION: Virtually all of your time in Campeche will be spent within the confines of the old city walls. You'll certainly pass one of the old baluartes as you come toward the center of town, which is the modernistic Plaza Moch-Couoh on the waterfront, next to which rises the modern office tower called the Edificio Poderes or Palacio de Gobierno, headquarters for the State of Campeche. Next to this is the futuristic Cámara de Diputados, or Casa de Congreso, or state legislature's chamber, which looks somewhat like an enormous square clam.

The city's two best hotels are within sight of the Palacio de Gobierno on the waterfront.

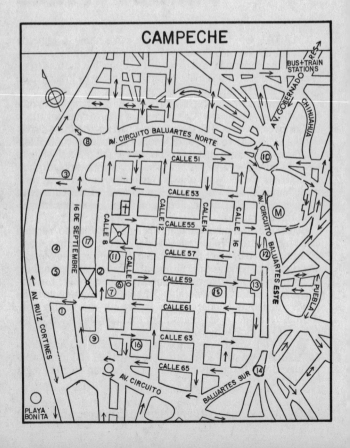

CAMPECHE

ARRIVING BY AIR: Campeche's connections by air are minimal, with one daily flight to and from Mexico City. Sometimes there is a shuttle service to Mérida. If you happen to arrive by air, you'll have to take a taxi (1,500 pesos, $3), or walk from the airport out to the intersection of Avenidas Héroes de Nacozari and López Portillo, where you can catch a bus ("China Campeche") for the trip into town.

ARRIVING BY BUS: First- and second-class buses arrive and depart from the terminal on Avenida Gobernadores, corner of Calle de Chile, about four blocks northeast of the **Baluarte de San Pedro (10).** You can walk to the center of town from here if your bags are not too heavy (turn left as you leave the station). Otherwise, a taxi to the hotels will cost a little over a dollar.

ARRIVING BY TRAIN: Campeche's train station is about 1¼ miles (2 km) northeast of the downtown waterfront, on Avenida Héroes de Nacozari, which intersects Avenida de los Gobernadores. A taxi should cost about 1,200 pesos ($2.40) to the center.

FINDING AN ADDRESS: Unlike most towns in Mexico, Campeche boasts a systematic street-naming plan whereby streets that run roughly north to south have even numbers, and those running east to west have odd numbers. Thus along Calle 14 you will cross in succession Calles 51, 53, 55, 57, etc., and if you turn right off Calle 14 onto Calle 51 you will cross Calles 12, 10, 8, etc., in your course down 51. Not to confuse you further, but the streets are numbered so that numbers ascend toward the south and west. After you get downtown and walk around for five minutes you'll have the system down pat. Bus, train, and airport terminals are all a good distance from downtown, and as Campeche is hardly a good town to negotiate by bus, I would recommend a taxi to get you from the various depots to the center.

TOURIST INFORMATION: The State of Campeche operates a convenient and helpful **Tourist Office (1)** (tel. 981/6-6068 or 6-6767) on the waterfront near the Palacio de Gobierno. Look for the modernistic bulwark with a slender vertical sign ("Turismo") on top. When you get to the structure, don't walk up the ramp toward the sign, but rather walk around to the right to reach the entrance, which faces the sea. Hours are 8 a.m. to 2:30 p.m. and 4 to 8:30 p.m., closed Sunday. They speak some English and are very helpful.

USEFUL FACTS: Look for the **Correos** (post office) in the **Edificio Federal (3)** (tel. 981/6-2134) at the corner of Avenida 16 de Septiembre and Calle 53, near the Baluarte de Santiago. The **telegraph office** is here as well.

Campeche's Hotels

Though Campeche's tourist trade has largely dried up, there are still some good places to stay.

THE TOP HOTELS: Right at the center of town, on the waterfront, are the city's two best hotels.

The **Hotel El Presidente Campeche (4)**, P. O. Box 251, Campeche 24000 (tel. 981/6-2233 or 6-4611), is officially at Avenida Ruiz Cortines no. 51. Most of the 120 rooms and suites have views of the sea, and all have the four-star luxuries: air conditioning, color television, servi-bar, and a terrace for sunrise-watching. Other luxuries include a swimming pool, fenced parking lot, plus a nice restaurant, bar, coffee-shop, and discothèque. Prices are quite happily low for all this: 11,385 pesos ($22.77) single, 12,535 pesos ($25.07) double, 14,835 pesos ($29.67) triple, tax in. Junior suites cost $3 to $5 more per room.

Just south of El Presidente is Campeche's old standby, the 100-room **Hotel Baluartes (5)**, Avenida Ruiz Cortines no. 61, Campeche 24000 (tel. 981/6-3911). This was the city's original luxury digs, but it's been extensively modernized, and now has all of the posh services of its neighbor, including air conditioning, swimming pool, and many rooms with sea views. Prices are less: 9,660 pesos ($19.32) single, 10,695 pesos ($21.39) double, 12,650 pesos ($25.30) triple, tax in.

A BUDGET CHOICE: At the other end of the price spectrum is the convenient **Hotel America (6)**, Calle 10 no. 252, Campeche 24000 (tel. 981/6-4588 or 6-4576), near the corner with Calle 59, a block east of the picturesque "Sea Gate" of the former city walls. The hotel charges 3,853 pesos ($7.70) for a double room overlooking the interior court, equipped with screens against the bugs and a private shower.

Campeche's Restaurants

The best all-around restaurant choice in Campeche is the **Restaurant Miramar (7)**, Calles 8 and 61, very near the town hall building. The decor is simple but pleasant, with lots of light-colored stone and some dark wood and ironwork. The menu offers typical Campeche seafood dishes: fried, breaded shrimp (ask for "camarones empanizadas") for 1,450 pesos ($2.90), ceviche

or fish and vegetable cocktail for 1,000 pesos ($2), arroz con cala-
mares (squid and rice) for slightly more, and for dessert, queso
napolitana, a sort of very rich, thick flan.

The **Restaurant del Parque (11)**, overlooking the zócalo on
Calle 57, is a beautifully white, cool, open place with a cozy air
about it, due in part to use of incandescent (not flourescent) lighting. Stereo music, caned chairs, and a tempting menu add to the
attractions. Have soup, a fish dinner, and dessert for about 2,900
pesos ($5.80); or dine for less on enchiladas or crêpes. Shrimp
platters are available, but they'll run your meal tab up.

What to See

"Campeche" is derived from the Mayan name Ah Kim Pech.
Founded in 1531, later abandoned, and refounded by Montejo
the Younger in 1540, it became the springboard for the Montejo's
conquest of Yucatán.

Campeche's dearth of tourists is a blessing, in a way, because it
allows you to see this charming old city without the crowds.

CITY WALLS AND BULWARKS: As the busiest port in the region during the 1600s and 1700s, Campeche was a choice prize to pirates,
who attacked it repeatedly starting as early as 1546. The Campe-
chanos, eventually tired of the depredations, began construction
of the city's impressive defenses in 1668. By 1704, all of the walls,
gates, and bulwarks were in place.

Today, seven of the bulwarks remain, and four are worthy of a
visit. Here's the rundown:

Baluarte de San Carlos

Southernmost of the seaside bulwarks, the **Baluarte San Carlos (9)** is near the modern Palacio de Gobierno at the intersection
of the Circuito Baluartes and the Avenida Justo Sierra, near
where Calles 63 and 8 meet. It's a good place to begin your tour,
as it is now set up as the Sala de las Fortificaciones (Chamber of
Fortifications). Models within the heavy stone walls, where once
Campechano soldiers and militia held off the pirates, show you
how the city looked in its glory days during the 1700s.

Admission is free after you sign the guest book. Hours are 9
a.m. to 1 p.m. and 5 to 7:30 p.m., every day.

Baluarte de la Soledad

Walk north along Calle 8, and you'll pass the Puerta de Mar, or
Sea Gate, the ancient entry to the city enclosure from the port
area. Just beyond the Puerta de Mar is the **Baluarte de la Soledad**

(17), or Bulwark of Solitude, just off the zócalo where Calles 57 and 8 meet. This bastion now houses the Sala de Estelas, or Chamber of Steles. The Mayan votive stones were brought from various sites in this ruin-rich state. Many are badly worn, but the excellent line drawings beside the stones allow you to admire their former glory. Admission is free, and hours are the same as for the Baluarte de San Carlos.

The Plaza

While you're in the area, take a stroll through Campeche's pretty little zócalo, or Plaza de la Independencia, complete with cathedral. Construction of the church was begun in 1540, though it was frequently interrupted, and not completed for over a century and a half.

Baluarte de Santiago

Walk north along Calle 8 and at Calle 51 you'll come to the **Baluarte de Santiago (8)**, northernmost of the seaside bulwarks, now fixed up as Campeche's Jardín Botánico (Botanical Gardens). This is the perfect place to take a breather in your walking tour, among the plants both common and exotic, on a bench in the cool shade. Want to learn about what you're seeing? The garden offers tours in English at 12 noon and at 4 p.m., Tuesday through Saturday; in Spanish almost every hour in the morning and evening.

Admission to the Jardín Botánico is 50 pesos (10¢). It's open Tuesday through Saturday from 9 a.m. to 8 p.m., Sunday from 9 a.m. to 1 p.m., closed Monday.

Baluarte de San Pedro

Head inland (east) on Calle 51, and at Calle 18 you'll see the **Baluarte de San Pedro (10)**, where there's a crafts showroom called the Exposición Permanente de Artesanías. Besides the bastion itself, you can look over the products of Campechano craftspeople. Hours are as at the Baluarte de San Carlos.

Other Baluartes

If you're not tired yet, make the complete circuit of the bulwarks. Follow Calle 18 south, passing the **Baluarte de San Francisco (12)** at Calle 57, then the **Puerta de Tierra (13)** (Land Gate) at Calle 59. The **Baluarte de San Juan (14)**, at Calle 65, is where you turn west toward the sea. The **Baluarte de Santa Rosa (18)**, at Calles 14 and 67 (Circuito Baluartes) is now a library.

Three blocks' walking brings you back to the Baluarte de San Carlos.

MUSEO REGIONAL DE CAMPECHE: Over the years, Campeche has moved its museum collections around quite a bit. The best of the lot have now come to rest in the **Museo Regional de Campeche (15),** in the former mansion of the Teniente de Rey (Royal Governor) at Calle 59 no. 36, between Calles 14 and 16.

The museum's displays are similar to those in the Palacio Cantón in Mérida. Pictures, drawings, and models are combined with original artifacts, bringing to life the ancient Mayan culture. The curious skull-flattening deformation of babies is shown in the most direct way: with an exhibit of the actual deformed skulls. Another highlight is the Late Classic (A.D. 600–900) Maya stele carved in a metamorphic rock that does not exist in Yucatán, but was brought hundreds of miles from its quarry.

A model of the archeological site at Becán shows Maya society in daily life. Other displays demonstrate Maya architecture, techniques of water conservation, aspects of their religion, commerce, art, and their considerable scientific knowledge.

Hours for the museum are 9 a.m. to 8 p.m. Tuesday through Saturday, 9 a.m. to 1 p.m. Sunday, closed Monday. Admission costs 100 pesos (20¢).

MUSEO DE CAMPECHE

Actually the restored **Templo de San José (16)** (St. Joseph Church), at the corner of Calles 10 and 63, this is the venue for many traveling art exhibits that come to Campeche. Drop by to see what's up.

STROLLING THROUGH CAMPECHE: One of this pleasant city's most enjoyable pastimes is simply to stroll along its colonial streets, particularly Calles 55, 57, and 59. Many of the buildings are in classic Mexican colonial style. Glance through a grand doorway to find a fine courtyard, or a Moorish colonnade, or a few high-ceilinged rooms. Remember that Campeche was a wealthy port. Its merchants could afford to build themselves the best, and to live in style.

Chapter XI

PALENQUE: FABULOUS JUNGLE CITY

LYING WEST of the mighty Río Usumacinta in the wild and mountainous jungle province of Chiapas, Palenque was a unique and eccentric outpost of Maya culture. Strictly speaking, it is not part of the Yucatán peninsula. But as a masterwork of Mayan art and architecture, it has no equal. With its great Temple of the Inscriptions built above a king's fabulous tomb, Palenque has intrigued archeologists, mythologists, and visitors for decades.

It's a long way from Cancún or Mérida to Palenque, but if you have the time, and a healthy interest in Mayan culture, you'll want to make the pilgrimage.

GETTING TO PALENQUE: The fastest way is by air, but you can also go by bus or car. You may end up going via Villahermosa, which is covered in the following chapter.

Arriving by Air

Palenque has its own little airstrip, but it serves mostly little chartered planes and the little scheduled planes that trundle over the mountains to San Cristóbal de las Casas.

You can charter a small plane in Cancún or Mérida to fly you to Palenque, but it will be pretty expensive.

The fastest way to reach Palenque by air is via Villahermosa from Cancún (daily evening flights, except Monday) or Mérida (daily morning flights). From Villahermosa you will have to rent a car, or catch a bus, to get to Palenque.

Arriving by Bus

From Mérida, the 372-mile (600-km) bus trip to Palenque can take as much as 10 or 11 hours. From Villahermosa, of course, it's much shorter, unless you inadvertently catch a second-class bus, which can take almost that many hours because it stops in every village and hamlet. See the following chapter for details.

When you arrive in Palenque, the first-class (ADO) bus station is on the main square, more or less across the street from the Hotel Lacroix. Second-class buses have an office on Avenida Juárez near the Pemex gas station, across the street from the Hotel Avenida, and not far from the Mayan statue you'll see at the fork as you enter the town.

Arriving by Car

Palenque is an eight-hour drive from Mérida, a five-hour drive from Campeche. The drive will be very hot, unless your car is air-conditioned.

ORIENTATION: From a Pemex station on Hwy. 186, a road turns right and heads for Palenque, 17 miles (27 km) off the main road. First you'll come to Palenque Junction (the railroad station), then a few miles later to a fork in the road—there's an incredibly dramatic statue of a Mayan here, so you can't miss it. Left at the fork takes you a mile or so into Palenque village with its bank, restaurants, hotels, stores, and ice house. A right at the fork takes you past several motels to Palenque ruins. A municipal bus is supposed to run between the town and the ruins every hour on the hour starting at 6 a.m., but in practice it's not very dependable. A taxi costs only about 750 pesos ($1.50), and might just be worth it. "Colectivos," minibuses or sedans, are the best buy and charge 100 pesos (20¢) per person.

Palenque's Hotels

There are no fancy or luxury lodgings at Palenque, though a number of places provide quite acceptable comfort. If you really want to sleep in luxury, you'll have to do so in Villahermosa, and drive out to Palenque for the day.

THE BEST PLACES: Several places qualify as the best available. **Chan-Kah,** Palenque, Chiapas 29960 (no phone), 2½ miles past the Mayan statue on the road to the ruins, is a collection of 18 rooms in little stone-and-wood bungalows, rustic in design but modern in comforts. Each has a ceiling fan (no air conditioning), and is priced at 11,500 pesos ($23) double. Chan-Kah has its own dining room.

Closest hotel to the ruins is actually a motel-style place named the **Hotel Las Ruinas,** Apdo. Postal 49, Palenque, Chiapas 29960 (tel. 934/5-0352, Monday through Friday, 4 to 7 p.m.), operated by a friendly gentleman named Prof. Ismael Corzo. A nice swimming pool serves as the motel's centerpiece; 32 rooms are arranged around it, all modern, bathroom-equipped, and all with ceiling fans for 4,000 pesos ($8) single, 5,000 pesos ($10) double. Here you're only a half mile from the ruins.

The **Motel Nututum** (or Nututun), Palenque, Chiapas 29960 (tel. 934/5-0100), is about two miles (three km) from the Mayan statue along the road to the ruins, and then left on the road through the jungle to Ocosingo, Agua Azul, and San Cristóbal. The setting is beautiful, right on the Río Tulija, which provides excellent swimming in the cool river waters. The 40 air-conditioned rooms are huge, each with two double beds. The tiled rooms have large closets, bathtub, and shower. Prices are in the moderate category, and swimming in the river after a hot day at the ruins is a bonus. Singles cost 7,556 pesos ($15.11); doubles, 9,143 pesos ($18.29); and triples, 10,730 pesos ($21.46). You can camp on the riverbank with your own equipment for 2,000 pesos ($4) per person. The hotel restaurant is inexpensive: most meals cost 1,500 to 3,000 pesos ($3 to $6), breakfasts cost 1,000 pesos ($2). The minibus (colectivo) will take you to the ruins from the hotel for 100 pesos (20¢).

In the village proper, facing the park, is Palenque's oldest hotel, the **Hotel Palenque,** Avenida Cinco de Mayo no. 15, Palenque, Chiapas 29960 (tel. 934/5-0188). It has had its ups and downs over the years; currently it seems to be up, because of the increased competition from newer hotels. Some of the Hotel Palenque's ancient rooms have been redeemed with paint, paper, and air conditioners, and the courtyard garden can be pleasant enough, but be sure you *inspect your room* before you take it—this is an "iffy" place. Rates are 3,800 pesos ($7.60) single, 4,200 pesos ($8.40) double, 4,990 pesos ($9.98) triple, with air conditioning and private shower. Some 30 new rooms are being added along the courtyard and may be completed soon.

A short distance back toward Villahermosa—only a half mile from the Maya-statue fork in the road, really—is the **Hotel Tulija,** Apdo. Postal 57, Palenque, Chiapas 29960 (tel. 934/5-0165), one of Palenque's more modern hotels with air-conditioned rooms going for 3,473 pesos ($6.95) single, 4,168 pesos ($8.34) double, 5,002 pesos ($10.01) triple. The hotel restaurant offers a six-course comida at midday for 1,200 pesos ($2.40), but the large-screen television may be more than one can endure. The hotel has a very nice swimming pool, and they take credit cards.

JUNGLE BUNGALOWS: Coming from Villahermosa, past the Hotel Tulija, and approaching the Mayan statue, you'll see an unpaved road on the left called Calle Merle Green. There's a camping area named Trailer Park Tulipanes at the beginning of the road.

At the far end of the dirt road is the **Hotel La Cañada** (tel. 934/5-0102), a group of cottages surrounded by dense woods and thus pretty secluded. Rooms can be a bit musty, but aren't bad. Price is 3,500 pesos ($7) single or 4,500 pesos ($9) double. Rooms 7, 8, 9, and 10 across the street from the office are particularly good values. Each is equipped with air conditioning and a huge ceramic bathtub. The jungle surrounding the rooms looks like the set of a Tarzan movie.

BUDGET HOTELS: All of Palenque's low-priced hotels are in the village proper, except for one, which is very near the Mayan statue.

The fanciest place to stay in Palenque Village is a bright fairly new mini-hotel called the **Hotel Casa de Pakal** (no phone), on the main street (Avenida Juárez) near the central park. Each of the rather small rooms here comes with a TV set, servi-bar, and piped-in music, plus that blessed air conditioning, for 3,900 pesos ($7.80) single, 4,950 pesos ($9.90) double. The hotel has a fancy restaurant called **El Castellano**.

Very near the Casa de Pakal is the slightly older **Hotel Misol-Ha** (tel. 934/5-0092), with a dozen or so small rooms still well kept. With a ceiling fan, you pay 2,570 pesos ($5.14) single, 3,150 to 3,650 pesos ($6.30 to $7.30) for two people. Many readers think this is the best lodging bargain in all Palenque.

The **Hotel Vaca Vieja,** Avenida Cinco de Mayo no. 42, at the corner of Calle de Chiapas (tel. 934/5-0377), is one of Palenque's newer hotels. A small, modern 12-room place on the far side of the park (walk around the park and past the big old Hotel Palenque), it is one of Palenque's best places to stay. Each room has a fan and nice tile shower and is immaculate. A little restaurant on the ground floor provides breakfast and dinner. The price is a reasonable 2,750 pesos ($5.50) single, 3,440 pesos ($6.88) double. There's only one mystery about this place: how did it get the name "old cow"?

A good choice for the starvation-budget reader is the **Hotel Lacroix,** Hidalgo no. 18 (no phone), facing the main square or park (as you come up Avenida Juárez into the center of town, turn left at the park, then right, and the hotel is down a block on the left-hand side behind the church.) Darkish and simple rooms are kept cool by shady trees, fans, and breezes, and each opens onto a cool veranda overlooking lush gardens of palms and banana plants. Primitive murals decorate the place, and prices are low: 2,500 pesos ($5) single or double. As you might imagine, the eight-room Lacroix is often full-up.

If you stand head-on, staring in rapture (or horror) at the Mayan statue at the fork in the road, then turn left and head down Calle Merle Green past the Trailer Park Tulipanes, you'll see the **Hotel Tulipanes** (tel. 934/0230) right next to it, on the left-hand side of the road. The "hotel" is actually several small buildings with very simple but adequate rooms, with private baths, renting for 4,000 pesos ($8) double. Each room has a ceiling fan.

Palenque's Restaurants

Hardly a culinary mecca, Palenque has mostly very basic, no-frills eateries. Two restaurants stand out, however, as having at least an interesting jungle ambience. Both are on Calle Merle Green, near the Mayan statue.

The first is **La Selva,** down Calle Merle Green on the left-hand side (tel. 5-0363). Though the restaurant has a thatched roof, this shelters a fairly refined and accommodating place to dine. Main-course dishes such as carne asada (grilled beef) and lomo de cerdo (pork chops) cost only 1,000 pesos ($2). Figure that a full meal will cost twice that amount. Surprise of surprises, La Selva has a very respectable (for Palenque) assortment of Mexican wines. You'll enjoy your meal here. Frequently live music is provided for diners' enjoyment. The rooms you can see from your table are operated by Hotel La Cañada next door.

Speaking of La Cañada, in the hotel's quaint dirt-floored restaurant, you can get a tasty supper of chicken tacos or quesadillas, with a cold bottle of beer, for 950 pesos ($1.90); meat entrees cost twice that amount. Near the restaurant, a two-story thatched "club" throbs to disco music. It never seems to be crowded, although it's the ideal setting for a *Night of the Iguana* romance.

Even if you do not stay or dine along Calle Merle Green, a stroll along this shady street is enjoyable. Several interesting shops are busy making and selling quality reproductions of Mayan art.

In the village proper, look for restaurants around the central park. The **Restaurant Maya** (no phone), facing the park near the Correos (post office), is breezy, open, and family-run, but tends to be a bit expensive for what you get. Main courses cost from 650 to 1,000 pesos ($1.30 to $2), but a daily comida corrida is priced at only 800 pesos ($1.60).

Next door to the Maya is the **Restaurant Nicte-Ha** (no phone), less cool but with advantages of its own: you get more food for less money. Daily special plates are priced at 700 pesos ($1.40), other dishes even less. Quality of food and service (such as it is) seems to be about the same in both places, so make your choice on the basis of coolness, attractiveness, and price.

Visiting Ancient Palenque

Palenque, now protected in the Parque Nacional Palenque, is one of the most spectacular of the Maya ruins with its roof-combed temples ensconced in lush vegetation high above the savannahs. It was a ceremonial center for the high priests during the Classical Period (A.D. 300–900), with the peak of its civilization being somewhere around A.D. 600–700. Pottery found during the excavations shows that there was a very early, pre-Classic people living here as early as 300 B.C. Alberto Ruíz Lhuillier, the archeologist who directed some of the explorations, states that because of "the style of its structures, its hieroglyphic inscriptions, its sculptures, its works in stucco and its pottery, Palenque undoubtedly fell within the great Maya culture. Yet its artistic expressions have a character all their own which is evident in the absolute mastery of craftsmanship, turning the art of Palenque into the most refined of Indian America."

See above, under "Orientation," for transportation details.

HOURS: The Palenque ruins are open from 8 a.m. to 5 p.m., although the crypt (see below) closes at 4 p.m. The entrance fee to the National Park is 50 pesos (10¢), on Sunday 25 pesos (5¢), and it will cost you another 25 to 50 pesos (5¢ to 10¢) to park your car. By the way, a quarter mile back toward town from the parking lot, on the right-hand side (as you approach from town) is a path leading into the Cascada Motiepa, a cool, beautiful waterfall good for cooling the feet and resting the soul. Watch the mosquitos, though.

The small museum (open 8 a.m. to 5 p.m.) has a chronological chart of Maya history, and a modest collection of votive figurines, pieces of statuary, and stones with calendar glyphs. Entrance is free once you have paid for access to the park. Be sure you save your ticket.

Plan to spend a whole day in these wonderful surroundings. When you're tired of looking at ruins, grab your bathing suit and head for the gorgeous stream and falls near the tiny museum at the end of the dirt track that goes past the "Grupo del Norte" complex of structures. A sign by the stream informs you (in Spanish) that there is no bathing allowed, but downstream a ways is a large pool out of view.

GUIDES: The official price for a two- or three-hour tour of the ancient city is 5,000 pesos ($10). Some of the guides are quite knowledgeable.

TEMPLE OF THE INSCRIPTIONS: As you enter the ruins, the building to the right is the Temple of the Inscriptions, named for the great stone hieroglyphic panels found inside (most of them are now in the Archeological Museum in Mexico City) and famous for the tomb that was discovered in its depths in 1949. It took four seasons of digging to clear out the rubble that was put there by the Mayas to conceal the crypt. The crypt itself is some 80 feet below the floor of the temple and was covered by a monolithic sepulchral slab ten feet long and seven feet wide. You can visit the tomb, and so long as you're not a claustrophobe, you shouldn't miss it. The way down is lighted, but the steps can be slippery due to condensed humidity—watch it! This is the only such temple-pyramid (resembling the Egyptian pyramids) in the Americas!

OTHER BUILDINGS: Besides the Temple of the Inscriptions, there is the Palace with its unique watchtower, the northern group (Temple of the Count and Ball Court) and the group of temples beyond the Palace (Temple of the Sun, Temple of the Foliated Cross). The official guidebook has a detailed description of this site and is well worth the money. (For a summary of pre-Columbian history, see the Introduction of the book you're now reading.)

Chapter XII

VILLAHERMOSA: OIL BOOM TOWN

VILLAHERMOSA (pop. 250,000) always had some regional importance as the capital of the state of Tabasco. But since the discovery of extremely rich oil fields in the state, Villahermosa has been a veritable boom town. Huge amounts of money have cascaded in from petroleum investors and buyers of petroleum products. In a matter of a decade, Villahermosa has moved from being a sleepy state capital to a medium-sized city with growing pains.

First results of the boom were raw and undisciplined: frantic building of highways, offices, oil field infrastructure, and hotels kept the city in chaos. Now, however, things have calmed down a bit, and the city's leaders have had some time to smooth the rough edges and to add the nice touches that may well make this town a "beautiful city," as its name announces. The Regional Museum of Anthropology, the archeological museum-in-a-park called La Venta, the new park-like office and leisure developments, the pedestrian streets in the heart of town—all have added considerably to the enjoyment of life in this city. And all are the direct result of the wealth brought in by oil.

For the visitor to Yucatán, Villahermosa is a transit point. Whether you fly to Yucatán via Mexico City and plan a stop in Palenque, or whether you fly from Mérida or Cancún expressly to visit that fascinating city, you will spend little more than a night or two in Villahermosa.

You can spend a full day here seeing the sights and getting a sense of place, and you will enjoy it—except for the heat. I know of few other places in Mexico where the heat seems so persistent, moisture-laden, and intense. Remember this when you look for a hotel room, and get one with air conditioning. Also remember it when you plan your sightseeing excursions. Hike through the

Parque La Venta in the freshness of morning, and then take a siesta, or visit the air-conditioned regional museum, during the heat of the day. Save the evening for a stroll along the pedestrian streets and along the Río Grijalva, which cuts right through the center of town.

TRANSPORTATION: Because of its importance in regard to oil, and because it is a way-station on the long road from mainland Mexico to Yucatán, Villahermosa is well served by public transportation.

By Air

Mexicana, with offices at Tabasco 2000 Avenida 4 and Calle 13, (tel. 931/3-5044), has at least four flights a day to and from Mexico City. **AeroMéxico,** Periferico Carlos Pellicer 511, (tel. 931/2-6991), has nonstop flights to and from Cancún (six per week), Mérida (daily), Mexico City (two daily), and Oaxaca (daily).

Airport minibuses charge 750 pesos ($1.50) for the trip into town, whereas a taxi will charge 3,000 pesos ($6).

Coming into town from Villahermosa's airport, which is 6½ miles (10½ km) east of town, you'll come across a bridge over the Río Grijalva, and turn left to reach the Plaza de Armas.

By Bus

The **Central Camionera de Primera Clase** (first-class bus station, sometimes called the **A.D.O. terminal**) is on Avenida Javier Mina. To get to the Plaza de Armas, go out and turn right on Javier Mina, then go left for about six blocks to Avenida Madero. Turn right onto Madero, and the Plaza de Armas is about four blocks along.

The **Central Camionera de Segunda Clase** (second-class bus station) is on Hwy. 180/186 near the traffic circle bearing a statue of a fisherman. Buses marked "Mercado–C. Camionera" leave frequently from the bus station for the center of town.

From the first-class bus station, A.D.O. and Cristóbal Colón buses depart daily for Veracruz, Mexico City, and points along that route, to Oaxaca, and to Mérida (18 buses a day) via Campeche.

To Palenque, there are two first-class A.D.O. buses a day, leaving at 8 a.m. and 5:30 p.m., and returning at 12:15 and 5:00 p.m. Buy your reserved-seat ticket as far in advance as possible; price is 915 pesos ($1.83).

If you take a second-class bus, be sure to ask about arrival times. Sometimes these buses take hours and hours because of all the stops en route.

Make sure you tell them *which* Palenque—the town or the Zona Arqueológica—you want a ticket to. You can return to Villahermosa the same day, or stay overnight in Palenque village, or go on to Campeche and Mérida by bus. Buy your tickets in advance.

ORIENTATION: The hotels and restaurants I recommend are located on Hwy. 180 or off the three main streets running north and south: Madero, Pino Suárez, and the Malecón. Highway 180 skirts the city, so a turn onto Madero or Pino Suárez will take you into the center of town.

Your point of focus in town can be the **Plaza de Armas,** or main square, bounded by the streets named Zaragoza, Madero, and Juárez. The plaza is the center of the downtown district, with the Río Grijalva to its west and Hwy. 186 to its north. If Villahermosa can be said to have a main downtown thoroughfare, then it is **Avenida Madero,** running south from Hwy. 186 past the Plaza de Armas to the river, where it intersects with the riverside avenue, the **Malecón.**

The **Tourist Office** has recently relocated to the mall at Juárez no. 111 (tel. 931/2-3171 or 3-5762). A large sign in front trumpets TURISMO in green letters; you can't miss it. The office has an excellent map of the city and an enthusiastic, helpful staff. Hours are 9 a.m. to 3 p.m. and 3:30 to 8 p.m., Monday through Saturday.

Parking is available underneath the Plaza de Armas for 500 pesos ($1) for 24 hours. Enter on the Avenida Vásquez Norte side of the plaza.

Villahermosa's Hotels

Prices for hotel rooms in Villahermosa were once fairly high, when oil personnel had lots of money to spend. Now that oil prices have dropped, so have other prices in this town. You may be surprised at what is charged for a luxury hotel room.

UPPER BRACKET HOTELS: You'd expect to find Hyatt hotels in New York City, Cancún, Los Angeles, Acapulco . . . and Villahermosa? Yes, indeed. The **Exelaris Hyatt Villahermosa,** Avenida Juárez 106, Villahermosa, Tabasco 86000 (tel. 931/3-4444, or toll free 800/228-9000 in U.S.), has 215 luxurious rooms with all of the Hyatt comforts, priced at what can only be described as unluxurious prices: 17,855 pesos ($35.71), single or double.

Competing with the Hyatt for the upscale trade is the **Hotel Villahermosa Viva,** Paseo Tabasco 1201, Villahermosa, Tabasco,

86000 (tel. 931/2-5555), out on Hwy. 180/186. Here, a luxury double costs 12,167 pesos ($24.34), and still has that marvelous air conditioning you're going to crave.

The **Hotel Maya Tabasco,** Avenida Grijalva s/n, Villahermosa, Tabasco 86000 (tel. 931/2-1111), down by the river in the midst of town, has 100 air-conditioned rooms within walking distance of the center for 9,750 pesos ($19.50) single, 11,000 pesos ($22) double.

BUDGET HOTELS: The area around the intersections of Avenidas Juárez and Lerdo is now one of the best places to stay, for these two streets have been closed to cars and made into pedestrian malls. A modest place here is the **Hotel San Miguel,** Lerdo 315, Villahermosa, Tabasco 86000 (tel. 931/2-1500), where 30 rooms have been renovated, each with tiled bathroom and ceiling fan, and going for 2,900 pesos ($5.80) single, 3,350 pesos ($6.70) double with air conditioning. The lobby of the San Miguel is plain, but graced by one very important appliance: a super-cold water dispenser.

The aforementioned hotel, while adequate, may not be up to what you want after a long, tiring trip, so here are the alternatives. The fanciest place right downtown is the **Hotel Miraflores,** Reforma 304, Villahermosa, Tabasco 86000 (tel. 931/2-0054, 2-0486, or 2-0022), a modern establishment of glass, aluminum, and brightly colored plastic furniture equipped with virtually everything your heart could desire: elevator, central air conditioning, and television and refrigerator in every room. Price for all this luxury is 6,670 pesos ($13.34) single, 6,900 pesos ($13.80) double, 7,475 pesos ($14.95) triple.

The older **Hotel Manzur,** Madero 14, Villahermosa, Tabasco 86000 (tel. 931/2-2566), has older but well-kept accommodations, all air-conditioned of course. A double room here costs 6,095 pesos ($12.19).

Near the Bus Stations

Just off Hwy. 186, not far from the first- and second-class bus stations, is the **Hotel Ritz,** Avenida Madero 1013, Villahermosa, Tabasco 86000 (tel. 931/2-1836), one block in from the highway. Its three modern stories hold 40 good rooms at 4,315 pesos ($8.63) single, 4,859 pesos ($9.72) double, all with window air conditioners. While it's a block off the highway, the Ritz is not subject to any more noise than other Villahermosa hotels. Note, however, that this is not a choice particularly for those arriving late at night by bus—like other hotels in this city, it's almost sure to be full by early evening, at the latest.

Villahermosa Restaurants

Besides the hotel restaurants, there's the **Restaurant Los Pepes,** Madero 610, near the Plaza de Armas (tel. 2-0154), probably the cleanest of Villahermosa's open cafés, and highly recommended by the townspeople. Each of the tables is covered in colorful placemats, it's fairly cool with large ceiling fans. Almost every dish here costs between 800 to 1,300 pesos ($1.60 to $2.60), for liver, pork chops, chicken, and shrimp, and the menu is fairly extensive. One of the tastiest dishes is the filet tampiqueño at 1,300 pesos ($2.60), but starvation-budget devotees might stick to the turkey tamales—you get three good-size ones for 400 pesos (80¢). Open daily 7 a.m. to 11 p.m.; closed Sunday.

What to See

Two museums, one outdoors, one indoors, are cultural highpoints of any visit to this city.

PARQUE MUSEO LA VENTA: This is a lovely outdoor museum park located outside Villahermosa on Rte. 180 (take Paseo Tabasco northeast to Hwy. 180, turn right, and it's less than a mile on your right, next to the Exposition Park). As you walk through on a self-guided tour you'll see Olmec relics, sculptures, mosaics, a mockup of the original La Venta, and of course the colossal Olmec heads. These heads were carved around 1000 B.C., are 6½ feet high, and weigh around 40 tons. The faces seem to be half-adult, half-infantile with that fleshy "jaguar mouth" that is characteristic of Olmecan art. Even stranger is the fact that the basalt, for carving, had to be transported from the nearest source, which was over 70 miles from La Venta! A total of 13 heads has been found: five at La Venta, six at San Lorenzo, one at Tres Zapotes, and one at Santiago Tuxtla—all cities of the Olmecs. On your tour through the park, notice the fine stone sculptures and artistic achievements of the Olmecs, who set forth the first art style in Mesoamerica. Their exquisite figurines in jade and serpentine, which can be seen in the Regional Museum of Anthropology, far excelled any other craft of this period.

La Venta, by the way, was one of three major Olmec cities during the Preclassic Period (2000 B.C. to A.D. 300). The ruins were discovered in 1938, and there in the tall grasses were the mammoth heads. Today all that remains of the once-impressive city are some grass-covered mounds—once pyramids—some 84 miles (135 km) west of Villahermosa. All of the gigantic heads have been moved from the site. You'll see three heads in Parque La Venta.

Parque Museo La Venta is open from 8 a.m. to 5 p.m. every day: admission is 40 pesos (8¢) to nonresidents, 20 pesos (4¢) to residents.

REGIONAL MUSEUM OF ANTHROPOLOGY: Tabasco's Museo Regional de Antropologia Carlos Pellicer Cámara, was opened in February 1980 to replace the older Tabasco Museum. The new museum is architecturally bold and attractive, and very well organized inside. There is more space and therefore the number of pre-Hispanic artifacts on display has greatly increased to include not only the Tabascan finds (Totonac, Zapotec, and Olmec), but the rest of the Mexican and Central American cultures as well.

The museum is beautiful, with parquet floors, wood dividers, and numerous plants. There is a very open and airy feeling about this place. Take the elevator to the top of the museum and walk down past large maps showing the Olmec and Mayan lands. Photographs and diagrams make it all easier to comprehend, but the explanatory signs are all in Spanish. Look expecially for figurines that were found in this area and for the colorful *Codex* (an early book of pictographs).

The Regional Museum is a mile south of the center of town, right along the river's west bank, open Tuesday to Sunday from 9 a.m. to 8 p.m.; admission is 50 pesos (10¢).

Chapter XIII

USEFUL INFORMATION

THOUGH MEXICO is close to the United States and Canada in many ways, it is also vastly different. Lots of the simple daily chores you do at home without even thinking can become major obstacles to happiness when you attempt to do them in a foreign country. Pay telephones work differently; banks don't have those handy money machines; buses operate on very different rules; and the Mexican post office won't accept your postcards if they don't bear Mexican postage stamps.

The solutions to these and many other daily travel problems are found below, in alphabetical order.

ABBREVIATIONS: Apdo. = post office box; **Av.** = Avenida; **"C"** on faucets stands for *caliente* (hot) and **"F"** stands for *fría* (cold); **C.P.** = Codigo Postal (postal or "zip" code); **P.B.** in elevators is for Planta Baja, ground floor.

AUTO MECHANICS: Your best guide is the **Yellow Pages.** For specific makes and shops that repair them, look under *Automoviles y Camiones: Talleres de Reparación y Servicio;* auto-parts stores are listed under *Refacciones y Accesorios para Automoviles.*

I've found the Ford and Volkswagen dealerships in Mexico to give prompt, courteous attention to my car problems, and prices for repairs are, in general, much lower than in the U.S. or Canada. I suspect that other big-name dealerships—General Motors, Chrysler, and American Motors—give similar, very satisfactory service. Oftentimes they will take your car right away and service it in a few hours—a thing almost unheard of at home.

Mexico imports lots of American cars of all makes, and the country manufactures a tremendous number of Volkswagens (using the old 1600 engine).

BANKS (See also "Money"): In Mexico, banks tend to be open from 9 a.m. to 1:30 p.m., Monday through Friday.

Large airports have currency-exchange counters that stay open as long as flights are arriving or departing.

Many banks south of the border have an employee who speaks English.

For the fastest and least complicated service, traveler's checks or cash are the best things to carry. You can usually get a cash advance on your credit card in 20 minutes or less. Personal checks may delay you for weeks—the bank will wait for it to clear before giving you your money. For money by wire, see "Money."

BRIBES: Called *propina* (tip), *mordida* (bite), or worse, the custom is probably almost as old as mankind. Bribes exist in every country—as one sees upon picking up a daily newspaper—but in Third World countries the amounts tend to be smaller and collected more often.

BUSES: Bus travel is the most popular form of transportation in Mexico. More and more foreign tourists are choosing to travel this way, and so here's a glossary of bus terms you'll find useful:

Autobus	Bus
Camión	Bus or Truck
Directo	Nonstop
Equipajes	Baggage (claim area)
Foraneo	Intercity
Llegadas	Gates
Local	Bus that originates at this station (see "Paso")
Paso, de paso	Bus originating somewhere else that will pass through this station; stops if seats are available.
Primera	First (class)
Recibo de Equipajes	Baggage claim area
Sala de Espera	Waiting Room
Sanitarios	Toilets
Segunda	Second (class)
Sin Escala	Nonstop
Taquilla	Ticket window

When traveling by bus, it's best to buy your ticket (and thus reserve your seat) a day in advance, or even more than a day in the case of very long-distance and international buses, and those running on holidays.

CAMERAS AND FILM: Both are more expensive than in the States; take full advantage of your 12-roll film allowance, and bring extra batteries. A few places in resort areas advertise developing for color film, but it might be cheaper to wait till you get home.

If you're really into the sport, bring an assortment of films at various ASA/DIN speeds as you will be photographing against glaring sand, in gloomy Mayan temples, in dusky jungles, through hazy humidity. The proper filters are a help, as well.

CAMPING: It's easy and relatively cheap south of the border if you have a recreational vehicle or trailer, a bit less easy if you're tenting. Some agencies selling Mexican car insurance in the U.S. will give you a free list of campsites if you ask. The AAA has lists of sites. The *Rand McNally Campground & Trailer Park Guide* covers Mexico.

Campgrounds here tend to be slightly below the standards of northern ones (with many attractive exceptions to this rule, though). Remember that campgrounds fill up just like hotels during the winter rush-to-the-sun and at holiday times. Get there early.

CAR RENTALS: The car-rental business in Mexico is as far flung and well developed as in Europe and the U.S., with the usual problems and procedures. As elsewhere, it's good to reserve your car in advance in Mexico, an easy task when you fly into the country, as most airlines will gladly make the reservation for you.

With a credit card (American Express, VISA, MasterCard, and so forth) rentals are simple if you're over 25, in possession of a valid driver's license, and have your passport with you. Without a credit card you must leave a cash deposit, usually a big one.

You can save yourself some money by renting only as much car as you *need:* make sure that the company you select offers the VW Beetle or Datsun—usually the cheapest car—if that will do, and make sure they will have one on hand to rent you. (Sometimes they'll say they do over the phone, but when you arrive at the office the cheapest cars will be "all booked up" for two weeks, etc.)

Don't underestimate the cost of renting a car. The total amount you'll be out-of-pocket for a short one-day trip to, say, Tulum and Xel-ha (59 miles, or 95 km, south of Cancún), might be in the range of $60. Take your time when you look over the company's rates, estimate the total distance and time, and allow a generous margin for side trips, wrong turns, etc.—those kilometers are expensive!—and then add up all of the charges you'll have to pay before the clerk starts filling out a rental contract.

Your completed estimate should look something like this, based on a total of 225 kilometers (95 down, 95 back, 35 for wrong turns), for the very cheapest car offered (these figures have been rounded off):

Basic daily charge	$14
Kilometers, 225 @ 12¢	27
Full collision insurance	6
Subtotal	$47
IVA tax @ 15%	7
Gas @ 95 pesos (19¢)/liter	5
Grand Total	$59

Yes! In my experience, to rent a VW Bettle in Yucatán, especially in Cancún, costs about $60 per day, all in. You can save a bit of money on this daily average if you rent by the week with unlimited mileage. But however you cut it, rental costs in Mexico are much, much higher than at home.

Once you've made up your mind to rent a car, finding a rental office is a snap. Rental desks are set up in the airports, in all major hotels, and in many travel agencies. The large firms like Avis, Hertz, National, and Budget have rental offices on main streets as well.

CLOTHES FOR TRAVEL: Mexico tends to be a bit more conservative in dress (except for the capital) so shorts and halter tops are not generally acceptable except at seaside resorts. Cool clothes are needed at all times for Yucatán. A raincoat is a good idea (a fold-up plastic one will do) for the rainy season (middle of May through September) when it rains almost every afternoon for an hour or so. For more hints on clothing, see the Introduction to this book.

CLOTHING SIZE EQUIVALENTS: You'll want to try on any clothing you intend to buy, but here are some equivalents in case you're buying gifts for friends. Note that women's blouse sizes are the same in the U.S. and Mexico.

Women's						Men's			
Dress		Shoes		Collar		Jacket		Shoes	
U.S.	Mex.	U.S.	Mex.	U.S.	Mex.	U.S.	Mex.	U.S.	Mex.
6	36	5	35	14	36	38	48	8	41
8	38	5.5	35.5	14.5	37	40	50	8.5	41.5
10	40	6	36	15	38	42	52	9	42
12	42	6.5	36.5	15.5	39	44	54	9.5	42.5
14	44	7	37	16	40	46	56	10	43
16	46	7.5	37.5	16.5	41	48	58	10.5	43.5
18	48	8	38	17	42	50	60	11	44
20	50	8.5	38.5	17.5	43	52	62	11.5	44.5
22	52	9	39	18	44	54	64	12	45

CRIME: It's getting to be more of a problem in Mexico—which is to say that there was not much of a crime problem before. Although you will feel physically safer in most Mexican cities than in comparable big cities at home, you must take some basic, sensible precautions.

First, remember that you're a tourist, and a tourist is a mark. Beware of pickpockets on crowded buses and in markets. Guard your possessions very carefully at all times; don't let packs or bags out of sight even for a second (the big first-class bus lines will store your bag in the luggage compartment under the bus, and that's generally all right, but keep your things with you on the less responsible village and some second-class buses on country routes).

Next, if you have a car, park it in an enclosed or guarded lot at night. Vans are a special mark. Don't depend on "major downtown streets" to protect your car—park it in a private lot with a guard, or at least a fence.

Women must be careful in cities when walking alone, night or day. Busy streets are no problem, but empty streets (even if empty just for afternoon siesta) are lonely places.

As to the police, in the past they have been part of the problem, not part of the solution. Although Mexico no doubt has dedicated and responsible officers, the general impression is that police have little training and fewer scruples. If you have the misfortune to be robbed, you should go to the police and report it, and get them to certify a report of the loss (you may have to write up the report yourself). But don't expect much sympathy, and even less action.

All these warnings having been stated, let me repeat that the prudent person need feel no more danger in Mexico than at home; most of the time you'll feel in less danger.

CUSTOMS AND DUTY-FREE GOODS: Coming to Mexico, Customs officials are very tolerant as long as you have no drugs (that is, marijuana, cocaine, etc.) or firearms. You're allowed to bring two cartons of cigarettes, or 100 non-Cuban cigars, plus a kilogram (2.2 pounds) of smoking tobacco; the liquor allowance is 1 liter of anything, wine or hard liquor.

Reentering the **U.S.**, you're allowed by **federal law** to bring in a carton (200) of cigarettes, *or* 50 cigars, *or* two kilograms (total, 4.4 pounds) of smoking tobacco, or proportional amounts of these items, plus one liter of alcoholic beverage (wine, beer, or spirits). If you bring larger amounts of these things, you will have to pay federal duty and internal revenue tax. *But wait!* Your quotas will also be subject to **state laws** (that is, of the state in which you reenter the U.S.). The state law may not allow you to bring back *any* liquor, which means *you will have to pour it out*. It's not simply a matter of paying duty, it's a matter of absolute quotas—or no quotas at all—for some states. This liquor quota is most strictly applied at the border posts, less strictly at airports not near the border.

Here are the limits for liquor in the states that border Mexico, from information supplied by the Distilled Spirits Council, Washington, D.C.:

Arizona: You may not import more than the federal duty-free limit; any amounts over the limit will be destroyed.

California: You may bring in a "reasonable amount" of liquor for each adult, for personal use only (not for resale or as gifts).

New Mexico: You may bring in a reasonable amount duty-free.

Texas: All liquor brought into Texas is subject to state tax; for amounts of hard liquor over one quart, you must have a permit from the state liquor authorities.

Canadian returning-resident regulations are similar to the U.S. ones: a carton of cigarettes, 50 cigars, two pounds (not kilos) of smoking tobacco, 1.1 liters (40 ounces) of wine or liquor, *or* a case of beer (8.2 liters). All provinces except P.E.I. and the Northwest Territories allow you to bring in more liquor and beer —up to two gallons (nine liters) more—but the taxes are quite high.

DOCTORS AND DENTISTS: Every embassy and consulate is prepared to recommend local doctors and dentists with good training and up-to-date equipment; some of the doctors and dentists even speak English. See the list of embassies and consulates under "Embassies" (below), and remember that at the larger ones a duty officer is on call at all times.

DRUGSTORES: The word is *farmacia*, and they will sell you just about anything you want, with prescription or without. Most are open every day but Sunday, from 8 a.m. to 8 p.m.

If you need to buy medicines outside of normal hours, you'll have to search for the *farmacia de turno*—pharmacies take turns staying open during the off hours. Find any drugstore, and in its window should be a card showing a schedule of which farmacia will be open at what time.

ELECTRICITY: Current in Mexico is 110 volts, 60 cycles, as in the U.S. and Canada, with the same flat-prong plugs and sockets. Light bulbs may have bayonet bases, though.

EMBASSIES: They provide valuable lists of doctors, lawyers, regulations concerning marriages in Mexico, etc. Contrary to popular belief, your embassy cannot get you out of a Mexican jail, provide postal or banking services, or fly you home when you run out of money. Consular officers can provide you with advice on most matters and problems, however. Here's a list of embassies, all of which are in the capital, Mexico City. Consulates in Cancún and Mérida are covered in the chapters on those cities.

Canada

The Canadian Embassy in **Mexico City** is at Schiller 529, in Polanco (tel. 905/254-3288). Hours are Monday through Friday from 9 a.m. to 1 p.m. and 3 to 5 p.m.; at other times the name of a duty officer is posted on the embassy door.

United Kingdom
   The British Embassy in **Mexico City** is at Río Lerma 71, at Río Sena (tel. 905/511-4880 or 514-3327).

United States
   The American Embassy in Mexico City is right next to the Hotel María Isabel Sheraton at Paseo de la Reforma 305, corner of Río Danubio (tel. 905/211-0042).

HOLIDAYS, PUBLIC: Banks, stores, and businesses are closed on national holidays, hotels fill up quickly, and transportation is crowded. Here are the holidays celebrated in Mexico:

January 1	New Year's Day
February 5	Constitution Day
March 21	Birthday of Benito Juárez
March–April (moveable)	Holy Week (closures usually Good Friday through Easter Sunday)
May 1	Labor Day
May 5	Battle of Pueblo, 1862 (Cinco de Mayo)
September 1	President's Message to Congress
September 16	Independence Day
October 12	Columbus Day (Mexico: Day of the Race)
November 20	Mexican Revolution Anniversary
December 24–25	Christmas Eve (evening); Christmas Day

INFORMATION: Before you leave home, you can get tourist information from any of the Mexican government tourist offices listed in Chapter I of this book. Once you're in Mexico, drop in to the tourism information offices mentioned in the text for each city or area.

LAUNDRY: All hotels can make some arrangements to have your laundry taken care of. Small laundries can be found in all but the tiniest villages. Coin laundries exist in all cities of any size—just ask at your hotel or a tourism information office.

MAIL: Mail service south of the border tends to be slow (sometimes glacial in its movements) and erratic. If you're on a two-week vacation, it's not a bad idea to buy and mail your postcards in the Arrivals lounge at the airport to give them maximum time to get home before you do. Be sure to use Mexican postage stamps!

General Delivery (Poste Restante)

If you don't use American Express, have your mail sent to you care of *Lista de Correos,* (City), (State), (Country). In Mexican post offices there may actually be a "lista" posted near the Lista de Correos window bearing the names of all those for whom mail has been received. If there's no list, ask, and show them your passport so they can riffle through and look for your letters.

You'll have to go to the central post office—not a branch—to get your mail, if the city has more than one office.

Glossary

Words you'll need to know include these:

Aduana	Customs
Buzón	Mailbox
Correo Aereo	Airmail
Correos	Postal Service
Entrega Immediata	Special Delivery, Express
Estampillas	Stamps
Giros Postales	Money Orders
Lista de Correos	General Delivery, Poste Restante
Oficina de Correos	Post Office
Paquetes	Parcels
Por avion	Airmail
Registrado	Registered Mail
Seguros	Insurance (insured mail)
Sellos	Stamps (sometimes rubber stamps)
Timbres	Stamps

METRIC EQUIVALENTS: Mexico uses the metric system, as in Canada, Europe, and most of the rest of the world. Here are some conversion tables to help you in your shopping and traveling.

1 inch = 2.54 centimeters
1 foot = 30.5 centimeters
1 meter = 39.37 inches
1 mile = 1.6 kilometers

1 kilometer = 0.62 miles
1 pound = 0.4536 kilograms
1 kilogram = 2.2 pounds
1 U.S. gallon = 3.79 liters
1 liter = 0.26 U.S. gallons

Approximations

Here are a few handy rules of thumb. A pound is slightly less than half a kilogram. A meter is a little more than a yard (three feet). A gallon is almost four liters.

An easy way to convert kilometer distances into miles is to multiply the kilometer distance by 0.6; another way of doing the same thing is to think in 3s and 5s, 6s and 10s; 3 miles is about 5 kilometers, 6 miles is about 10 kilometers, so 100 kilometers is about 60 miles.

Temperature

Use of the metric system includes use of the Celsius (centigrade) thermometer. Here are some reference points:

Fahrenheit		Celsius
−40		−40
0		−18
32	Water freezes	0
50	Cool weather	10
68	Comfortable weather	20
88	Hot weather	30
98.6	Body temperature	37
104	Very hot weather	40
212	Water boils	100

MONEY (See also "Banks"): The dollar sign ($) is used to indicate pesos in Mexico. As many establishments dealing with tourists also quote prices in dollars, confusion is cleared up by the use of the abbreviations "Dlls." for dollars, and "m.n." (*moneda nacional*—national currency) for pesos, so "$1,000.00 m.n." means 1,000 pesos. Banks often charge a fee for changing traveler's checks, or give a rate of exchange below the official daily rate. Hotels usually exchange below the official daily rate as well. The bank that writes your traveler's checks (American Express, First National City, etc.) will give you the best rate of exchange.

In recent years it has been normal for the exchange rate on traveler's checks to be better than that for cash dollars—you actually get something back for your penny-on-the-dollar investment in safety.

Canadian dollars seem to be most easily exchanged for pesos at branches of Banamex and Bancomer.

Credit Cards

You'll be glad to know that Mexico is well into the age of living on the little plastic card, and that you will be able to charge some hotel and restaurant bills, almost all airline tickets, and many store purchases. You can get cash advances of several hundred dollars on your card. However, you can't charge gasoline purchases in Mexico at all.

VISA, MasterCard (which is "Carnet" in Mexico), American Express, and their affiliates are the most widely accepted cards. You may not see your card's logo in a shop window or on a travel agency door, but don't worry—the Mexican equivalents such as Bancomer and/or Bancomatico will do just as well.

NEWSPAPERS AND MAGAZINES: For American travelers in Mexico the English-language newspaper *The News* is an excellent buy at about 25¢, more on Saturday. It carries many Stateside columnists as well as newsworthy commentaries, and a calendar of the day's events including concerts, art shows, plays, etc. A Spanish-language paper, *Excelsior,* has a daily partial page in English.

Newspaper kiosks in larger Mexican cities will carry a selection of English-language magazines—*Time, Newsweek,* and the like.

POST OFFICE (See "Mail").

SIESTA: The custom of having a copious, long lunch and taking a rest during the heat of the day is still well entrenched south of the border. You may notice it less in mountainous areas and in the big cities, where life seems to plow onward from morning to evening without a break. But in coastal towns and hot climates, expect banks, offices, consulates, and museums to take a somewhat lengthy break for lunch You'd be well advised to do the same.

TELEPHONES: Local calls in Mexico are very inexpensive. There are two types of coin phones: in one the slot at the top holds your coin (20 or 50 centavos, or one peso—any will work) in a gentle grip until your party answers, then it drops; if there's no answer or a busy signal you can pluck your coin from the slot. The other type is the sort where you insert a coin which disappears into the bowels of the machine, and drops into the cashbox when your call goes through, or into the return slot if it doesn't (after you hang up). This type of phone is often jammed, and your coin won't drop, so that when your party answers you will hear them but they won't hear you. Try from another pay phone.

Long Distance

Long-distance calls in Mexico are as expensive as local calls are cheap. And *international long distance calls tend to be outrageously expensive,* even if you are calling *collect* to the U.S., Canada, or Britain: a 20-minute call from a Mexican hotel to the U.S. or Canada can easily cost $50 or $60! To find out estimated charges *(tarifas)* and area codes *(claves)* you don't know, dial 07.

To call the U.S. or Canada collect, dial 09, and tell the *operadora* that you want *una llamada por cobrar* (a collect call), *telefono a telefono* (station-to-station), or *persona a persona* (person-to-person).

If you don't want to call collect, you'll have to go to a *caseta de larga distancia,* or call from your hotel, as it's impracticable to load hundreds of small coins into a pay phone. Your hotel will levy a service charge—perhaps a percentage!—on top of the already exorbitant rate. Ask in advance what they'll add on. At a caseta you pay just the call charge.

From a caseta or hotel, dial 95 + Area Code + number for the U.S. and Canada, or 98 + Area Code + number for anywhere else in the world.

To call long distance (abbreviated "lada") within Mexico, dial 91 + Area Code + number. Mexican area codes *(claves)* are listed in the front of the telephone directories, and in the hotel listings for each area in this book.

Calling to Mexico from Abroad

I've included Mexican Area Codes in all important telephone numbers so that you can call long distance within Mexico, or to Mexico from the U.S. and Canada (and, for that matter, from the rest of the world). Mexico's *claves* (Area Codes) and numbers are sometimes shorter than those up north, but they work just as well. Until the Mexican system is fully integrated with that in the U.S. and Canada, you may have to ask the operator for assistance in calling.

Saving Money in Mexico

You can save up to 29% by calling in off-peak periods. The cheapest times to call are after 11 p.m. and before 8 a.m. any day, and all day Saturday and Sunday; the most expensive times are 8 a.m. to 5 p.m. weekdays.

TIME ZONE: The entire Yucatán peninsula, like most of Mexico, uses Central Standard Time all year round (Daylight Saving Time is not used). That means that it's the same hour in Mérida or Cancún as it is in Chicago, New Orleans, or Houston. But when it's 12 noon in Yucatán, it's 1 p.m. in New York and Miami, or 11 a.m. in Santa Fe or Salt Lake City, or 10 a.m. in Seattle or Los Angeles.

TIPPING: When it comes to tipping, you should throw out the iron 15% rule right away south of the border, no matter what other travel literature may say. Do as the locals do: for meals costing $2 to $3 or under, leave the loose change; for meals costing around $4 or $5, leave from 6% to 10%, depending on service. Above $6 to $7, you're into the 10% to 15% bracket. Some of the more crass high-priced restaurants will actually add a 15% "tip" to your bill. Leave nothing extra if they do.

Bellboys and porters will expect about 25¢ per bag. You needn't tip taxi drivers unless they've rendered some special service—carrying bags or trunks, for instance.

TRAVELER'S DIARRHEA: This is the doctors' term for diarrhea from which many tourists suffer, although others seem immune. It's not only unclean food or water that's to blame, but also the change of eating habits and environment. If your condition becomes serious—fever and chills, stomach pains—do *not* hesitate to call a doctor. Diseases far more serious than Traveler's Diarrhea are on the loose down here. To neglect a potentially serious ailment, because of the belief that Traveler's Diarrhea is painful but not dangerous, could be an unhappy mistake. Also, it is advisable, no matter how serious your illness, to consult a doctor before buying or taking any kind of drug. For more information on Traveler's Diarrhea, refer to Chapter I, under "Health and Medicaments."

WATER: Most hotels have decanters or bottles of purified water in the rooms and the snazzier hotels have special taps marked *"Aqua Purificada."* Virtually any hotel, restaurant, or bar will bring you purified water if you specifically request it.

YOUTH HOSTELS: Mexico has some beautiful government-built and supported hostels, at very low prices. For a list, write to **SETEJ,** Hamburgo 273, in Mexico City (tel. 905/211-0743). A source of information on inexpensive youth hostel tours is the **Agencia Nacional de Turismo Juvenil,** Glorieta del Metro Insurgentes, **Local** C-11, México 6, D.F. (tel. 905/525-2699 or 525-2974).

Chapter XIV

SPEAKING SPANISH

YOU'LL BE SURPRISED at the number of Mexicans you'll meet who are fluent in English. It is, after all, the most important language in Mexican tourism, commerce and industry, science, banking, and diplomacy. English is taught in most Mexican high schools and colleges.

But many people not involved in these fields have no reason to learn English (or to remember the English they learned in school), and so the time will come when you'll need a Spanish word or phrase in order to make yourself understood. This chapter should fill the need nicely, if you're on the average one- or two-week trip.

Should you plan a long trip in Yucatán, I'd suggest picking up a good Spanish phrase book. If you pick up a copy of **Frommer's Fast 'n Easy Phrase Book,** you'll be getting a real bargain. For only $6.95, you get over 400 pages of words and phrases, not just in Spanish, but in the three other languages most often encountered by international travelers: French, Italian, and German. Pocket-size despite its impressive length, bound in a durable Perma-travel cover, this is the phrase book you'll be able to use not just on your trip to Yucatán, but to Europe, the Caribbean, and Canada as well. It's a good, long-term investment.

Berlitz Publications puts out a handy pocket-size phrase guide with copious background notes on cultural matters, social customs, and "body language." In effect, it's a guidebook to the language and culture attuned to regional dialects, as its title, **Latin American Spanish for Travellers,** reveals. It's available in most bookstores.

Bueno. Here's your first lesson in Spanish, the one most visitors find necessary first: the numbers.

Numbers

1 **uno** (ooh-noh)	15 **quince** (keen-say)	kewn-tah)
2 **dos** (dose)	16 **dieciseis** (dee-ess-ee-says)	60 **sesenta** (say-sen-tah)
3 **tres** (trayss)	17 **diecisiete** (de-ess-ee-see-ay-tay)	70 **setenta** (say-ten-tah)
4 **cuatro** (kwah-troh)	18 **dieciocho** (dee-ess-ee-oh-choh)	80 **ochentz** (oh-chen-tah)
5 **cinco** (seen-koh)	19 **diecinueve** (dee-ess-ee-nway-bay)	90 **noventa** (noh-ben-tah)
6 **seis** (sayss)	20 **veinte** (bayn-tay)	100 **cien** (see-en)
7 **siete** (syeh-tay)	30 **treinta** (trayn-tah)	200 **doscientos** (dos-see-en-tos)
8 **ocho** (oh-choh)	40 **cuarenta** (kwah-ren-tah)	500 **quinientos** (keen-ee-ehn-tos)
9 **nueve** (nway-bay)	50 **cincuenta** (seen-	1000 **mil** (meel)
10 **diez** (dee-ess)		
11 **once** (ohn-say)		
12 **doce** (doh-say)		
13 **trece** (tray-say)		
14 **catorce** (kah-tor-say)		

Useful Phrases

		Pronounced
Hello	**Buenos días**	bway-nohss dee-ahss
How are you?	**¿Cómo está usted?**	koh-moh ess-tah oo-sted
Very well	**Muy bien**	mwee byen
Thank you	**Gracias**	grah-see-ahss
You're welcome	**De nada**	day nah-dah
Goodbye	**Adiós**	ah-dyohss
Please	**Por favor**	pohr fah-bohr
Yes	**Sí**	see
No	**No**	noh
Excuse	**Perdóneme**	pehr-doh-neh-may
Give me	**Déme**	day-may
Where is?	**¿Dónde está?**	dohn-day ess-tah
the station	la estación	la ess-tah-see-own
a hotel	un hotel	oon oh-tel
a gas station	una gasolinera	oon-nuh gah-so-lee-nay-rah
a restaurant	un restaurante	oon res-tow-rahn-tay
the toilet	el baño	el bahn-yoh
a good doctor	un buen medico	oon bwayn may-dee-co

the road to . . .	**el camino a . . .**	el cah-mee-noh ah . . .
To the right	**A la derecha**	ah lah day-ray-chuh
To the left	**A la izquierda**	ah lah ees-ky-ehr-dah
Straight ahead	**Derecho**	day-ray-cho
I would like	**Quisiera**	keyh-see-air-ah
I want	**Quiero**	kyehr-oh
to eat	**comer**	ko-mayr
a room	**una habitación**	oon-nuh hab-bee-tah-see-own
Do you have?	**¿Tiene usted?**	tyah-nay oos-ted
a book	**un libro**	oon lee-bro
a dictionary	**un diccionario**	oon deek-see-own-ar-eo
How much is it?	**¿Cuánto cuesta?**	kwahn-toh kwess-tah
When	**¿Cuando?**	kwahn-doh
What	**¿Qué?**	kay
There is (Is there?)	**¿Hay . . .**	eye
Yesterday	**Ayer**	ah-yer
Today	**Hoy**	oy
Tomorrow	**Mañana**	mahn-yawn-ah
Good	**Bueno**	bway-no
Bad	**Malo**	mah-lo
Better (best)	**(Lo) Mejor**	meh-hor
More	**Más**	mahs
Less	**Menos**	may-noss
No Smoking	**Se prohibe fumar**	seh pro-hee-beh foo-mahr
Postcard	**Tarjeta postal**	tahr-hay-tah pohs-tahl
Insect repellent	**Rapellante contra insectos**	rah-pey-yahn-te cohn-trah een-sehk-tos

Do you speak English?	¿Habla usted Inglés?
Is there anyone here who speaks English?	¿Hay alguien aquí qué hable Inglés?

I speak a little Spanish	Hablo un poco de Español.
I don't understand Spanish very well.	No lo entiendo muy bien el Español.
The meal is good.	Me gusta la comida.
What time is it?	¿Qué hora es?
May I see your menu?	¿Puedo ver su menú?
What did you say?	¿Mande? (colloquial expression for American "Eh?")
I want (to see) a room	Quiero (ver) un carto (una habitación)
for two persons	para dos persones
with (without) bath	con (sin) baño
We are staying here only one night (one week)	Nos quedaremos aqui solamente una noche (una semana).
We are leaving tomorrow.	Partimos mañana.
Do you accept traveler's checks?	¿Acepta usted cheques de viajero?
Is there a laundromat near here	¿Hay una lavandería cerca de aquí?
Please send these clothes to the laundry.	Hágame el favor de mandar esta ropa a la lavandería.

Menu Terms

almuerzo	lunch	frito	fried
cena	supper	poco cocide	rare
comida	dinner	asado	roast
desayuno	breakfast	bien cocido	well done
el menu	the menu	milanesa	breaded
la cuenta	the check	veracruzana	tomato and green olive sauce
tampiqueña	thinly sliced meat		
cocido	boiled	pibil	roasted
empanado	breaded		

BREAKFAST (DESAYUNO)

jugo de naranja	orange juice	huevos motuleños	egg on ham with tortilla, cheese, and tomato sauce
cafe con crema	coffee with cream		

pan tostado	toast	**huevos poches**	poached eggs
mermelada	jam	**huevos fritos**	fried eggs
leche	milk	**huevos pasados al agua**	
te	tea		soft-boiled eggs
huevos	eggs	**huevos revueltos**	scrambled
huevos rancheros	fried eggs		eggs
	on a tortilla, covered with	**tocino**	bacon
	tomato sauce	**jamón**	ham
huevos cocidos	hard-boiled		
	eggs		

LUNCH AND DINNER

antojitos	Mexican specialties	**caldo de pollo**	chicken broth
caldo	broth	**frijoles refritos**	refried beans
sopa	soup	**menudo**	tripe soup
sopa de ajo	garlic soup with egg	**médula**	bone marrow soup
sopa clara	consommé	**salchichas**	knockwurst
sopa de lentejas	lentil soup	**taco**	filled fried tortilla
sopa de chicaros	pea soup	**torta**	sandwich
sopa de arroz	rice pilaf (not	**tostada**	crisp fried tortilla
	soup!)	**enchilada**	filled tortilla
pozole	meat-hominy stew	**tamales russos**	cabbage rolls

SEAFOOD (MARISCOS)

almejas	clams	**merluza**	hake (type of cod)
anchoas	anchovies	**ostiones**	oysters
arenques	herring	**pescado**	fish
atún	tuna	**mojarra**	perch
calamares	squid	**pez espada**	swordfish
camarones	shrimp	**robalo**	sea bass
caracoles	snails	**salmon**	salmon
caviare	caviar	**salmon ahumado**	smoked
corvina	bass		salmon
huachinango	red snapper	**sardinas**	sardines
jaiba	crab	**solo**	pike
langosta	lobster	**trucha**	trout
lenguado	sole		

MEATS (CARNES)

ahumade	smoked	**callos**	tripe
alambre	shish kebab	**venado**	venison
albondigas	meatballs	**conejo**	rabbit
aves	poultry	**cordero**	lamb
bistek	steak	**costillas de cerdo**	spareribs
cabeza de ternera	calf's head	**faisan**	pheasant
cabrito	kid (goat)	**filete milanesa**	breaded veal
carne	meat		chops
carne fría	cold cuts	**filete de ternera**	filet of veal
cerdo	pork	**ganso**	goose
chiles rellenos	stuffed peppers	**pavo**	turkey
chicharrón	pigskin cracklings	**higado**	liver
chorizo	spicy sausage	**jamón**	ham
chuleta	chop	**lengua**	tongue
chuleta de carnero	mutton chop	**lomo**	loin
chuletas de cordero	lamb chops	**mole**	chicken in spicy
chuletas de puerco	pork chops		bitter-chocolate sauce
paloma	pigeon	**pollo**	chicken
pato	duck	**res**	beef
pechuga	chicken breast	**riñones**	kidneys
perdiz	partridge	**ternera**	veal
pierna	leg	**tocino**	bacon

VEGETABLES (LEGUMBRES)

aguacate	avocado	**espinaca**	spinach
aceitunas	olives	**frijoles**	beans
arroz	rice	**hongos**	mushrooms
betabeles	beets	**jicame**	sweet
cebolla	onions		yellow turnip
champiñones	mushrooms	**lechuga**	lettuce
chicharos	peas	**lentejas**	lentils
col	cabbage	**papas**	potatoes
col fermentada	sauerkraut	**pepino**	cucumber
coliflor	cauliflower	**rabanos**	radishes
ejotes	string beans	**tomate**	tomato

elote	corn (maize)	**verdura**	green
entremeses	hors d'oeuvres	**zanahorías**	carrots
esparragos	asparagus		

SALADS (ENSALADAS)

ensalada de apio	celery salad		
ensalada de frutas	fruit salad	**guacamole**	avocado salad
ensalada mixta	mixed salad	**lechuga**	lettuce salad
ensalada de pepinos	cucumber salad		

FRUITS (FRUTAS)

chavacanos	apricots	**higos**	figs
ciruelas	yellow plums	**limon**	lime
coco	coconut	**mamey**	sweet orange fruit
duraznos	peaches	**mango**	mango
frambuesas	raspberries	**manzanas**	apples
fresas	strawberries	**maranjas**	oranges
con crema	with cream	**pera**	pear
fruta cocida	stewed fruit	**piña**	pineapple
granada	pomegranate	**plátanos**	bananas
guanabana	green pear-like fruit	**tuña**	prickly pear fruit
		uvas	grapes
guayabas	guavas	**zapote**	maple-sugary fruit

DESSERTS (POSTRES)

arroz con leche	rice pudding	**helado, nieve**	ice cream
brunelos de fruta	fruit tart	**macedonia**	fruit salad
coctel de aguacate	avocado cocktail	**nieve**	sherbert
		pastel	cake or pastry
coctel de frutas	fruit cocktail	**queso**	cheese

compota	stewed fruit	**torta**	cake
flan	custard	**leche tipo bulgar,**	yogurt
galletas	crackers or cookies	**lavin**	

BEVERAGES (BEBIDAS)

agua	water	**leche**	milk
brandy	brandy	**licores**	liqueurs
café	coffee	**manzanita**	apple juice
café con crema	coffee with cream	**refrescas**	soft drinks
café negro	black coffee	**ron**	rum
cerveza	beer	**sidra**	cider
ginebra	gin	**sifon**	soda
hielo	ice	**té**	tea
jerez	sherry	**vaso de leche**	glass of milk
jugo de naranja	orange juice	**vino blanco**	white wine
jugo de tomate	tomato juice	**vino tinto**	red wine
jugo de toronja	grapefruit juice	**refresco**	soft drink

CONDIMENTS AND CUTLERY

aceite	oil	**pan**	bread
azucar	sugar	**bolillo**	roll
copa	goblet	**pimienta**	pepper
cilantro	coriander	**sal**	salt
cuchara	spoon	**taza**	cup
cuchillo	knife	**tenedor**	fork
epazote	Mexican tea	**tostada**	toast
mantequilla	butter	**vinagre**	vinegar
mostaza	mustard	**vaso**	glass

PREPARATION AND SAUCES

asado roasted
cocido cooked
bien cocido well-done
poco cocido rare
empanado breaded
frito fried
al horno baked
milanesa Italian breaded
mole poblano hot red peppers and cocoa sauce with raisins and spices
a la parilla grilled
pibil sauce of tomato, onion, red pepper (hot), cilantro, vinegar; wrapped in a banana leaf

poc chuc pork leg cooked with onions, cilantro, sour oranges, and served with black beans
relleno negro stuffed ground pork, pimiento, olives, eggs, epazote, salt, vinegar and tomato stuffing
blanco the above with raisins cinnamon, and capers
tampiqueño thinly sliced meat
veracruzana tomato and green olive sauce

Date_____

**PRENTICE HALL PRESS
ONE GULF + WESTERN PLAZA
NEW YORK, NY 10023**

Friends:

Please send me the books checked below:

FROMMER'S $-A-DAY GUIDES™

(In-depth guides to sightseeing and low-cost tourist accommodations and facilities.)

☐ Europe on $25 a Day $12.95
☐ Australia on $25 a Day $10.95
☐ Eastern Europe on $25 a Day $10.95
☐ England on $35 a Day............... $10.95
☐ Greece on $25 a Day................ $10.95
☐ Hawaii on $45 a Day $10.95
☐ India on $15 & $25 a Day $9.95
☐ Ireland on $30 a Day............... $10.95
☐ Israel on $30 & $35 a Day $10.95
☐ Mexico on $20 a Day $10.95

☐ New Zealand on $25 a Day $10.95
☐ New York on $45 a Day............. $9.95
☐ Scandinavia on $50 a Day........... $10.95
☐ Scotland and Wales on $35 a Day..... $10.95
☐ South America on $30 a Day $10.95
☐ Spain and Morocco (plus the Canary
   Is.) on $40 a Day $10.95
☐ Turkey on $25 a Day (avail. Nov. '87) . $10.95
☐ Washington, D.C. on $40 a Day $10.95

FROMMER'S DOLLARWISE GUIDES™

(Guides to sightseeing and tourist accommodations and facilities from budget to deluxe with emphasis on
the medium-priced.)

☐ Alaska (avail. Nov. '87) $12.95
☐ Austria & Hungary $11.95
☐ Belgium, Holland, Luxembourg $11.95
☐ Egypt........................... $11.95
☐ England & Scotland $11.95
☐ France.......................... $11.95
☐ Germany........................ $11.95
☐ Italy............................ $11.95
☐ Japan & Hong Kong $12.95
☐ Portugal (incl. Madeira & the Azores) . $11.95
☐ South Pacific (avail. Oct. '87)....... $12.95
☐ Switzerland & Liechtenstein $11.95
☐ Bermuda & The Bahamas........... $10.95
☐ Canada $12.95
☐ Caribbean $12.95

☐ Cruises (incl. Alaska, Carib, Mex,
   Hawaii, Panama, Canada, & US) $12.95
☐ California & Las Vegas $11.95
☐ Florida.......................... $10.95
☐ Honeymoons (US, Canada, Mexico, &
   Carib) (avail. Nov. '87) $12.95
☐ Mid-Atlantic (avail. Nov. '87) $12.95
☐ New England $11.95
☐ New York State (avail. Aug. '87)...... $11.95
☐ Northwest $11.95
☐ Skiing in Europe $12.95
☐ Skiing USA—East $10.95
☐ Skiing USA—West $10.95
☐ Southeast & New Orleans........... $11.95
☐ Southwest....................... $11.95
☐ Texas........................... $11.95

TURN PAGE FOR ADDITIONAL BOOKS AND ORDER FORM.

THE ARTHUR FROMMER GUIDES™

(Pocket-size guides to sightseeing and tourist accommodations and facilities in all price ranges.)

FROMMER'S TOURING GUIDES™

(Color illustrated guides that include walking tours, cultural & historic sites, and other vital travel information)

SPECIAL EDITIONS

ORDER NOW!

In U.S. include $1.50 shipping UPS for 1st book; 50¢ ea. add'l. book. Outside U.S. $2 and 50¢ respectively.

Enclosed is my check or money order for $_____

NAME_____

ADDRESS_____

CITY_____ STATE_____ ZIP_____

It's 2 am.
It's far from home.
It's more than
a tummyache.

American Express Cardmembers can get emergency medical and legal referrals, worldwide. Simply by calling Global Assist.℠

What if it really is more than a tummyache? What if your back goes out? What if you get into a legal fix?

Call Global Assist – a new emergency referral service for the exclusive use of American Express Cardmembers. Just call. Toll-free. 24 hours a day. Every day. Virtually anywhere in the world.

Your call helps find a doctor, lawyer, dentist, optician, chiropractor, nurse, pharmacist, or an interpreter.

All this costs nothing, except for the medical and legal bills you would normally expect to pay.

Global Assist. One more reason to have the American Express® Card. Or, to get one.

 For an application, call 1-800-THE-CARD.

Don't leave home without it.℠